Sujata Moorti is Professor of Gender, Sexuality and Feminist Studies at Middlebury College, Vermont. She is currently completing a manuscript, 'iFeminism: Social Media and Activist Re-Imaginings,' analyzing the transnational socialities enabled by digital media. Her publications include *Color of Rape: Gender and Race in Television's Public Spheres* (2003) and two co-edited volumes. She has also written extensively on the South Asian diaspora and critical race theories.

Lisa M. Cuklanz is Professor of the Communication Department at Boston College. She is former department chairperson and form Director of Women's and Gender Studies at Boston College. Her research focuses on representations of gendered violence in media. She is the author or editor of five books as well as dozens of other publications. Her work has appeared in journals including *Critical Studies in Media Communication, Communication Quarterly, Journal of Gender Studies, Women's Studies in Communication,* and *Communication Studies.*

'Moorti and Cuklanz's book illustrates the necessity and value of analyzing those kinds of long-running, well-watched TV series often disqualified from academic canons. Their study of *Law & Order SVU* brilliantly illuminates its hybridization of melodrama and police procedural, the ways it indexes shifts in US rape culture and its production of what the authors call a "misogynist feminism."'

Diane Negra, Professor of Film Studies and Screen Culture, University College Dublin

'Setting a US drama in relation to global issues, Moorti and Cuklanz provide yet another deep and insightful analysis of contemporary mainstream popular culture. Through *Law & Order: Special Victims Unit*, Moorti and Cuklanz conduct the utterly necessary task of bringing together an optic of race, gender, and the global to bear on this massively popular television show with a global audience. This book will immediately become a major resource for those researching and teaching in issues of television studies – once more underscoring that television is by no means dead. As well as this book, previous work by Moorti and Cuklanz makes an absolutely essential contribution to studies of gender, race, media, and violence.'

Angharad N. Valdivia, Professor of Media and Cinema Studies, University of Illinois at Urbana-Champaign

Library of Gender and Popular Culture

From *Mad Men* to gaming culture, performance art to steam-punk fashion, the presentation and representation of gender continues to saturate popular media. This new series seeks to explore the intersection of gender and popular culture, engaging with a variety of texts – drawn primarily from Art, Fashion, TV, Cinema, Cultural Studies and Media Studies – as a way of considering various models for understanding the complementary relationship between 'gender identities' and 'popular culture'. By considering race, ethnicity, class, and sexual identities across a range of cultural forms, each book in the series will adopt a critical stance towards issues surrounding the development of gender identities and popular and mass cultural 'products'.

For further information or enquiries, please contact the library series editors:

Claire Nally: claire.nally@northumbria.ac.uk
Angela Smith: angela.smith@sunderland.ac.uk

Advisory Board:

Dr Kate Ames, Central Queensland University, Australia

Prof Leslie Heywood, Binghampton University, USA

Dr Michael Higgins, Strathclyde University, UK

Prof Åsa Kroon, Örebro University, Sweden

Dr Niall Richardson, Sussex University, UK

Dr Jacki Willson, Central St Martins, University of Arts London, UK

**Library of Gender
& Popular Culture**

Published and forthcoming titles:

Ageing Femininity on Film: The Older Woman in Contemporary Cinema
Niall Richardson
All-American TV Crime Drama: Feminism and Identity Politics in Law & Order: Special Victims Unit
Sujata Moorti and Lisa Cuklanz
Beyoncé, Feminism and Popular Culture
Kirsty Fairclough-Isaacs
Female Bodies and Performance in Film: Queer Encounters with Embodiment and Affect
Katharina Lindner
Framing the Single Mother: Gender, Politics and Family Values in Contemporary Popular Cinema
Louise Fitzgerald
Gay Pornography: Representations of Sexuality and Masculinity
John Mercer
Gender and Economics in Popular Culture: Femininity, Masculinity and Austerity in Film and TV
Helen Davies and Claire O'Callaghan (eds)
Gendering History on Screen: Women Filmmakers and Historical Films
Julia Erhart
Girls Like This, Boys Like That: The Reproduction of Gender in Contemporary Youth Cultures
Victoria Cann
Love Wars: Television Romantic Comedy
Mary Irwin
Masculinity in Contemporary Science Fiction Cinema: Cyborgs, Troopers and Other Men of the Future
Marianne Kac-Vergne
Paradoxical Pleasures: Female Submission in Popular and Erotic Fiction
Anna Watz
Positive Images: Gay Men and HIV/AIDS in the Popular Culture of 'Post-Crisis'
Dion Kagan
Queer Horror Film and Television: Sexuality and Masculinity at the Margins
Darren Elliott-Smith
Queer Sexualities in Early Film: Cinema and Male-Male Intimacy
Shane Brown
Steampunk: Gender and the Neo-Victorian
Claire Nally
Television Comedy and Femininity: Queering Gender
Rosie White
Television, Technology and Gender: New Platforms and New Audiences
Sarah Arnold
Tweenhood: Femininity and Celebrity in Tween Popular Culture
Melanie Kennedy

Sujata Moorti and Lisa Cuklanz

ALL-AMERICAN TV CRIME DRAMA

FEMINISM AND IDENTITY POLITICS IN *LAW & ORDER: SPECIAL VICTIMS UNIT*

BLOOMSBURY ACADEMIC
LONDON • NEW YORK • OXFORD • NEW DELHI • SYDNEY

BLOOMSBURY ACADEMIC
Bloomsbury Publishing Plc
50 Bedford Square, London, WC1B 3DP, UK
1385 Broadway, New York, NY 10018, USA
29 Earlsfort Terrace, Dublin 2, Ireland

BLOOMSBURY, BLOOMSBURY ACADEMIC and the Diana logo
are trademarks of Bloomsbury Publishing Plc

First published in Great Britain by I.B. Tauris 2017
Paperback edition published by Bloomsbury Academic 2022

Copyright © Sujata Moorti and Lisa Cuklanz, 2017

Sujata Moorti and Lisa Cuklanz have asserted their right under the Copyright, Designs and Patents Act, 1988, to be identified as authors of this work.

For legal purposes the Acknowledgements on p. ix constitute
an extension of this copyright page.

All rights reserved. No part of this publication may be reproduced or transmitted in any form or by any means, electronic or mechanical, including photocopying, recording, or any information storage or retrieval system, without prior permission in writing from the publishers.

Bloomsbury Publishing Plc does not have any control over, or responsibility for, any third-party websites referred to or in this book. All internet addresses given in this book were correct at the time of going to press. The author and publisher regret any inconvenience caused if addresses have changed or sites have ceased to exist, but can accept no responsibility for any such changes.

A catalogue record for this book is available from the British Library.

A catalog record for this book is available from the Library of Congress.

ISBN: HB: 978-1-7845-3429-5
PB: 978-1-3502-5895-2
ePDF: 978-1-7867-3161-6
ePUB: 978-1-7867-2161-7

Series: Library of Gender and Popular Culture

To find out more about our authors and books visit
www.bloomsbury.com and sign up for our newsletters.

Contents

	Acknowledgments	ix
	List of Figures	xi
	Series Editors' Foreword	xiii
	Introduction: All-American Crime Drama	1
1	A Very American Story	14
2	Family Matters: Criminal Mothers and Fathers	50
3	The Violence of Race	75
4	A Foreign Affair: The Global Turn to Gaze at the Self	105
5	Images of Truth: The Science of Detection	134
6	Paratexts and the Afterlife of *SVU*	170
	Conclusion: The Story Continues	201
	Notes	208
	Bibliography	234
	Index	246

Acknowledgments

This manuscript has had a long history and there are a number of people whose contributions have made it possible. We want to thank audiences in the numerous places we presented our research for their comments and suggestions.

Our research assistants have helped us keep track of the 350-odd episodes and the paratextual elements that proliferate on the internet. Thank you Laverne Blackman, Christine Bachman-Sanders, Jackie Park, Emily Pedowitz, Alex Strott and Erin Work at Middlebury College, as well as Shauyi Tai, Erin Maloney, Katharine Burkland, Rebecca Kelly, Christine Suchy and Emily Mervosh at Boston College.

The time required for much of the research and writing for this manuscript was generously supported through a Research Incentive Grant at Boston College. A significant portion of this manuscript was crafted in the Allen Room of the New York Public Library. Thank you Jay Barksdale for making this possible. Thanks also to the numerous interlocutors who helped us refine our arguments.

Above all, we thank our families for their patience as we worked through this manuscript and seemingly never-ending episodes of *SVU*.

List of Figures

1.1	Detectives Eliot Stabler and Olivia Benson, the protagonist cop-duo for the first 12 seasons.	19
1.2	A DVD cover displaying the *SVU* ensemble cast from the first season.	27
1.3	The recurring cast from seasons 4–5.	28
1.4	The new cast from season 15.	29
3.1	Tennis superstar Serena Williams appeared in 'Brotherhood' (5: 12) as Chloe Spears, a college basketball player.	79
3.2	In 'Ballerina' (10: 16), renowned actor-comedian Carol Burnett appeared as a retired ballerina.	80
3.3	Former boxing champion and convicted rapist Mike Tyson appeared as a guest actor in 'Monster's Legacy' (14: 13).	88
5.1	Medical Examiner Melinda Warner often provides scientific backing to the detectives' hunches.	138
5.2	Actor-comedian Kathy Griffin guest stars as leader of the lesbian activist group LesBeStrong in 'P. C.' (11: 13).	164
6.1	Mariska Hargitay's image from the opening credits in the first season.	173
6.2	The youthful feminine image of Hargitay featured in the first season was replaced with a more masculine style, popular with some fans, in season 3.	173
6.3	Hargitay's image in the opening credits of season 15.	174
6.4	This image from the episode 'Loss' (5: 4) features an intimate gaze between Olivia Benson and Alex Cabot, alibied by Benson's effort to staunch the flow of blood from Alex's shoulder after a gunshot wound from close range.	190

Series Editors' Foreword

The Library of Gender and Popular Culture presents a critical engagement with a variety of media, including TV, films, magazine culture and internet phenomena. In Sujata Moorti and Lisa Cuklanz's study, we witness the ways in which media representations of sexual assault and the penal system feature in the NBC series *Law & Order: Special Victims Unit*. As with many of the books in this Library, this study is enhanced by the positioning of the fictional texts in their production and 'real world' contexts. The research presented here asks some key questions about women's representation in the modern world, and addresses the anxieties associated with sexual violence and trauma as represented in US popular culture. As we progress through the twenty-first century, such issues are increasingly important: internet interventions such as Everyday Victim Blaming (http://everydayvictimblaming.com) and the SlutWalk campaigns testify to the pressing issue of violence against women, whilst the concept of rape culture has entered our critical and popular cultural vocabulary. As such, this volume in our series is a fascinating and timely account of the nexus between media, women and gendered violence.

– Angela Smith and Claire Nally

Introduction

All-American Crime Drama

Over the past few years, public discussions of rape and sexual assault have become quite commonplace in the US. These conversations have bubbled up around spectacular instances of sexual violence, such as the Abu Ghraib scandal or the Jerry Sandusky case, as well as more general and ongoing issues, such as the prevalence of sexual assaults on college campuses. The debates that have dominated the media have tried to disentangle the causes for the prevalence of sexual assault from the experiences of victims and have also sought to formulate some solutions to what has often been described as an 'epidemic.' Very seldom do these media representations explicitly spell out the ways feminist ideas have shaped the contours of these discussions. The long-running NBC series *Law & Order: Special Victims Unit* (hereafter *SVU*) echoes these conversations even as it seems to have initiated some of them. In September 1999, when the series first aired, *SVU* appeared daring and unique for realigning the police procedural by focusing exclusively on crimes pertaining to sexual assaults. Critics dismissed the series as trite and sensational and few of the early reviewers could have predicted its resilience and continued success 16 years later. Its signature features seem to have seeped into the weft and warp of millennial popular culture. Over its long run *SVU* has offered sensational and sobering accounts of the prevalence of sexual assaults in the US; the series has tracked the shifts in legal definitions as well as the problems associated with the penal system. These fictional narratives of sexual assault have, on a weekly basis, asserted that the police and legal systems offer the best, if flawed, possible solutions. *SVU* offers a wealth of information about American understandings of sexual violence and possible ways to address it. This book hones in on *SVU* to offer an understanding of the prevalent media images of sexual assault and equally importantly of the police procedural, a television staple.

With its putative focus on solving crimes of sexual assault and rape, *SVU* is different from other police procedurals primarily because it engages with a topic that has been of enduring concern for feminists. *SVU*'s popularity raises important questions about how the detective genre accommodates a weekly chronicling of sexual violence, trauma, and victimization. Can we read the thematizing of rape in *SVU* as an achievement of the goals of twentieth-century women's movements? Does this televisual representation signify a new understanding of sex and sexuality? Does *SVU* alter taken-for-granted understandings of the prime time series? We contend that *SVU* has become a key site from which new understandings of sexual violence are being crafted, and this is the primary focus of our analysis in the chapters that follow. *SVU* reflects simultaneously twentieth century and millennial transformations in social responses to sexual assaults. The series sutures together a multiplicity of feminist understandings of sexual violence with anti-feminist meanings to articulate a theory wherein the term sexual assault becomes a capacious category of crime but the definition of the sexual criminal remains slippery.

Set in New York City the series speaks to American anxieties and American attitudes. Yet, *SVU* has been enormously popular outside the US, so much so that a Russian production company purchased the rights to create an adaptation of the series. Most viewers around the world, however, watch the American show on NBC affiliates or the internet; there is a significant body of scholarship examining its popularity in countries such as South Korea. It is intriguing that a series centered not just on the US but specifically New York City would find resonance outside. We set aside these questions in our analysis. Instead, we offer a symptomatic reading of the episodes to tease out themes relevant to our analysis. Internet sites and various social media offer a detailed accounting of all of the minutiae

Introduction

pertinent to the series. We do not aspire to compete with them or offer a hagiographic account of the series. *All-American TV Crime Drama* offers a critical reading of the series: tracking how *SVU*'s engagement with rape and sexual violence has shifted over the course of 16 seasons, exploring how its representations of 'identity issues' – that is gender, race, national identity, and sexuality – have altered, and mapping the ways in which shifting media ecologies have shaped the narratives.

SVU is an American prime time series par excellence. A spinoff of the popular *Law & Order* series, it is shaped by the institutional imperatives of commercial network television. Each episode runs between 42 and 44 minutes; each scripted storyline is constructed to accommodate at least five commercial breaks and the pacing is designed to ensure that audiences return after the breaks. Hewing close to the rules of episodic television, most of the narrative arcs are contained within the space of a single storyline. During ratings seasons though the storylines inevitably include cliffhanger endings. *SVU* is a melodrama in that it rehearses repeatedly the contestation between good and evil; it also stages the restoration of the social order. The storylines are a curious mix of the lurid aspects typical of 'true crime' stories and dazzling displays of new forms of criminality. As an enduring police procedural *SVU* reveals how network programming has responded to the innovations offered by cable and internet productions. Its visual grammar has been altered by the changing media ecology. Although *SVU* has eschewed the aesthetics of the glossy, color-saturated crime drama, starting in season 13, the series finally switched to digital film. In narrative terms, episodes have started to play with temporality and have started to enfold multiple storylines. Above all, with its continued focus on the prosecution of sexual assaults the series offers insights into current definitions of crime and criminality. It makes no claims to being realistic, but like any popular culture product it offers insight into dominant understandings. Its portrayal of sexual criminality and victimhood resonates with a significant portion of the television viewing audience. Like the larger society from which it emanates, *SVU* reveals who has the power to seek justice, who lacks the power to defend themselves against accusations of sexual criminality, who can seek immunity from the law, and so on. In short, *SVU* limns the prevailing contours of social citizenship. It is for these reasons that we call *SVU* an All-American TV crime drama; it addresses sexual crimes from within the perspective of the well-defined contours of the American police procedural.

Produced by Dick Wolf, the series makes no pretensions to being new or innovative. Instead *SVU* thrives in its adherence to the rules of prime time programming. Wolf rejects the term 'franchise' to describe the panoply of programming bearing the *Law & Order* title. He prefers the term 'brand,' instead, and has sought longevity and profits. Wolf's business acumen has ensured that his 'brand' has developed a life outside of network television.[1] It is commonplace to joke that on any given weekend one could watch wall-to-wall *SVU* episodes. Thus, one must reckon with *SVU* not just as a network production, but as one that has acquired sturdy legs beyond its initial broadcast. Over the last decade the series and NBC have become adept at using social media such as Twitter and Facebook to 'create a buzz' about *SVU* episodes. This marketing apparatus in conjunction with fan-audience productions has created an *SVU* transmedia world that has shaped our analysis.

Although the show is associated with Wolf, no single author can be credited for its episodes since they are products of an ensemble of numerous writers and production staffers. Neal Baer was the showrunner for 12 years and his training as a medical doctor has shaped some of the storylines. Similarly, the new showrunner Warren Leight brings his experiences in theater to bear on the more recent seasons. As we discuss in the chapters that follow, the staff have been very nimble in incorporating current affairs into the storylines. They have also woven in the latest scientific findings about diseases and trauma. These flourishes give the series a continual sense of newness and vibrancy.

SVU has increasingly become associated with the figure of the lead protagonist Detective (now Sergeant) Olivia Benson, played by Mariska Hargitay. While the series has not been critically acclaimed, Hargitay and other actors have been praised repeatedly for their skill. Hargitay has received numerous awards for her performance as the Lead Actress in a Drama Series. More recently, though, as *SVU* has continued to be renewed television critics have started to praise it as 'nuanced' and as offering a 'meta-commentary on pop culture, contributing intelligent, critical dialogue to the sensationalised current events it appropriates' and calling attention 'to our cultural lust for violence.'[2] Others have singled out its portrayal of sexual assault as being, 'at once prurient and cathartic, exploitative and liberating.'³ Yet, amid these graphic depictions of violence Olivia Benson, the lone remaining cast member of the original ensemble, has remained a touchstone figure, resilient and vulnerable. This female lead figure is unique within the context of US crime drama and the broader landscape of American network programming. In the chapters that follow, we discuss the significance of her character in greater detail.

Mapping the Book

How does one write about a series such as *SVU* with over 350 episodes? How do we contain the analysis? Where do we draw the boundaries? This project began a long time ago and its publication is homage to the continued relevance of the long-lived prime time series. When it first started we were both intrigued in different ways by the possibility of an entertainment show centered on sexual violence. We were trepidatious about the series' capacity to depict sexual violence: how would *SVU* entice viewers to make a weekly commitment to watch sexual assault; would it sensationalize rape; would it undo years of feminist activism; would it make television headlines by crafting a new grammar for representational practice? Over its tenure, we can now say yes and no to most of the preceding questions.

Working from within the interdisciplinary fields of cultural studies and feminist media studies, our analysis teases out the affective power of the show. Analyzing the specificity of *SVU* narratives, our book engages with interlocutors in feminist and queer theories, critical race theories, as well as theories of popular culture. While theoretically grounded, thick textual and visual analyses serve to highlight the televisual codes that characterize contemporary crime dramas. In *SVU*, crime becomes the fertile terrain from which contemporary attitudes toward feminism are articulated. We signal how the storylines become the staging ground for new, millennial understandings of sexual violence. An individual episode may privilege one (or more) particular definition of feminism. Cumulatively though *SVU* offers a cacophony of feminisms. It hews neither to the tenets of postfeminist television nor backlash feminism. The prime time series has become a key site of popular culture where feminist opinions are aired, even if they are ultimately disavowed.

We concur with numerous television scholars who have cautioned against attributing a singular meaning to any show. Especially in a series of this length, we contend that inevitably the meanings and visions generated by *SVU* are polymorphous and heterogeneous. Depending on the axis of analysis taken to examine *SVU*, the viewer will find new understandings of rape, national identity, and citizenship. Thus in each of the chapters that follow we have honed in on one particular entry point into the series in order to interrogate how it addresses sexual assaults, the kinds of feminisms the storylines engage with, and the resulting understanding of crime, criminality, and justice. For instance, in Chapter 2, 'Family Matters' we examine episodes that focus on sexual assaults within families to underscore the ways in which the series gives voice to a misogynist feminism. In Chapters 3 and 4, we turn our analysis to episodes that highlight race and global concerns, respectively. Since *SVU* has successfully competed with a raft of forensic dramas, in Chapter 5 we analyze how the series engages with questions of scientific truth and illustrate how this perspective affords a new understanding of popular culture's quest for certitude on the vexing questions of race, gender, and sexuality. Such an engagement with different vectors of analysis offers a rich and provocative reading of the series and is particularly suitable for a show of *SVU*'s durability. This multifaceted analysis, along with the paratexts that we examine in Chapter 6, also sheds light on the particularities of contemporary prime time television programming.

Chapter Outline

In the first chapter, 'A Very American Story,' we offer a broad overview of the series and its signature features, situating these characteristics within a broader televisual landscape. We also map out the shifts in social understandings and laws related to rape. We single out the ways in which today's neoliberal policies have had an impact on sexual assaults. Since *SVU* is a police procedural we offer a brief context of the debate about prison policies and the discussions about punishment that have come to dominate in the US. This chapter lays the groundwork for the detailed analyses that follow. We illustrate why *SVU* is a useful vantage point from which to observe the formation of a new theory of sexual violence; one that emerges from the contestation between the residual feminisms of the 1970s and the emergent neoliberal millennial feminism.

In the second chapter, 'Family Matters: Criminal Mothers and Fathers,' by using gender as the point of entry into narratives we direct readers' attention to the multiplicity of feminisms the series engages with. Feminists have long pointed out that the domestic realm has been a key institution for the maintenance of patriarchy. Contradicting sentimental claims of the joys of the hearth and the home, feminists have highlighted the power imbalances central to family structures, especially in the context of sexual assaults. At first glance, *SVU* seems to have incorporated rigorously these insights. Storylines repeatedly thematize the family as the primary site of gendered violence, with children as the victims. However, a closer analysis reveals that there is a twist in this feminist parable. In *SVU* episodes, it is the mother figure who is often criminalized, producing what we call the monstrous maternal. When there is an abusive father, he is often exonerated for the crimes he commits against children. Through a comparative analysis of episodes featuring criminal fathers and mothers we show that in *SVU* women's maternal power has much more potential to harm, whereas fathers' damages to their children are more distant, more limited, or more marginalized. The family-centered storylines become a key site from which the series articulates a misogynist feminism, an understanding of the causes of sexual assault that borrows from feminism even as it denigrates femininity. In addition, a number of storylines engage with anti-feminist ideas about sexual assault and often present men as the victims of feminism.

The next two chapters need to be read together if we wish to comprehend the role race and racial difference play in the series over the seasons. *SVU* storylines engage with a predominantly white cast; multicultural New York City is often relegated to a colorful backdrop for the actions of the detectives. In Chapter 3, 'The Violence of Race,' we single out the ways in which the series, operating within this limited scenario, represents the intersections of race, gender, and sexual violence. By examining the series' engagement with issues of race and racism, we argue that *SVU* advocates a color-blind feminism; individual storylines help resurrect insidious myths about rapists of color even as they seemingly disavow them. Women of color are for the most part absent in *SVU*; if they appear it is most often as silent or already dead victims. Men of color are portrayed in more problematic ways but most often very sympathetically. The form of race-thinking *SVU* promotes makes sense only when we juxtapose it with the series' depiction of the foreign criminal (and victim). In Chapter 4, 'A Foreign Affair: The Global Turn to Gaze at the Self,' we focus on the limited number of storylines that engage with a global concern. In storylines from the post 9/11 era, the foreigner becomes the site through which the series articulates a number of American anxieties. We contend that the figure of the foreign criminal becomes a site of displacement, as domestic concerns about race and racism are sublimated onto the body of the foreign criminal. Through this process, the series helps naturalize the surveillance practices and the policing gaze characteristic of the millennial security state. Simultaneously, the foreign victim is repeatedly presented as someone who needs to be rescued and brought into the embrace of a liberal, global sisterhood. The race episodes and the global episodes together reveal the limited ways in which the series repackages old ideas about the US as an exceptional state. Our analyses in these chapters underscore the ways in which national identity mediates *SVU*'s understanding of sexual assault. Together these two sections highlight the productive ways in which *SVU* taps into a variety of feminist understandings of sexual assault.

The three chapters that examine the series' content through the lenses of gender, race, and national identity underscore forcefully *SVU*'s capacity to generate a multiplicity of meanings. Feminists have long focused on the intersections of gender, race, and class to understand the multifaceted nature of oppression and inequality. We have instead devoted a chapter each to underline how *SVU*'s engagement with feminism, feminist concerns about sexual assault, and its definition of sexual assault radically shifts and morphs when the storyline centers on gender, race, or national differences. In the remainder of the book, we return to these themes but also highlight how the series has responded to changes in the media ecology, shifts in network programming, and the impact of new technologies.

SVU's long run has accompanied the growth of popular forensic crime dramas such as *NCIS* and *CSI*. While *SVU* remains committed to the gritty police procedural, it too participates in a mode of science-thinking which promotes an optical empiricism. In Chapter 5, 'Images of Truth: The Science of Detection,' we highlight the ways in which the series turns to images of science to secure its truth claims about crime and criminality. By repeatedly airing storylines that argue that criminal activity is the result of one's brain configuration, the series resurrects the idea of biology as destiny. In effect the series undoes the feminist adage that rape is about power and instead it re-centers a biological explanation of the rapist as an exceptional, perverted individual. We single out the ways in which *SVU* uses 'realistic' images of science to mobilize these arguments. These ideas about biological claims of difference are highlighted in the few *SVU* episodes that engage with trans subjects. In these storylines, images of the brain are mobilized to highlight the truth about sex differences. The scientific optic is largely invisible in storylines engaging with gay subjects and instead the series participates in a broader discourse of tolerance. Cumulatively, these episodes offer a nuanced account of sexuality but resurrect binarized ideas about sex, sexual identity, and gender difference. Specifically in this chapter, we highlight *SVU*'s capacious definition of sexual assault and the complicated ways in which the series continually engages with the entanglements of feminist and anti-feminist understandings.

Over the course of the lengthy run of *SVU*, a wide range of audience responses has emerged. Chapter 6, 'Paratexts and the Afterlife of *SVU*,' outlines some of the many forms of participatory culture, paratexts, and popular culture responses to *SVU*, including lesbian fan fiction, Mariska Hargitay's Joyful Heart Foundation website, social media engagements, and Lisa Jackson's HBO documentary *Sex Crimes Unit* (2011). The chapter illustrates the tremendous breadth of audience responses as well as the ways in which the series itself has engaged with feminist discourses. We show here the significant afterlife of the series in a range of forms and influences through productions within popular and participatory cultures.

We recognize *SVU*'s status as a prime time network program. Expecting a popular series from a commercial network to offer a coherent feminist perspective would be foolhardy. Nevertheless throughout this project we have resisted the urge to recast *SVU* as ventriloquizing the dominant ideology. In the conclusion we reiterate the multiple ways in which the series engages with feminist ideas. Even in episodes where the storyline's conclusion may endorse anti-feminist understandings, we highlight the series' ability to simultaneously air feminist viewpoints. From within this cacophony of feminisms the series crafts an internally contradictory millennial theory of sexual assault. This prime time theory of sexual assault is inchoate and protean. It emerges from a heady entanglement of a range of feminisms and anti-feminist ideas about gender, sexuality, and sexual assaults. As we underscore repeatedly in our analysis, individual episodes foreground one of several competing understandings of sexual assault. Similarly the majority of episodes clearly identify victim and victimizer, even as the storylines offer a number of causes of sexual assault. In the accretion of storylines over the seasons, *SVU* has created an understanding of sexual assault as a 'heinous' crime but is less clear on identifying a criminal. The series has highlighted constituent elements of rape culture and has cultivated skepticism towards a range of social institutions by highlighting their capacity for creating the conditions where sexual assaults become possible. Such ambivalence would normally be praiseworthy because it hints at the complexity of sexual assault, something that cannot be neatly resolved in the space of 44 minutes. However, the generic limits of the crime drama which push towards a moral resolution also help produce a key element of *SVU*'s theory of sexual assault: it is a crime without a criminal or at best an ill-defined and unpunished criminal. To be clear, the majority of *SVU* episodes conclude with the apprehension of a criminal, but by highlighting a number of institutions and structures that contribute to rape culture and remain unpunished, in its totality the series cultivates the sense of sexual assault as a crime with no end in sight and with an ill-defined cause. In the pages that follow, we flesh out how the crime drama arrives at this paradoxical position.

An Emblematic Episode

As we completed this manuscript, in February 2015, *SVU* aired an episode, 'Devastating Story,' thematizing sexual assaults on US college campuses. The storyline borrowed liberally from an ongoing news scandal: *Rolling Stone* magazine had published in December 2014 a cover story entitled 'Rape: A Campus Story.' The essay offered a searing account of a University of Virginia student's gang rape at a fraternity party. Building on the nationwide conversation about the inadequate responses within higher education institutions, the essay's publication resulted in news media engagement with the concept of rape culture. The University of Virginia suspended the fraternity cited in the essay and conducted a belated investigation into the rape charge. In the weeks following the publication of the essay, journalists from other news outlets started to pick holes in the account. By February 2015 the essay had been discredited completely for its shoddy journalism. *Rolling Stone* withdrew the essay, the University of Virginia reinstated the suspended fraternity, and rape counselors warned of potential negative consequences on rape claimants.

'Devastating Story' dipped into this toxic brew of shoddy journalism and contestations over rape, while borrowing elements from other ongoing news events. The *SVU* account has a young college student reluctant to press charges against her rapists, who are members of a popular fraternity and of the hockey team. But propelled by the interests of an unscrupulous television news host and the guidance of a feminist professor, the student's version of a gang rape is publicized. The chief of police orders Special Victims Unit detectives to investigate a case in which no formal charges are made. The ensuing storyline echoes many of the themes that followed the publication of the *Rolling Stone* essay. Significantly, the episode initially limns the contours of rape culture, the inadequacies of campus responses to sexual assault claims, and the virulent forms of masculinity that often prevail in fraternities. As the rape claimant's account is called into question, the narrative shifts to wholeheartedly condemn the feminist professor. The episode permits the series to offer a meta-commentary on news media practices; it condemns the sensational practices of television journalism even as the series positions itself on a higher moral ground. For the purposes of our analysis what is more relevant is the singular attention paid to the feminist professor, who served as an informal advocate to the rape claimant. Professor Dillon is distinguished from the rest of the predominantly white cast by her hatred of men and her ability to throw around terms such as 'phallocentric choice of language' at the SVU detectives. By the narrative's end 'Devastating Story' draws audience sympathies for the college student who appears to have been sexually assaulted but is unable to seek judicial redress because she let herself be duped by Professor Dillon. The feminist professor is presented as ruthless in her desire to eliminate rape culture and quite uninterested in the particular circumstances of the rape claimant: 'It doesn't matter what happened to her. What matters is it happens every day … This isn't about the boys. This is bigger than all of us. This is about eliminating rape culture once and for all.' In her disregard for truth and justice, pursuits central to the crime drama, the feminist professor emerges in 'Devastating Story' as the real problem. The fraternity members are presented as having their reputations damaged beyond repair, while the feminist professor's unscrupulous desire to change rape culture helped 'set the clock back 30 years.' In striking contrast to Professor Dillon, Olivia Benson is self-reflexive, attentive to her faults, and, above all, consistently concerned about the welfare of the rape claimant. The sergeant is the caring, protective persona who embodies an ideal police force.

This ability of the series to air within the space of a single episode multiple understandings of sexual assault, engendering sympathy for victims even as it encourages skepticism toward rape claims, and ultimately presenting the police and the judiciary as the bulwarks against crime, are the elements that draw us to *SVU*. In the following chapters, we pay specific attention to how the series represents sexual crime and criminality. In 'Devastating Story' the nature of crime and criminality shift over the course of the episode. At the onset, young, white men and college administrators are presented as criminals and the series airs mainstream understandings of sexual assault that were first publicized by the 1970s women's movement. By episode's end though the immoral actor in the storyline turns out to be an overzealous feminist, who unlike the SVU detectives is unconcerned by real crime but more interested in righting the wrongs of patriarchy. This episode encapsulates for us some of the key ideas we want to capture in the book: how *SVU* depicts sexual assault, rape victims' claims, and feminist understandings of gender-based violence as well as judicial responses. 'Devastating Story' presents the rape claimant *and* her assailants as sympathetic and repugnant figures, they are each simultaneously victim and victimizer, caught in a web of gender politics not of their own making. The rape claimant transforms her experience of an acquaintance rape into a sensational gang rape to gain the attention of the media and campus administrators. The fraternity residents adhere to rigid codes of violent masculinity and are also victimized by an overzealous judicial system (and feminist ideology) that seeks quick solutions to a deeply entrenched cultural problem. All of the characters in the episode, except for the SVU detectives, are distasteful figures. 'Devastating Story' is emblematic of how the series pits multiple understandings of sexual assault against each other.

Introduction

At the end of 44 minutes, men, women, feminism, and new media technologies are all depicted as contributing factors in contemporary rape culture. Sexual assault itself emerges as a crime without a real criminal. In this book we trace how a series about rape crafts this millennial theory of sexual assault, a crime with multiple causal factors but no individual, identifiable criminal. As we document in the chapters that follow, the series' depiction of rape has not remained static. Rather, we believe that in the early seasons *SVU* was forthright in voicing a liberal feminist position. More recently though, even as the series airs feminist voices it undermines them by producing a fungible definition of sexual violence.

A few stylistic clarifications are required. The series and the detective squad are both referenced as Special Victims Unit (SVU). When we refer to the series we italicize the term *SVU*, but when we address the squad per se the term remains without italics. When we isolate a single storyline we include the name followed by information in parentheses about the season it appeared and the episode number within that season. Thus, 'Devastating Story' would be referenced as 'Devastating Story' (16: 14). As is true with many forms of popular culture, we are concerned with allusions to events and ideas that may no longer hold currency; this is a particularly acute concern in the case of *SVU*, which draws on and reworks contemporary news events. Rather than provide a long explanation of the original event, as we have done previously, we have posted citations in our notes directing readers to additional materials. In the following chapters, we map out the different vectors along which the series engages with feminist ideas about sexual assault.

1

A Very American Story

Hi my name is Alexis I'm 10. Ive been a big Law & Order svu fan my entire life. and the woman who plays Olivia Benson (Mariska Hargitay) really inspires me to try my hardest to achieve my dreams and when I'm older I wanna come to newyork and work in the svu squad.and if you know her or if she sees this I want her to know that her character made me who I am today. She made me strong and independent before that I was so shy but she made me get rid of that shy person ...[1]

This fan comment in a feminist magazine encapsulates the structure of appreciation that has evolved for *SVU*. Although the youth of the fan may be unusual, the emotions she evokes offer some explanation for the series' continuing success 18 years after it was first launched in 1999. The admiration for the female detective and the work conducted by this once largely unknown branch of the police propels our analysis in this book. By virtue of its focus on sexual assault, the series engages with feminist concerns. Rather than espouse a consistent stance towards feminism, the series has offered a multitude of positions, sometimes hostile to the ideology and the women's movement and at other times permitting a prime time airing of feminist ways of thinking about how the body, violence, and sex intersect. It is this complicated engagement with feminism that renders *SVU* remarkable. This prime time series has become a site from which a new millennial understanding of sexual violence, albeit inchoate and protean, is being crafted.

In the chapters that follow, we contend that *SVU* offers a cacophony of feminist understandings of sexual violence while operating within a postfeminist televisual setting, one that assumes that feminist goals have been attained and so sexism is impossible. The makers of the series do not espouse a feminist stance, but through the narration of sexual assaults individual episodes engage with the ideology that has enabled such a discussion. Due to its longevity, *SVU* is a site from which we can observe shifting understandings of sexual assault, from an era when the slogans 'No means No' and 'rape is about power, not sex' dominated public discussions to more recent conversations about 'legitimate' rape. The series offers a vantage point from which to observe how neoliberal societies address feminism, crime, and the state. As we discuss later in this chapter, the tendency to privatize state functions in neoliberal societies has produced new understandings of sexual violence. Similarly, the feminism that has emerged under such conditions, neoliberal feminism, centers on a subject who accepts full responsibility for her own well being and self care with no expectation of structural change.[2]

In a television landscape that has changed dramatically since its debut season, it is easy to forget that *SVU* marked the beginning of the crime drama franchise, a phenomenon that exploded with the popularity of *CSI* (CBS, 2000–2015) and *NCIS* (CBS, 2003–present). Buoyed by the success of the original *Law & Order* series, NBC asked producer Dick Wolf for a spinoff, which resulted in *SVU*, a scripted series dedicated to crimes of sexual assault and rape. In the 18 years that followed, the original *Law & Order* series as well as various other spinoffs have gone off the air but *SVU* maintains its popularity and is the lone remnant of a once thriving *Law & Order* franchise.[3] *SVU* was recently extended for a seventeenth season, making it one of the longest-running prime time series in US television.

With its 'ripped from the headlines' storylines, *SVU* centers on cases undertaken by a police unit modeled after the New York City Police Department's Special Victims Unit.[4] Although in recent seasons, the storylines have devoted considerable time to the judicial processes involved in prosecuting crimes of sexual assault, *SVU* remains primarily a police procedural. Shot on location in New York City, *SVU* shares several of the signature elements of the franchise: scene-setting labeling accompanied by the chung-chung, two-note signature sound; hand-held camerawork; sudden shifts in scenes; and 'the succession of close-up interview scenes that begin in media res.'[5] The solemn voice over that begins every episode declares the gravity of the crimes under consideration:

> In the criminal justice system, sexually-based offenses are considered especially heinous. In New York City, the dedicated detectives who investigate these vicious felonies are members of an elite squad known as the Special Victims Unit. These are their stories.

In the 44-minute storylines that follow, the series has seemingly explored every possible variation on the phrase sexual assault; it has tackled hot-button issues and adopted controversial positions in narrating sexual violence. The appeal of a weekly narration of sexual assault has now been well established, but the longevity of the series is derived as well from the franchise's unique syndication policy, repurposing, whereby episodes are first aired on the network and later on the USA cable channel.[6] In this book, we parse out some of the ways the series maintains viewer interest.

Rising from a Stupor

In the US, *Law & Order* (1990–2010) is credited with reviving network interest in crime dramas. While this genre has been a staple of television schedules, since the 1990s crime dramas have populated the prime time program in greater numbers (competing with reality television shows for viewers) and have addressed crime and punishment through a range of innovations.[7] Scholars have contended that the efflorescence of this genre in the new millennium serves as a public forum to work 'through the trauma of living in a violent culture.'[8] Crime dramas are symptomatic of a wound culture, wherein the very notion of sociality is bound to the public display of torn and wounded bodies. They are representative of a pathological public sphere, in which stranger intimacy and vicarious violation become models of sociality.[9] Others argue that contemporary crime dramas address the war on terror not so much as a political question but as a mode of addressing a visceral threat to the nation.[10] These assessments have produced significant scholarly debate. For our purposes, what is most relevant is that crime dramas and their popularity are inciting widespread academic and network interest. These television programs speak to and reflect prevalent structures of feeling.

Law & Order established certain features that have become key to television crime drama in the ensuing two decades. The ripped-from-the-headlines narrative style, which the series proudly proclaimed, helped modify the crime drama genre. The franchise pivots on storywriters' ability to cull news stories for ideas of crime and criminality. Although the writers modify the news events, often melding a few in a single episode, the franchise does not hide its indebtedness to 'true crime.' Consequently, the storylines tend to focus on the unique and the exceptional. These journalistic qualities are the bedrock of the franchise's claims to realism. Ironically, each episode includes a disclaimer that characterizes the storyline as fictional in that it 'does not depict any actual person or event.'[11] The hand-held cameras and the focus on gray, gritty New York locales compound the sense of verisimilitude. Apart from these stylistic innovations, narratively the original *Law & Order* addressed in a single episode the policing and judicial aspects of crime solving, thus offering insights into the multifaceted 'war on crime' waged in the US. Often the storylines offered none of the satisfaction of moral resolution normally associated with crime dramas; the police always apprehended a culprit but the legal processes inevitably revealed the systemic nature of the problem (or at least the shared responsibility for the problem). Further, unlike previous crime dramas the original *Law & Order* eschewed any exploration of the private lives of its protagonists; the ensemble cast sought audience identification through their job performance (as cops and lawyers). Each episode was self-contained with no loose threads or continuing plot lines.

SVU is distinguished from other crime dramas and *Law & Order* by its subject matter, which reprised decades-long feminist discussions of violence against women. In addition, this spinoff series was primarily concerned with the detectives who pursue crime and criminals. *SVU* also marks its difference from other series in the franchise by highlighting the effects of the job on its protagonists' private lives. Increasingly, too, individual narratives are not contained within the space of a single episode. In effect, *SVU* offers a significant variation on the signature features of the franchise even as it maintains continuity with the genre.

Rewriting a Masculine Genre

SVU has used its casting choices as well to rewrite the format of the televised crime drama. For the first 12 seasons, the male–female cop protagonists of Detectives Elliot Stabler (Chris Meloni) and Olivia Benson (Mariska Hargitay) marked a radical shift in televised police procedurals (see Figure 1.1). Since season 15, Benson has been promoted as the commander of the squad. In 2015, there are other television policewomen who head departments but the gender shift in leadership is still significant in terms of the police procedural, as we discuss below.[12]

When crime dramas migrated from radio to television in the 1950s, they featured the lone male cop trying to restore the social order by tracking down evil (*Dragnet*, NBC, 1951–9, 1967–70 and *Untouchables*, ABC, 1959–63). These shows provided audiences with an insider's perspective into the world of detection – the storylines foregrounded organizational structures, the jargon used by the police as well as the technical and legal concerns that shaped cop work. While the early shows were whodunits, by revealing the identity of the criminal at the beginning and spending an entire episode divulging how the crime was committed and how the police would arrest the criminal, *Columbo* (NBC, 1971–8; ABC 1989–2003) offered a different perspective within this well-established genre. Steven Bochco's *Hill Street Blues* (NBC, 1981–7) offered the next major innovation to the genre. Instead of foregrounding a single police officer, *Hill Street Blues* offered viewers an ensemble cast of recurring characters. Any given episode was devoted to a number of intertwining storylines and the show thematized the blurred boundaries between the home and the work sphere. Drawn by the popularity of *Hill Street Blues*, many cop shows started to feature ensemble casts, however *Cagney & Lacey* (CBS, 1982–8) and *Miami Vice* (NBC, 1984–9) foregrounded a cop duo as their protagonists. The dual protagonist narrative device permits storylines to explore the tensions generated by a pair of mismatched police officers with radically different temperaments working together on a case. *Cagney & Lacey*

A Very American Story

Figure 1.1: Detectives Eliot Stabler and Olivia Benson, the protagonist cop-duo for the first 12 seasons. Screenshot of *Law & Order: SVU*, NBC, 1999.

elaborated on this narrative structure by showcasing two women police officers. Responding to a number of workplace reforms initiated by the Civil Rights Act of 1964 as well as pressure from various women's groups, the CBS series illustrated how the police procedural is transformed by having two women as its lead characters. Julie D'Acci's excellent analysis of the series illuminates how the show was able to focus on the sexism women experienced within the police force and the individual difficulties they encountered in balancing work and family life.[13] By contrast *SVU* remains parsimonious in its casting innovations and exemplifies what Todd Gitlin has identified as network television's recombinant strategies, incorporating elements of a successful program with minor modifications.[14] *SVU* gambles on the popularity of the cop-duo genre even as it draws on some of the characteristic features of the ensemble cast of characters. The presence of a heterosexual pair elaborates on the teamwork and conflicts inherent in the dual cop structure, but also adds the frisson of a possible office romance.

The dual cop structure has been deployed historically to offer two contrasting personalities and their different approaches to policing. This generic conceit helps literalize the good cop–bad cop format wherein one officer is an empathetic figure while the other is dour. Such a pairing also allows shows to thematize different attitudes toward law and order institutions, with one officer adhering to the rules while the other tends to be skeptical of procedures and constantly breaks them in the pursuit of justice. Together, though, such a pairing restores faith in existing judicial systems and institutions. *SVU*'s pairing of Benson and Stabler (and later other partners) reiterates many aspects of this narrative formula. However, the two do not serve as foils to each other but throughout the series oscillate between the positions of good and bad cop. They are each skeptical of policing processes at any given point and one partner has to recuperate the other back into the fold. Once the series had established itself, storylines highlighted conflicts between the two protagonists. They are nevertheless shown as being devoted to each other. In season 7, Benson requests a new partner, believing their partnership is no longer working ('Fault' 7: 19). The two detectives are reunited soon and regain the equilibrium that characterized their professional lives until the Stabler character is written out at the end of season 12.

Olivia Benson's presence as a competent professional complicates quite dramatically the trajectory of this dual-protagonist procedural. She is introduced in the pilot episode as a newcomer to the special victims squad and yet is depicted as polished, proficient, and self-sufficient. Benson is also consistently portrayed as an empathetic and compassionate officer, zealous but seldom overbearing. Storylines repeatedly remind viewers that Benson's mother's unsolved rape, which resulted in her birth, motivates her in this difficult job. She is able to connect with victims to elicit information and to persuade reluctant victims to help the police and themselves in ways that her male counterparts are unable to achieve. The female police officer often voices feminist understandings of rape but never addresses police work from such a perspective. As was true for her television predecessors and most contemporary postfeminist television, *SVU* storylines erase any structural barriers or workplace sexism even as they highlight the struggles Benson encounters in bringing her insights and experiences to bear on her detective work.[15]

We make a brief digression here to offer some definitional clarity. The term postfeminism has acquired a chameleon-like quality over the past two decades, as scholars have struggled to demarcate changes in media representations of women and feminist discourses. In many instances, the 'post' marks a periodization, signaling a passage of time. In these understandings postfeminism refers to an ill-defined moment from the 1980s, once the so-called second wave of feminism ends. A second stream of thought uses the term to argue that central tenets of feminism have already been incorporated in society and thus sexism and misogyny are things of the past. A number of media scholars have argued for a complex understanding of the term, which has resulted in a third school of thought. These scholars signal the contradictory and contentious ways in which television representations engage with feminist concerns, entangling feminist and anti-feminist themes.[16]

Our analysis of *SVU* is designed to unpack the heterogeneous and paradoxical terrain of feminism that the series articulates, including postfeminism. We contend that *SVU*'s episodic structure and its ripped-from-the-headlines narrative style defies a singular understanding of feminism. From season to season, and episode to episode, the feminisms espoused by the series and the protagonists vary radically. Even a single character such as Benson adopts internally contradictory stances. This is perhaps most visible in the physical appearance of the female detective. In the early seasons, Benson's persona was coded as masculine. Her hair was cropped close to the contours of her face. She was always clad in monochromatic shirt and trousers, often topped with a leather bomber jacket. Over the seasons the length of her hair has grown, and for a while she appeared in dresses and accentuated her femininity. But she has since reverted to her uniform of trousers, which emphasize her authority as the chief of the unit.[17] These stylistic shifts align with particular understandings of feminism: liberal, girlie, and lean-in feminisms respectively.[18] Like most women of postfeminist noir that Linda Mizejewski analyzes, Benson is double coded in a manner that 'objectifies and fetishizes' her but also 'ascribes to her a historically specific subjectivity, power, and agency.'[19]

SVU contains the signature features of embedded feminism that Susan Douglas has isolated: there is no question that Benson and her female cohorts belong in the squad and they take for granted the gains made by feminism for women.[20] Benson rarely experiences sexism among her immediate colleagues; the squad seems to be always-already feminist. (Officers in other precincts and suspects sometimes tend to focus on her womanliness and utter sexist statements). However, within the squad Benson does not develop friendships with other women; she is presented as content with male camaraderie. For most of the series, she is also shown as being single, unable to balance professional success and a happy, domestic life. These character traits of the lonely, dedicated detective serve to shore up the cop drama genre. As the series progresses we see her grow into her position and as we write this manuscript she now heads the unit and is the mother of an infant.[21] She is also the lone remnant of the original ensemble cast and has thus become the central figure associated with the series.

There are other aspects of Benson's persona that are more problematic from a feminist perspective. In recent seasons, Benson's femaleness, her womanly body and feminine characteristics, become impediments to her work. For instance, she is abducted on a few occasions, assaulted (with the woman in distress scenario highlighted repeatedly in recent seasons), and in other instances she becomes so emotionally invested in her cases that she jeopardizes them. Benson, nevertheless, represents what Melissa Schaub has identified as the female gentleman of British detective fiction.[22] She embodies many of the characteristics associated with the middle-class masculinity central to police procedurals: she is competent, courageous, and self-reliant. She is also represented as a haunted persona, initially by her mother's rape and her desire to track down the rapist (her biological father), and throughout by her own maternal desires. In later seasons, she seeks to connect with her newly discovered half-brother. As we write this manuscript, Benson is learning to leaven her workplace responsibilities with the demands of being a parent to a young baby. Although Benson displays some of the sentimental characteristics in which televisual maternity is portrayed, as is the case for her male counterparts, parenting responsibilities make her a better detective. This lead protagonist who has become both a magnet for viewer identification and a lightning rod for audience criticism and discontent, simultaneously disrupts and maintains conventions of televisual femininity. Over the duration of the series Benson has displayed a complicated and fungible feminism.

Benson's uniqueness in a male–female cop duo gains salience through paratextual elements. When the series began in 1999, the televisual landscape lacked strong female cops. Similarly, women experienced many hurdles to success and achievement in the workplace and Benson's ability to blend seamlessly into a male-dominated arena served as a metaphor for larger social longings. Today in the audience imaginary *SVU* is closely associated with the figure of Mariska Hargitay, the actor who gained national recognition for this role.[23] The actor herself has been transformed by her role. In the early seasons she volunteered at shelters and trained as a rape crisis advocate to gain a better understanding of sexual assault victim's experiences. In 2004, she helped found the Joyful Heart Foundation, a non-profit organization geared to assist sexual assault victims. She has become a passionate advocate against wartime rape, highlighting the problem in war-torn countries. To some extent the star persona she plays on screen has merged with her off-screen life.

Overall, Benson's character embodies many elements scholars have identified as central to a postfeminist sensibility.[24] She never claims the feminist label but her very presence in the male-dominated precinct as well as the assignments she undertakes are the result of the women's movement. She is a vocal advocate for rape victims and often becomes the mouthpiece for feminist understandings of sexual assault. Simultaneously she has also been fetishized and objectified. We contend that she is one of the nodal points for the series' articulation of its complicated and heterogeneous feminisms.

The Male Foil

The good cop–bad cop formula of police procedurals requires the staging of two characters as radically different. *SVU* destabilizes this premise by not associating a particular character as the good or bad police officer but rather allowing its protagonists to cycle through these roles.[25] In any given episode, Benson and her partner occupy one of these binarized positions and all of the detectives on the squad get to play the bad cop at some point. Benson's male partners, first Stabler and then Nick Amaro (Danny Pino), have consistently been portrayed as the traditional male detective but with some important variants.

Stabler's personality underwent a dramatic arc during his tenure in the series. In the opening seasons he was depicted as a warm, loving family man, which produced some discordant intertextual meanings. When *SVU* debuted, the actor Christopher Meloni had gained critical acclaim for his role in the HBO prison drama, *Oz* (1997–2003), where he played a rapist murderer incarcerated in a maximum-security prison. In his *SVU* avatar, Meloni played a white heterosexual, a father of four children, and a Catholic who repeatedly blurred the public–private divide by introducing family concerns into the workplace. For audiences familiar with *Oz*, Stabler was the antithesis of the other character, Chris Keller. *SVU* establishes Stabler's credentials as a good cop in the pilot episode; a former Marine, he volunteered to serve in the squad because 'sexually-based crimes are a major law enforcement problem,' and he wanted to make a dent in the depravity he encountered daily.[26] Stabler thus maintained historical continuity with televisual cops such as the protagonists of *In the Heat of the Night* (CBS, 1988–1994) and *Hill Street Blues* who while cynical were nevertheless idealistic enough to believe that they and their jobs make the world a better place. Yet Stabler's character also marks several departures that made him and his successors unique.

Stabler is presented as a sensitive and complexly motivated character. Although a senior detective, he is shown repeatedly learning the new skills he needs to bring to the job to successfully pursue instances of sexual assault. His character often served as the mouthpiece through which the series articulated and generated complicated understandings of sexual assault. He is another key figure through which the series' engagements with feminism are proffered. In the totality of the series, Benson's feminism is embodied in her persona and her experiences. She also will repeat feminist mantras such as 'No means No,' but Stabler's character is the one whose consciousness is raised through the practice of detection. He learns feminist modes of understanding and thinking about sexual violence.

Stabler's experiences in the squad have shaped his family life, making him more protective of his daughters. In many instances, like Benson, Stabler too overidentified with individuals associated with a case. Thus in later seasons he was repeatedly investigated for lapses in professionalism or for ignoring police procedures in the pursuit of suspects. Stabler often undertook dangerous assignments; he was injured a number of times, and sometimes tortured, while conducting his job. He is depicted as being on the verge of a divorce, which produces a crisis in faith. In season 8, he is also shown as being drawn romantically to his temporary partner, Detective Dani Beck (Connie Nielsen), while Benson is on an undercover assignment. Over and over again he was disillusioned with existing law and order institutions but he was also repeatedly folded back into the police family. He was violent and aggressive, and he served as the pivotal figure demonstrating the platitude that the line dividing the police from the criminal is blurred and often transgressed. In sharp contrast to the early seasons, by the end of his term in *SVU* Stabler is depicted as a victimized male, damaged by the laudable yet restrictive mandate of the work conducted by the squad.

The Benson–Stabler pairing endured over 12 seasons with the two officers presenting complex and complementary characters. Once Meloni left the series, Detective Amaro, a Latino officer, took over as Benson's partner. Like his predecessor, Amaro too is depicted as a devout Catholic and family man who is angry and emotionally vulnerable. Apart from Amaro's Spanish skills, there are very few traits that distinguish him from Stabler, so we could conceive of him as a continuation of the male partner archetype. As Benson has taken command of the unit, *SVU* has not abandoned the dual cop structure. Instead, other characters now re-enact the roles occupied by Benson and Stabler.

SVU is an ensemble procedural where Benson and Stabler were supported by a varying and often diverse group of detectives, assistant district attorneys, medical examiners, and psychologists – the storylines seldom deepen the biographies of these other characters so their additions or departures do not alter the trajectory of the series. The SVU squad is depicted in the familiar manner of a nuclear family with Captain Cragen (Dann Florek) as the benign patriarch who has to often rein in his unruly wards, the detectives.[27] The dynamics within this workplace family shape the investigation of sex crimes.

Thematizing Multiculturalism

As a result of the conventions of the workplace family, *SVU* has been populated with women and people of color, and has offered a visual paean to multiculturalism.[28] From its opening credits *SVU* walks a tightrope of foregrounding Benson and Stabler as the protagonists even as the ensemble cast of characters draws attention to the teamwork necessary in the police force. This having it both ways extends to casting choices. From the pilot episode, the regular cast has included a female assistant district attorney, an African-American detective, and a series of eccentric male cops, including Richard Belzer who reprises his role as John Munch, a Jewish detective who is always ready with a conspiracy theory (see Figure 1.2).[29] The visual appeal of this brand of multiculturalism is accentuated by the opening credits, which include a highly stylized group photo of the ensemble cast, just before the screen is emblazoned with the name of the show in red, white and blue, underscoring the American identity of the show. In the opening seasons, Detectives Benson and Stabler were in the center of the profile (with the latter a step ahead to indicate his seniority), flanked by the other main detectives, including the Captain. In the ensuing years, the number of people in the photo has ebbed and flowed with the African-American detective Monique Jeffries (Michelle Hurd) giving way to rap star Ice-T playing the role of Detective Odafin Tutuola.[30] Similarly the photo has at various times included the Asian-American psychiatrist, Dr. David Huang (B. D. Wong, who comes out to his colleagues as gay in season 13), the African-American medical examiner, Melinda Warner (Tamara Tunie), the Native American detective Chester Lake (Adam Beach) for one season, and in some seasons the ADA, all the while Benson and Stabler were presented in the center (see Figure 1.3). These shots of 6–10 people showcase the range of identities presented in the series. The shots capture how the central cast of characters in the series has expanded and shrunk over time. Once Stabler left the series, from season 13, Benson has been the focal point of this group photo flanked by colleagues, who include a white woman officer, Amanda Rollins (Kelli Giddish), and a Latino detective, Nick Amaro (see Figure 1.4).[31] For the first 12 seasons the series offered a series of white women assistant district attorneys, who were replaced by a white male (for season 12) and since season 13 by a Latino ADA (Rafael Barba played by Broadway actor Raul Esparza). These figures appear intermittently in the opening photograph. As the cast has shifted, so has the diversity profiled in this opening shot; over the seasons the medical examiner and the psychiatrist were foregrounded and now have receded from view. While cast changes may be routine, especially in a series of such longevity, the changes in the still photo offer an abbreviated understanding of the series' fidelity to a multiracial appearance. They also offer clues to the shifts in the series' commitments, as we discuss in the forthcoming chapters. This diversity of characters comes to stand in for the nation as each episode begins with the ensemble standing in a police precinct. The photo reveals as well the shifting demographics in the US

Figure 1.2: A DVD cover displaying the *SVU* ensemble cast from the first season. From left to right: Detectives Monique Jeffries, Eliot Stabler, Brian Cassidy, Olivia Benson, Captain Cragen, and Detective John Munch.

Figure 1.3: The recurring cast from seasons 4–5. From left to right: Detectives Odafin Tutuola, John Munch, Olivia Benson, Captain Cragen, Detective Eliot Stabler, Psychiatrist Dr. David Huang, and Assistant District Attorney Alexandra Cabot. Screenshot of *Law & Order: SVU*, NBC, 2002.

and the particular ethnic groups network television courts during the new millennium. In later chapters, we elaborate on how this visual multiculturalism shapes *SVU*'s capacity to address concerns pertaining to race, sexuality, and the nation.

It is worth noting that despite its visual multiculturalism the series fails at what critics have termed the Bechdel test: do two or more named women characters talk to each other about something other than a man?[32] As we have noted previously, despite working in a male-dominated profession Benson is depicted as being content with male camaraderie. The series alludes to a warm relationship between Benson and the recurring figures of female ADAs as well as the medical examiner. But these relationships are rarely highlighted within the diegetic space of the series. The feminisms proffered by the series are reminiscent of Teresa de Lauretis' observation of a feminism without women. As we illustrate in Chapter 6, viewers though have made up for *SVU*'s failure at the Bechdel test by producing fictional friendships and romantic relationships between Benson and her female colleagues. These trans-media elements amplify feminist

Figure 1.4: The new cast from season 15. From left to right: Assistant District Attorney Rafael Barba, Captain Cragen, Detective Nick Amaro, Sergeant Olivia Benson, Detectives Amanda Rollins and Odafin Tutuola. Screenshot of *Law & Order: SVU*, NBC, 2013.

aspects contained within the storylines or sometimes revisit the series through feminist eyes.

City as Actor

New York City itself is a key but unobtrusive character in the *Law & Order* franchise.[33] The city, especially the borough of Manhattan, is as much of a protagonist as are the human characters. Scholars have singled out the representation of New York City in series as diverse as *Sex and the City* (HBO, 1998–2004) and *Girls* (HBO, 2012–present) to highlight how this particular setting echoes themes of postfeminism and neoliberal policies.[34] On *SVU* the city makes a complicated presence. It is a place of freedom and safety as well as a site of decadence, corruption, and perverted self-expression. Since the new millennium it has also become the city that can best represent the US as a vulnerable state, one susceptible to terrorism. As in other crime dramas the hand-held camera work highlights the gritty aspects of the city and accentuates the noir elements associated with police procedurals. At the same time the storylines integrate aspects of the global metropolis so that it is not merely a backdrop but integral to the commission and prevention of crime. In effect, New York City serves as emblematic of the US. However, both the camera work and the narratives remind us ceaselessly that this is simultaneously a unique, exceptional city.[35]

The idea of New York City being a stand-in for the nation and unlike any other American city is captured from the opening credits. As the voice over to the show highlights that the special victims unit is located in New York City, the accompanying visuals underscore this specificity. The credits begin with an overhead view of a light-emblazoned night shot of a traffic-clogged avenue. As the aerial camera zooms in to ground level, each of the recurring characters of the series is depicted against an architectural icon. Thus, we see Christopher Meloni against the gothic architecture of the turn-of-the-century police headquarters, followed by Mariska Hargitay profiled against a row of brownstones (as characteristic of the city as its skyscrapers). As the show introduces other recurrent characters, between profiling the individual figures, the camera zooms into various brightly lit streets resembling the blurry features of a video game. The opening credits end with the camera circling around the Brooklyn Bridge showcasing the panoramic Manhattan landscape, almost as though we are entering the borough and the SVU precinct from across the bridge. The presence of landmark buildings over which the camera lingers, such as the Empire State or the Chrysler buildings, punctuates the uniqueness of New York City. The energy and dynamism of the city serve as condensation symbols for American exceptionalism.[36] Despite the many physical changes that have occurred in New York City over the past 16 years, the images of places in the opening credits have remained unchanged except for a shot of the World Trade Center Towers, destroyed in the 2001 attacks, which were cut from the sequence in season 3.

In the pilot episode, 'Payback' (1: 1) the storyline highlights clichéd and unusual features of the city. The episode centers on a murdered cab driver and thus from the opening shots the storyline highlights the emblematic yellow cab that is commonly associated with the city. The narrative leads the viewer through both the bustling glass-and-steel encased high-rises of midtown Manhattan and the seeming quiet of residential brownstones. The city itself features in a manner that highlights its centrality to the series. As the detectives try to identify the murder victim, they visit a diner (a key signifier of the US in the global imaginary), where they encounter a multicultural cast of characters including a Sikh cab driver who helps them identify the Serbian murder victim. Unlike the recurrent figures of the SVU unit, these bit players are representative of the immigrant base of the city, underscoring the American claim to be a melting pot of cultures. The city's vastness, as hinted through the different locales the police visit, indicates the ease with which people can disappear. New York City visually captures the daunting task the police face in apprehending criminals. The hurried camera work in the credit sequence as well as the way in which different locales of the city are introduced through staccato on-screen identification markers underscore the dynamism and vitality of the city.[37] Simultaneously, when the camera lingers on Central Park or the rivers viewers are introduced to a tranquility that will be soon disrupted.

Like the iconic buildings and the photogenic landscape that pepper every episode, the soundscapes assert the specificity of New York City. Every episode has its fair share of the distinctive police sirens and ambulance wails. These recurrent sonic registers, as much as the visuals, locate the narrative firmly in the city. The seemingly ambient soundscapes also underscore the fear and vulnerability which is central to the crime drama.

SVU's narrative location in a metropolis taps into a rich cultural archive of meaning. Dick Wolf characterizes the series' aesthetic quality as that of 'raw naturalism' and sharply in contrast to the glossy set up of *CSI*.[38] It is also different from the representations of the modern city in the cinematic imaginary (and in crime drama) as a place of arrival (into modernity). In cinematic narratives the city is a condensation symbol for the alienation characteristic of modernity.[39] The televisual city breaks away from this archive. On *SVU*, New York City is simultaneously a global metropolis, offering a new iteration of millennial modernity, and a thoroughly American city with a locally inflected understanding of violence. The city thickens the narrative with local color and also with identities and concerns particular to that urban setting. Consequently, sexual assault on the series appears as a malaise particular to the metropolis, but also one that exceeds it.

In representational terms, the gritty, crowded streets along with camera pans of iconic buildings help maintain the ripped-from-the-headlines affective structure of the narratives and repeatedly cue the indexicality of the city. A few issues pertaining to production are worth noting: for the first 12 seasons, the series was filmed in 35 mm with motion picture cameras. *SVU* switched to the digital format in season 13. Exterior shots of the city have always been shot on location. The interior scenes of the squad room and court scenes were shot in New Jersey until 2010. Since then the indoor shots have been filmed at Chelsea Piers in the city. The shooting of the series has become such an integral part of the city that websites listing daily events include the location of *SVU* filming.

The storylines tap into New York's reputation as a key node in terms of the global economy, global culture, and global crime. For instance, episodes based on the exploitative sweatshop industry are set in crowded Chinatown streets while those on trafficking are situated in tony upper east side houses. The global drug trade industry is shown both in the piers and in the run-down apartments of black and Hispanic neighborhoods. The global mix of populations is signaled often by the prevalence of esoteric cultural practices, whether it is Santeria or female genital mutilation, in different locales. Central Park and the various elite universities within Manhattan feature frequently as sites of crime and also as homes of the upper-class criminal elements. Similarly, narratives that feature the detectives at airports or the visual representation of the various bridges help secure the globality of the metropolis.

The disparities central to New York City, which locate the narratives firmly on American soil, serve the crime drama elements of *SVU* very well. Repeatedly crime victims are identified as poor, disenfranchised, hardworking New Yorkers. The criminals, on the other hand, are frequently the rich, upper-class, privileged New Yorkers, who are recast not as engines of growth but of corruption. New York City is figured as decaying and a crucible of hope. Notwithstanding the grid structure of the city, its television representation transforms it into a labyrinthine maze that criminals and the dispossessed exploit. As we illustrate in subsequent chapters, by repeatedly highlighting the presence of the homeless or other marginal subjects, such as the trans population inhabiting the meatpacking district, *SVU* draws attention to ideas of social citizenship.[40]

The city portrayed in *SVU* is one characterized by sexual diversity. As we discuss in our chapters, the storylines inevitably present non-monogamous (heterosexual) sex as non-normative. The series offers the space for a discussion of BDSM, barebacking, and other 'transgressive' sex but the frames of the crime drama necessarily categorize these sex acts as deviant, if not criminal. Nevertheless, the focus on sexual violence along with these alternative sex acts offers a tacit challenge to heteronormativity. The format and the content of the series inevitably raise questions about New York City and futurity. The following chapters highlight how the city serves as a very productive site for reworking American anxieties and recrafting ideas of sexual assault.

Prime Time Assaults

SVU features sex crimes to showcase the activities of the police, however it does not offer a hagiographic account of policing institutions. *SVU*'s investments in its representation of sexual assault are aligned with the state and not with the feminist impetus of raising collective consciousness. This is not a new phenomenon but it is a significant variant from past televised practices.

In police procedurals from the 1980s US television, rape was a narrative device that permitted the inclusion of some titillating scenes and presented the detective as a heroic vigilante. Narratives featured brutal stranger attacks that were accompanied by extreme violence: victims were rendered mute and helpless by the attack and detectives avenged rape by capturing and killing the perpetrators. In effect, rape storylines showcased the talents of male detectives and enabled a reinscription of hegemonic masculinity, as Lisa Cuklanz has pointed out.[41] These storylines did not focus on female experiences of violation, survival, consciousness raising, or empowerment. Women became bit players in stories that were ostensibly about their violation.

By the 1990s, some crime dramas started to focus instead on survivors' experiences, even as they showcased detectives' policing skills. Scholars have repeatedly highlighted the limits of these crime drama rape narratives, especially their inability to incorporate feminist understandings that had already been circulating for at least two decades. For instance, Sarah Projansky argues that a postfeminist sensibility dominated prime time representations of women. She documents how postfeminist culture declares feminism is no longer necessary and displaces actual feminist rhetoric and representations, constraining the potentials of televisual treatments of rape, which fail to deal complexly with the subject or to account for its social context.[42] Feminism was often ventriloquized by the male protagonists, as Sujata Moorti has pointed out.[43] In sum, over the decades, victim voices and perspectives have been rare and feminist ideology concerning rape even more rare. Rape narratives in detective genres have focused primarily on men and masculinity, and the central and often sole cause of rape is a character defect of the individual perpetrator. Of all the elements of feminist understandings of rape, the idea that women do not ask for or deserve violent rape is the only one consistently voiced on prime time. Rape scenes have often been depicted in graphic detail that sometimes objectified the victim while emphasizing her lack of consent.

SVU's portrayal of sexual assault shares continuities and departures from this representational grammar. We believe that more than other crime dramas, because of its putative focus on sexual assault, *SVU* offers insights into the ways in which US society negotiates and redefines understandings of this phenomenon. Over its many seasons, *SVU* has not offered a singular understanding of the crime. Rather the series has laid bare the contradictions and complexities that are central to the 'contested concept.'[44] As we document in the following chapters, some of the storylines hew closely to the 1970s feminist understandings of rape while others undercut and undermine them, often castigating the women's movement. Informed by Raymond Williams' formulations, we contend that *SVU* offers simultaneously insights into the residual culture of 1970s liberal feminist engagement with sexual assault and into the emergent cultural formation of the twenty-first century wherein gender-based violence has been redefined primarily as a state concern.[45] *SVU* engages with feminist ideas in a manner that few other prime time shows do. The series offers a vantage point from which we can observe a neoliberal feminist understanding of sexual assault coming into formation. Simultaneously, the series permits the airing of a multiplicity of feminisms, borrowing elements from 1970s feminist efforts and postfeminist media culture of the late twentieth century; the logic of carceral feminism pervades the series as do elements of anti-feminism. Without intending to, *SVU* serves as a platform from which a millennial theory of sexual violence is being crafted. In the early seasons, the storylines recapitulated understandings of sexual violence that feminists espoused in the 1970s and 1980s. Episodes articulated a deep sympathy for sexual assault victims and several storylines presented sexual assaults as symptomatic of patriarchy. In more recent seasons, storylines have foregrounded false rape claimants and the series has helped cultivate skepticism about sexual assault. These ideas have jostled with notions of male victimization and the biological underpinnings of criminality. A consistent thread through the years has been an abiding faith in punishment as the only solution to sexual violence. This blend of ideas, which prioritize state efforts over social change, helps the series craft an inchoate but new understanding of sexual assault that we delineate in the individual chapters.

SVU crafts an understanding of sexual violence that is disarticulated from social systems of gender. In the early seasons, the series presented a fairly complicated understanding of the interplay of violence, sex, and bodies. In more recent seasons, the generic limits of crime dramas and the postfeminist televisual landscape have helped produce a new understanding of sexual assault. It is presented as a heinous crime, which can affect women, men, children, heterosexuals, gays, and lesbians. This 'democratizing' impulse has also redefined the cause of sexual violence. The series now offers it as a suspect category: rape claimants are depicted frequently as lying. The assailants themselves are presented as predators, perverts, or pathologically ill. The causes of sexual assaults are increasingly presented as individual idiosyncrasies, rather than as a symptom of social structures. Consequently the response to sexual violence has been more violence, incarceration rather than rehabilitation.

The rest of this chapter sets the backdrop for the cacophony of feminisms the series enables by exploring different but interrelated aspects of the phenomenon. First, we trace the changes in understandings of sexual assault that have occurred in the US since the 1970s. Second, we offer a brief summary of the rise of the neoliberal state during the same period and its impact on police practices, which numerous scholars have termed as the formation of the penal state. We conclude this section by highlighting how shifts in sexual assault policy and neoliberal formations have intersected to articulate new forms of feminisms, including neoliberal feminism, which is a mode of thinking wherein some feminist impulses are incorporated into neoliberal state practices. By separating these intertwined aspects for analytical purposes, our aim in this chapter and in this book is to illustrate the vantage point *SVU* offers into the contours of an emergent neoliberal feminism, one that has facilitated the expansion of the prison population. Over the 16 years then, we argue that *SVU*'s continued success allows us to track several aspects of society, crime, and feminism:

- how understandings of sex crimes have become mainstream and expanded;
- changes in the carceral state and investments in policing and correctional facilities;
- the emergence of neoliberal formations, particularly with respect to race, punishment, and sexual assaults.

We conclude this chapter by mapping out very briefly some of the key innovations *SVU* enacts in the representation of sexual assault.

Feminism and Rape

At the most basic level, twentieth century feminist movements redefined understandings of rape. They helped transform it from an invisible crime into a social concern enabled by patriarchal structures.[46] The US feminist movement of the 1970s defined rape as a political, not an individual, problem. Feminists sought to call attention to the realities of violence in women's lives and how rape was used as a tool to subordinate women to men. Sexual violence, in this vision, was linked to the lack of equal rights and women's inability to participate in the public sphere. Embodying the slogan that the personal is political, speak-out rallies of the 1970s helped victims recognize that their experience of sexual assault was not an individual problem but rather was a systemic concern. These rallies also helped demystify popular rape myths. The feminist focus on sexual assault was motivated by a desire to transform collective consciousness and to mobilize activism.

Consciousness-raising sessions became the fulcrum to imagine collective action and political solutions to the subordination of women. Simultaneously, feminists helped recalibrate common-sense understandings of rape and sexual violence; they initiated legal reforms; and they trained the police to prosecute sexual assaults differently. This concerted and multipronged approach was productive in ensuring new laws related to rape and sexual assault as well as a revised approach to the trial process. Most notably, the legal definitions of rape have been repeatedly modified since the 1970s, making it more expansive and simultaneously more specific. For instance, marital rape is now recognized in all 50 states of the US as a crime and acquaintance rape is recognized legally. However, the specific understanding of the parameters of sex crimes varies vertiginously across states, as does the concept of consent. For instance, in 2012 the federal government modified its definition of 'forcible rape' to make it inclusive of same sex assaults as well as forms of bodily violation that could not be encompassed in the traditional definition of rape.[47]

Feminist efforts undoubtedly have redefined rape as a crime. Concomitantly though the concepts of sex crime and the sex offender have expanded in ways that do not always coincide with (liberal) feminist understandings. For instance, in several states the category of sex offender includes public urination, the exposure of genitalia, and people who text half-naked photos of themselves.[48] *SVU* highlights the capaciousness of this category, not always in a critical way but as aiding the detectives in the pursuit of criminals.

A raft of new legislation pertaining to sex crimes was enacted in the 1990s and 2000s.[49] These laws relate to the regulation and monitoring of those deemed to be sex offenders. As the category of sex crime has expanded, those who are monitored by the state and registered as sex offenders has expanded exponentially. *SVU* storylines foreground how these surveillance practices assist detectives. In more recent seasons, episodes have started to question the usefulness of some of the practices. Overall, within the US there is a significant diversity in the definition of sex crimes and in more recent years rape has been reclassified as either sexual assault or aggravated sexual assault. *SVU* storylines undertake interesting narrative maneuvers to integrate these issues.

Concurrently, laws pertaining to the prosecution of rape trials have also undergone rapid transformations over the past four decades. There now exist laws to delimit the kinds of evidence mobilized in the trial process. In the international arena sexual assaults committed in conflict zones are now prosecuted as war crimes.[50] These legal reforms have altered the ways in which rape victims/survivors can address their assaults. Several *SVU* episodes highlight rape law reform in the domestic and international arenas, but seldom reference particular laws. Similarly, feminist activism has resulted in the police and medical services using rape kits to collect evidence routinely. This empirical evidence is often used in court cases as well. *SVU* has thematized the backlog in testing these rape kits, which has stymied efforts to prosecute assailants. Even as feminists worked with different state institutions to enable the prosecution of sexual assaults they also helped establish a network of shelters and crisis centers to offer immediate and long-term assistance to sexual assault victims. The initial aim of these feminist efforts was to raise collective consciousness and thereby change the underlying social conditions that enable sexual assaults. However, in recent decades rape crisis centers are no longer autonomous but integrated with state institutions. Consequently, these programs are less oriented towards enabling social change and have been realigned to offer short-term solutions to physically violent situations. Some scholars contend that since the 1990s, rape crisis centers have become a primary means through which the government regulates and monitors sexual assault victims.[51] *SVU* captures some of these energies, although rape shelters are never discussed. The recurrent figure of Sister Peg who assists prostitutes and operates a homeless shelter is the closest the series comes to referencing rape shelters.

In an analogous fashion, feminist activism from the 1970s is responsible for the establishment of sex crimes prosecution units. These organizations brought together the policing and judicial arms under one roof and were dedicated to the prosecution of sex crimes. These umbrella organizations recognized that the police and lawyers needed special training to deal with sex crimes. The New York City Police Department was among the first sites to establish a Sex Crimes Investigation Squad in 1972 (with funds from a federal grant) as well a 24-hour hotline called the Sex Crimes Assistance Unit, which was staffed by female officers. The two units were integrated within the Special Victims Unit in the 1990s.[52] In 1974, the Manhattan district attorney's office established the Sex Crimes Unit to focus on the prosecution of sex crimes. The NBC series *SVU* is modeled on an amalgam of these units; we signal some of the differences in Chapter 6. As we write this book, the media in the US have been covering the prevalence of sexual assaults on college campuses, rape as a weapon of war in different war-torn regions, gang rapes in towns small and big, as well as various celebrities assaulting their wives/partners. This ongoing coverage reveals both how much has been accomplished by feminists in redefining rape since the 1970s and how much more needs to be done. Through an assessment of *SVU* our book contributes to the growing body of scholarship on representations of gender-based violence. We are reluctant to identify the relationship between *SVU*'s representations of sexual assaults and the handling of sexual assaults in the US in causal terms; the series undoubtedly amplifies ideas already circulating in society even as it, on occasion, becomes the fulcrum for enabling social change. What is significant though is that *SVU*'s presence on the airwaves has been accompanied by a more vigorous and nuanced national discussion about the prevalence of sexual assaults.

Birth of the Prison State

In an analogous timeline, understandings of crime and criminality have shifted in the US since the 1970s. As several scholars have noted, by 1973 the prison population in the US was at a statistical low.[53] In addition, policy makers and scholars were arguing for decarceration practices, contesting the usefulness of penal punishment. Michel Foucault and other scholars have noted that the birth of the prison permitted a modern form of governmentality, wherein torture and visible bodily harm gave way to the loss of freedom. Prisons, in effect, became a central facet in the exercise of biopower by the modern state.[54] By the 1970s, however, in the US criminologists questioned the efficacy of prisons as a deterrent mechanism. They offered community-based rehabilitative solutions as more productive options in a nation with low crime rates. Paradoxically, in this climate of skepticism the US prison population started to expand and grew five-fold in 25 years to reach a total of over 2.3 million people in 2011 (with an additional 4.8 million on parole or probation), making the US the country with the largest incarcerated population in the world. Under the aegis of the 'war on crime' and 'war on drugs' initiatives, the prison population grew, with people of color overrepresented in this category. However, government statistics registered a steady crime rate and more recently a persistent decline in crime rates. Most scholars associate the growth in the prison population with the emergence of a slew of laws that have made imprisonment the only option for even minor crimes. In addition, changes in criminal policies, such as mandatory sentences, have helped contribute to the growth of the prison population. Scholars tend to underline the vastness of the prison system through a range of analogies. For instance, Loic Wacquant points out that if correctional services were to constitute a state, it would be the fourth most populous one in the US. There is now a consensus that this enormous carceral system is a uniquely American and modern phenomenon. In these discourses the terms penal state and carceral state are used interchangeably, and we do the same.

Marie Gottschalk points out that the expansion in the prison population has not been driven so much by an increase in crime as it has by how we respond to crime.[55] Fear of crime is now regarded as a problem in and of itself, distinct from actual crime and victimization. This partially accounts for how the prison has emerged as a core political institution. Criminologist David Garland contends that state attitudes toward crime control and prison from the 1970s to the present confound social theories of punishment and its historical development. The decline of the rehabilitative model over the retributive one has been one of the most significant changes in the penal system over the last four decades. Wacquant has argued in a number of essays and books that the growth of the prison population is a product of neoliberal society. He believes that the ascent of the penal state is a response to the dislocations provoked by the withdrawal of state support and by the imposition of precarious wage labor as a new norm of citizenship for those at the bottom of the class structure.[56] *SVU* storylines repeatedly thematize the contestation between the two models of punishment, most often securing the call for retribution.

In opposition to these developments, there is now a vibrant movement advocating for the abolition of prisons. Michelle Alexander has characterized the growth in prison population, especially the over-representation of people of color, as constituting a new Jim Crow era.[57] Alexander and other scholars have pointed out that African Americans comprise almost 40 percent of prison inmates and one in three black men can expect to go to prison. As we illustrate in Chapter 3, this is in sharp contrast to *SVU*'s representation of criminals. Critically examining the causes for this disproportionate incarceration of black men, Wacquant, Alexander, and Gottschalk contend that the growth of the prison state has undermined the social gains made by the civil rights movement.

Advocates of the prison abolitionist movement have pointed out the poor living conditions of the prison system, the onerous laws in place that ensure incarcerated people remain under the jurisdiction of the law and order system long after they have served their sentence, as well as the ways in which incarceration serves to accentuate inequalities. Significantly for our analysis of *SVU*, abolitionists have highlighted how the state under the aegis of the prison system has now become the wielder of violence. Rather than change attitudes or behaviors, prisons exacerbate violent behavior, especially since, often, criminals are victimized within jails. Thus, if the feminist movement of the 1970s was primarily about addressing the harms (and violence) of patriarchy, the existing prison system is seemingly at odd with those goals.[58]

With its ripped-from-the-headlines storylines, *SVU* offers a useful perch from which to observe the shifts in the criminal justice system, or what Garland describes as the expressive logic of the carceral state. At the same time, we also explore how the representational grammar of the police procedural often produces contradictory narratives, espousing a rehabilitative rather than a retributive logic. *SVU*'s continued popularity speaks to the show's ability to tap into a rich vein of popular, paradoxical responses to crime, criminality, and prisons.

Neoliberal Feminism

Scholars have identified the 1970s as the start of the neoliberal era, a time when the state started to redefine its relationship with citizens as well as the concept of governance (which has increasingly resulted in the withdrawal of state support for many social projects). Neoliberalism has increasingly become a catch-all term to describe any number of social and economic changes that have occurred since the 1970s. Informed by the arguments of David Harvey and Loic Wacquant, we understand neoliberalism as the array of structures emerging from economic deregulation and policies fostering of social insecurity.[59] Strikingly the paradox of neoliberal penality is that the state reasserts its responsibility, potency, and efficiency in the narrow register of crime management at the very moment when it proclaims and organizes its own irrelevance on the economic front. Thus, even as state services shrank under the governing logic of neoliberalism, the growth of the prison system in the US helped the state grow in new arenas.

Nancy Fraser has argued that many aspects of the liberal feminist movement of the 1970s have become immiserated in the logic of the neoliberal state; in particular she argues that unwittingly feminism has become a handmaiden to the neoliberal state.[60] The various feminist approaches to sexual assault have become reduced to those of law reform and policing efforts. Kristin Bumiller makes a stronger argument, pointing out that sexual violence has been appropriated by the neoliberal state. The feminist campaign against sexual violence was driven by the logic of social reform. However, by relying on the coercive power of the state to ensure women's safety the same campaign became complicit in neoliberal agendas. Bumiller has documented the ways in which a myopic focus on the criminalization of rape and domestic violence during the 1990s contrasted with grassroots and early second-wave feminist concerns about women's social and economic empowerment. Arguing that the neoliberal carceral imperative has had a devastating impact on the ways that feminist engagement with sexual violence has been framed, Bumiller demonstrates that the reciprocal is also true: once feminism became fatally inflected by neoliberal strategies of social control, it could serve as an effective inspiration for broader criminalization campaigns.

Elizabeth Bernstein characterizes as carceral feminism those strands of the gender justice movement that move away from redistributive models of justice towards a politics of incarceration.[61] Some feminists perceive the punitive system of control as the best deterrent for men's bad behavior. Concomitantly they image women as victims with little agency and waiting to be rescued. This is exemplified in the anti-trafficking movement with its focus on rescue and restoration. This brand of feminism has coalesced with crime control even as it has embraced the language of women's empowerment and social justice. Activists' focus has shifted from the 'bad men inside the home to bad men outside the homes,' from the gender politics of the family to a focus on gender-based violence in the public sphere. *SVU* documents this repeatedly, as we show in Chapter 4.

Earlier in this chapter, we argued that Benson's character could be seen as espousing a heterogeneous and fungible form of feminism. Drawing on the above theories of feminism we can now describe the vulnerable and strong SVU detective as presciently promoting a lean-in feminism, one that requires women to balance their work–life responsibilities rather than seek institutional changes.[62] She has succeeded in her career without making any gender-based demands for changes within the SVU squad. As we have stated previously, she seems to thrive in male camaraderie and has shown no desire for female friendships. In season 13, once Amanda Rollins is introduced as a junior detective the series creates the possibility for a tentative female solidarity. Rollins tries to bond with Benson over their shared experience of sexual assault and protests the negative ways in which men in the squad describe rape claimants. Rollins turns to Benson for support exclaiming, 'They can't say that can they? I thought things had changed.' Benson shuts down these entreaties with a curt response that things have changed. In subsequent seasons, as Benson heads the unit she does not serve as a mentor for the junior detective. Rather she cultivates a distant relationship with Rollins and disavows any possibility of a shared set of gender-centered experiences.

Benson's espousal of feminism within the squad is one that does not endorse activism in the streets but instead sees the state, particularly law and order institutions, as the best solution to gender justice concerns. Janet Halley has described this as governance feminism, while Bernstein calls it carceral feminism.[63] If Benson's espousal of sexual assault victims can be characterized as feminist, it would fit best within these categories of governance or carceral feminism, a commitment to punitive systems of control. This is exemplified in her anguished response to sex trafficking and prostitution. In both instances she is a staunch advocate of the rescue and restoration efforts Bernstein describes as central to carceral feminism. Simultaneously, Benson espouses a retributive response to sexual assaults. In recent years she has become more self-reflexive, recognizing her capacity for over-zealousness. In 'Justice Denied' (13: 17), Benson recognizes her ability to coerce confessions from innocent people. She has a moral crisis about her interrogation practices, but this does not alter the overall trajectory of the carceral feminism she advocates.[64]

Her responses to sexual assault itself have varied over the seasons. While in the first two seasons she is presented as someone haunted by her mother's unsolved rape, by the third season she questions her mother's account, believing her to be an alcoholic liar. In different episodes, Benson repeatedly voices her fears that she has inherited her father's gene for violence and yet in others she seeks to convince criminals that they are not governed by their biology. Since 2010, Benson's character has been repeatedly kidnapped, held hostage, assaulted, and raped. Initially she refuses the label of assault victim and denies any trauma. Yet, in her encounters with rape victims she repeatedly espouses the importance of coming to terms with the assault and the ensuing trauma. She tells victims that pressing charges against assailants is part of the healing process. Starting in season 14, Benson comes to terms with her assault and starts to advocate self-defense classes and psychotherapy; thereby she offers a privatized solution to a systemic problem. In her espousal of (and modeling of) these individual solutions to sexual assault as well as the focus on self-care, she has come to exemplify strands of neoliberal feminism. The following chapters enumerate the different forms of feminism the series voices.

The Formula

Most television viewers are familiar with the *SVU* formula, but we offer here a brief overview of those aspects most relevant to our analysis. In general, episodes begin with the NYPD finding a dead body (and they call the SVU squad) or the SVU squad are asked to investigate a sexual assault. A lingering shot freezes over the crime scene before the credits roll. Until recent seasons, the sexual assault per se occurred outside of the diegetic space of the episode.[65] In their pursuit of the assailant, the detectives interrogate two or three suspects. With each new suspect the detectives' understanding of the sexual assault becomes more complicated and complex. An Australian critic offers an apt description of *SVU*'s narrative arc, which 'sticks to a tried and tested plot that begins a long way from where it ends and takes some time to get the nose pointed toward home.'[66] Most episodes end once the detectives have figured out the cause of the crime and identified the criminal; in more recent seasons the court proceedings following the arrest have taken up more narrative space. We can find only one episode, 'Doubt' (6: 8), which has an ambivalent ending with no clear account of crime or criminal. Since this episode is an anomaly, we focus on it to signal the parameters of the *SVU* formula.

The pre-credits section of this episode features a young white, seemingly inebriated woman in an altercation with a taxi driver, which culminates with her throwing a bottle at the vehicle. In a seamless transition, the police are shown on the scene and the section ends abruptly with the woman's declaration, 'I was just raped.' After the credits, Stabler and Benson are shown in situ with Myra Denning, a graduate student. Benson travels with Myra in an ambulance to the hospital while Stabler remains on site to interview potential witnesses. In what follows, the camera intercuts between these two sites rapidly: the ambulance/hospital figuring Myra and Benson, and the crash scene where Stabler speaks to witnesses. In contrast to the regular police who view Myra with suspicion since she 'suddenly outcries about a rape,' the SVU detectives are gentle and earnest. Once Stabler meets Ron Polikoff, Myra's advisor and professor, the rape as an indeterminate he said–she said narrative is developed through quick edits and cross-cutting shifts in scenes. Alternating between the hospital and the police precinct, and the voices of Myra and Ron, the episode sutures together the account of a sexual encounter that the woman characterizes as an assault and the man as rough but consensual sex, initiated at Myra's behest. Detectives Benson and Stabler split their affinities between the two protagonists and their radically different accounts of the event. The episode eschews the good cop–bad cop formula and instead helps viewers understand how the two detectives arrive at their different affiliations. Myra declares her attraction for her professor and points out 'I started it. I kissed him.' Benson assures her that she can still withdraw consent. Meanwhile, Stabler develops a growing sympathy for the professor who confesses that after a messy divorce, 'I was lonely and I wasn't thinking straight … she came at me like a bird hits your windshield.' While feminist scholarship on a professor–student sexual relationship may have highlighted power imbalances, the episode filters out these ideas by presenting both personae as equally distasteful and disreputable. Myra's roommate and her boyfriend aver that 'she chased after a man whose life is falling apart.' The SVU detectives discover that Ron had an ongoing relationship with another of his students, Myra's roommate.

The SVU detectives are unable to sort out the accounts and their emotional allegiances seem to shape their responses. Stabler believes Myra 'had buyer's remorse' and that her words could 'put him [Ron] in prison for ten years' while Benson reiterates that the graduate student exhibited symptoms characteristic of PTSD and hence was not faking her rape claims.

The female officer's sympathies are strengthened when Ron's lawyer offers the SVU squad a list of Myra's sexual partners, effectively bypassing the law and producing the rape claimant's sexual history as grounds for scrutiny. As the detectives seek to unravel the competing claims, the narrative undergoes further twists and turns, building suspense about the 'truth' of rape. First, Myra's lawyer claims that Stabler had inappropriately touched the rape claimant when he escorted her home. This allows the storyline to digress and explore Stabler's imploding family life; he is forced to reveal to Benson that he is separated from his wife and children. Nothing comes of Myra's sexual harassment accusation but this digression allows the storyline to align viewer sympathies with the familiar figure of Stabler and against the rape claimant. Next, the detectives discover that Myra was receiving a number of threatening emails for filing charges against Ron. With some technical help, the detectives are able to identify Ron's teenage daughter as the author of the emails. And in a final twist, Benson is called to Myra's apartment after a suicide attempt but the SVU detective soon figures out that this was a ploy performed to gain police sympathy as Myra was in no real danger of dying.

Rather than file charges based on forensic evidence and witness testimonials or dismiss the case, in an unusual move the SVU squad decide that since 'only Ron and Myra know what went on in the room' the lawyers would bring the evidence to a grand jury, which would decide if there was a legal case worth pursuing. Stabler and Benson are called to give evidence and in the process both start to doubt the people they had initially espoused. The episode ends with a grand jury trial to investigate the rape claim. Ron's lawyer makes an eloquent closing statement, wherein she presents feminist-initiated rape law reforms as victimizing men. In a didactic mode, characteristic of the early *SVU* episodes, the trial offers a quick history of feminist activism, but does it to indict women and feminism, a narrative feature that we discuss in the next chapter as constituting misogynist feminism:

> The crime of rape used to be hard to prove, even harder to convict. The victim was on trial, not her rapist. Then the laws changed. A woman's identity was protected, her sexual history excluded and rapists were rightly brought to justice. Now

perhaps the pendulum has swung too far. Women who have sex and later regret it are not entitled to call their partners rapists.

Myra's lawyer offers an equally passionate defense of the rape claimant, highlighting the emotional and physical vulnerabilities women experience:

> Believe me, rape is still hard to prosecute and it is still a nightmare for the victims. Ms. Denning has had to endure three separate sexual humiliations. Her teacher, a man she admired, raped her. In the hospital, she had to strip naked. She was photographed, poked, prodded, and then scraped, so the police could gather evidence. And finally she sat here and relived every sordid, painful detail. Her sex life dissected, her entire motivation called into question. So ask yourselves this: Why did she put herself through such hell if she wasn't telling the truth?

Like the defense lawyer, Myra's attorney too taps into language feminists have used to describe the de-humanizing procedures rape claimants have to endure. But while the defense pins the blame on excessive legal reforms, Myra's lawyer focuses on the humanity of the rape claimant, presenting her as a multiply wounded subject. The two statements allow the episode to air feminist claims in prime time, but by making them seem equivalent 'Doubt' sets up a false clash of feminisms, one that is victim centered and the other that focuses on the broader claims of American justice. While most episodes would then end with one of these positions being validated (even if the detectives disagree with it), in an unusual and unique turn the episode ends mid-sentence as the jury foreman intones, 'We find the defendant …'. With this unarticulated verdict the episode validates the ambivalences and attachments detectives Stabler and Benson espouse toward the rape claimant and the accused. It reinforces the sense that rape is a he said–she said dispute with unverifiable truth claims. 'Doubt' is also the only instance when NBC allowed viewers to communicate their own verdicts online.[67] The episode amplifies the notion that rape is a contested category; that viewers, like the jury can assess the available evidence to arrive at radically different truths about sexual assault claims. Rape thus is not about power but transformed into a hermeneutic reading of sex. 'Doubt' is noteworthy because more than most episodes it foregrounds the ambivalences and contestations that continue to shape contemporary understandings of sexual assault. It is also significant because of how it violates key aspects of the series' formula.

The majority of criminals on *SVU* tend to be white, wealthy heterosexuals; rape claimants are far more heterogeneous. As the following chapters outline, these depictions of rape and assailants are complicated and draw on several strands of feminism. In more recent seasons, *SVU* episodes have contained multiple plotlines that complicate the narration of sexual assault. For instance, 'Friending Emily' (14: 6) begins with two young sisters visiting New York City on a high school class trip when one of them is abducted by a child pornographer. A parallel plotline explores the complicated relationship between Detective Rollins and her sister, Kim, who decides to visit her unexpectedly. Even as Rollins pursues the child abductor she attempts to take care of Kim, who has a long history of addiction and is in a physically abusive relationship. In their pursuit of the child pornographer, technological obstacles repeatedly stymie the SVU detectives. They also encounter women who are part of the pornography ring and do not see it as criminal or abusive. It is only after successfully rescuing and recuperating these women that the detectives are able to arrest the pornographer. Meanwhile, the Rollins plotline ends with the detective shooting her sister's abusive boyfriend. The two parallel storylines allow the episode to map out complicated family dynamics and illustrate Tolstoy's belief that 'every unhappy family is unhappy in its own way.' An assault is central to both plot lines but they take on very different meanings in the two contexts. Such convoluted storylines help *SVU* outline many of the points we have made earlier about the capacious understanding of the term sex crime. They also help illustrate how a carceral form of justice is asserted as superior to other forms of punishment.

Despite the problematic terrain from which *SVU* operates – its putative (liberal) feminism[68] works in contradiction with the retributive model necessitated by the carceral state – it offers a useful vantage point from which to make sense of the shifts in our understanding of sexual assault as well as the neoliberal state. Rather than delve into the symbiotic relationship shared between popular culture and the state, our analysis is designed to elaborate on how the show's depiction of the carceral state normalizes certain practices of the retributive state. In the next chapter we explore in greater detail the mechanisms through which *SVU* narratives help to elaborate on notions of carceral feminism even as they espouse ideas central to the 1970s movement elaborating on the presence of the crime. Specifically we highlight how the series' focus on gender works against a feminist analysis of sexual assault.

2

Family Matters

Criminal Mothers and Fathers

Over the seasons, *SVU* has tended to offer a very multifaceted account of rape and sexual assault, often without depicting the actual violence on screen. The generic limits of crime dramas as well as episodic television's need to maintain viewer interest have shaped these portrayals. Thus, from the first season, storylines have refuted a binarized depiction of men as victimizers and women as victims. Episodes have shown women facilitating and sometimes enacting violence against both men and women. Storylines have also featured women as false rape claimants. In these false rape storylines, men emerge as victims not just of individual women, but of a society that has been dominated by an overzealous focus on sexual violence. Cumulatively, *SVU*'s representations of rape and sexual violence defy a singular definition. In this chapter, we map out some of the numerous and contradictory ways in which the series has depicted sexual violence within families. Since these scenarios draw attention to the family as a site of violence, at first glance they appear to articulate feminist concerns about a patriarchal space where male power is exercised and sometimes abused.[1] The majority of the familial storylines, however, tend to center on women and their misuse of power. Concomitantly, many familial episodes either ignore male power within the domestic sphere or exonerate men for their criminal actions. Unpacking the aesthetic and narrative devices *SVU* brings to bear on familial episodes, this chapter highlights the pressures that the televisual crime drama format deployed within on a feminist understanding of the family and rape.[2]

The combination of revelations of sexual abuses within the family unit along with frequent narrative turns against women as dangerous perpetrators, is reminiscent of what Angela McRobbie and Rosalind Gill have characterized as a postfeminist sensibility.[3] To use McRobbie's terms, in *SVU*, feminism is both 'taken into account' as well as 'understood as having already passed away.' The focus on sexual violence within the family assumes knowledge of domestic sphere abuses exposed and critiqued by feminists since the 1970s. However, the series' ready willingness to frame mothers as perpetrators announces the irrelevance of gender-based critiques of these phenomena.[4] Furthermore, combined with another set of narratives surrounding family-based violence perpetrated by fathers, *SVU* overshoots this postfeminist sensibility and veers into anti-feminism. Amid these paradoxical narrative turns, *SVU*'s family-centered storylines do not destabilize the heterosexual nuclear family but shore up its centrality to the maintenance of the social order.

Analyzing episodes from the first six seasons, in previous work we argued that *SVU* constitutes a new brand of televisual feminism, distinct from the lifestyle feminism of the 1970s and 1980s and the postfeminism of the 1990s. We characterized this as 'misogynist feminism'; *SVU* parses the televisual grammar of rape from a feminist perspective while simultaneously denigrating feminine qualities.[5] In repeated storylines, the series disparages the feminine even while promoting feminist condemnation of sexual assault. In crime dramas, which are traditionally associated with vindicating hegemonic masculinity, the vilification of feminine qualities and the association of women with horrific crimes within the family counteract the feminist perspective presented in many episode narratives in relation to rape and rape reform. We contended then that the cumulative effect of the anti-feminine traits makes the series appear more misogynist, or even anti-feminist, rather than feminist.[6] *SVU*'s misogynist feminism includes false claims of rape; negative portrayals of feminine characteristics such as intuition and emotion; criminal use of interpersonal power by women; and the figure of the monstrous mother.

Misogynist Feminism

A closer look at one early episode helps us establish the contours of the series' misogynist feminism in relation to these storylines. Set at the opening of a tony Manhattan hotel, 'Taken' (2: 8) begins with 17-year-old Siobhan Miller tumbling out of an elevator, apparently raped and beaten brutally. The visual evidence is uncontestable. Detectives Benson and Stabler arrest Russell Ramsey, a convicted sex offender whose fingerprints are found at the scene of the crime. In the didactic mode characteristic of the early seasons, the detectives assert that perpetrators tend to rape repeatedly; still they remain suspicious of the forensic evidence. As the narrative unfolds Benson is depicted as being blinded by Siobhan's version of events and unable to perceive the teenager as a criminal. The 'real' crime is solved when Benson overhears a Miller family conversation about how to share the proceeds of a lawsuit. SVU detectives finally unravel a family collaboration to frame Ramsey in a rape set up. The women in the Miller family are presented as the masterminds; one brutally beats Siobhan to produce visible 'evidence' of an assault, while the teenager herself seduces Ramsey after she finds his name on the sex offender registry. Unlike in 'Doubt' which we discussed in the previous chapter, 'Taken' goes beyond suggesting that rape is open to multiple interpretations. Instead it depicts a case where a rape claimant stages the assault so convincingly that an innocent man is convicted. By the narrative's end Siobhan, who at first elicited viewer sympathy, turns out to be a venal, mercenary character. The Miller men, including a much older brother, are bit players in an elaborate scam concocted by the women. This particular episode ends only after Benson has disavowed Siobhan. Within the space of a 43-minute storyline, a sympathetic female figure and rape victim turns out to be a dangerous character, whose femininity serves as a masquerade for criminality. This and other episodes exemplify our understanding of misogynist feminism. *SVU*'s criminal women deploy 'feminine' traits of empathy, intuition, passion, and nurturance to conduct crimes. But in spite of these episodes that 'criminalize' feminine characteristics and reverse the dynamics of gender and power, *SVU* as a whole maintains a feminist understanding of sexual assaults in broader terms. This self-contradictory double-movement is central to *SVU*'s misogynist feminism.

Reversal of Terms

The misogynist feminism of the series is exemplified in narratives of family-based crimes, which foreground the 'monstrous maternal.' We designate as the monstrous maternal a mother or surrogate figure (such as a grandmother, aunt, or sister who is a primary caregiver) whose parenting is so disordered as to cause serious harm to those under her care. Often the damage caused extends beyond the individual child to harm society at large, as when a damaged child becomes a criminal. Monstrous maternal figures most importantly commit crimes against their children in the forms of violence, neglect, and other abuses. Through psychologically or physically harming the children in their care, these maternal figures often create criminals who commit crimes against others. Building on a rich body of feminist scholarship on motherhood and maternity, we explore the ways in which *SVU* expands on a literary trope but we also develop how, in the context of rape, this recurrent figure becomes the flashpoint for a vivid articulation of anti-feminism. In this chapter, we reiterate our analysis of the recurring trope of the monstrous mother found in numerous *SVU* narratives, while expanding on the compounding and counterbalancing meanings generated through the show's narratives featuring abusive fathers. While feminist critiques of abuses of patriarchal power are sometimes included in *SVU* narratives, such critique is seldom sustained, as many stories ostensibly about paternal abuse turn instead to themes of false accusation, exoneration of the father, or even victimized masculinity.[7] Through numerous narrative devices, the series shifts focus away from harms caused by paternal abuses including sexual abuse. In consort with narratives blaming mothers for parenting harms and excesses, these stories lend further support to the irrelevance of feminist criticisms.

Repeatedly *SVU*'s family-centered narratives show women's abuse of power within the domestic sphere as more common as well as more damaging than patriarchal abuse of power. The domestic sphere set in the temporal present is primarily a site of dangerous feminine domination; there are quantitatively fewer stories about patriarchal abuses and these often involve memories from the distant past. The crimes of mothers against their children in *SVU* are more immediate and more physically and psychologically damaging than those of fathers. Abusive fathers as characters are marginalized, appearing infrequently and often as victims themselves, whereas abusive mothers are more central to the storylines in which they appear, and motherhood itself receives specific notice for its dangerous potential. While *SVU*'s stories of abusive mothers link criminality and bad mothering, stories of abusive fathers seldom make such a connection. On the contrary, a number of narratives work to explicitly exonerate fathers from apparent abuses or false claims of wrongdoing against their children. Suzanne Enck-Wanzer has observed similar patterns in news coverage of domestic violence. She summarizes scholarly findings that point to 'problematic ways in which narratives of domestic abuse circulate so as to exonerate men and find women as both culpable for their own abuse and responsible for redress.'[8] Similarly, *SVU* rarely offers an explicit condemnation of patriarchal power, while narratives centering on the harmful effects of maternal power abound.

We argue that these patterns of difference retain a tendentious ideological frame of gender polarization: traditional gender roles and meanings are reinforced and repeated no matter which parent is the abuser. Furthermore, while abusive mothers become the emotional focal point of narratives involving maternal harms, abusive fathers are repeatedly exonerated and absolved of their past crimes through a range of narrative strategies that marginalize their negative impact on their children. In *SVU* narratives, the real threat to vulnerable children, and to society at large, is more often maternal rather than patriarchal power. While episodes rehearsing the dangers of maternal abuse are featured consistently across the run of the series, narratives exploring real paternal harms to children have waned from the early to later seasons. By locating the cause of family as well as social problems with individual mothers while turning the focus away from problematic patriarchal actions and structures, the series privatizes systemic problems in a way characteristic of neoliberalism. At the extremes, false accusation narratives involving innocent or victimized fathers could be read as anti-feminist.

The Monstrous Maternal

The monstrous maternal storylines show *SVU* grappling with the limits of the detective-cop show genre. Barbara Creed analyzes the 'monstrous feminine' in horror films, revealing how women's sexuality is often presented as the root problem.[9] Her analysis is based on psychoanalytic film theory and furthers the idea that these horror narratives reveal male fears of the sexual power wielded by women. *SVU*'s 'monstrous maternal' similarly refers to maternal characterizations focusing on the dangerous potential of women's power, within narratives about mothering and caregiving rather than sexualized power.

Differences in cultural narratives of bad mothering versus bad fathering have been clearly explained in previous scholarship. In particular, the frequent emphases on the misuse of maternal power and its psychological effects on children are well documented. In *Motherhood and Representation*, E. Ann Kaplan argues that cultural dictates related to the necessity of self-sacrifice of mothers mean that maternal abuse is understood as more horrific, while father's abuse is more readily forgiven. Furthermore, mothers are more likely to be blamed for negative outcomes with their children than are fathers. She identifies two predominating types of 'bad' or 'evil' mothers in popular culture: the 'fusional' mother, and the over-indulgent mother.[10] (There exist no equivalents for bad fathers.) The former is overly possessive and hampers the development of her child's independent identity, while the latter lives a vicarious emotional life through the child.

Working from these insights, we have identified two kinds of monstrous mothers in *SVU* storylines: those who overlook their children's criminality through a misguided faith in their innocence, and those who are themselves criminals. In 'Soulless' (4: 25), a mother's misdirected commitment to her murdering son results in the death of his second victim. The mother's abjectly tearful testimony on the witness stand denies evidence of her son's sociopathy and previous murder of a young boy. She is unable to see that her son is a danger both to her and to others. Eventually, faced with undeniable evidence (a gift her son gave her was removed from his victim's body), she breaks down on the witness stand and admits to her mistakes. Significantly, the narrative focus shifts away from the criminal son to the mother, who is presented as the real threat to the social order. This theme is also repeated in 'Night' (6: 20) with the award-winning Angela Lansbury playing the role of an overprotective mother, who is in denial about her son's criminality. Here again narrative closure is attained not when the detectives apprehend the criminal, but when the mother recognizes her misguided faith in her son. In 'Born Psychopath' (14: 19), both parents are unable to make difficult decisions about the treatment of their psychopathic 10-year-old son, but the mother is more central to the narrative and is slashed by the son on one occasion and in another scene is locked in a laundry room. The abject status of the mother is highlighted over that of the father. Caring too much about the needs of their children, these mothers put themselves and others at risk. Bumiller characterizes this phenomenon as 'parentification,' wherein the parents (usually mothers) are over involved in caring for their children, to such an extent that they disregard their own needs.[11] The storylines we just discussed exemplify this concept of parentification. But *SVU* storylines go further by presenting parentification as the central cause for greater social harms, such as attacks on additional victims, as well. In a manner reminiscent of neoliberal discourses, in these narratives *SVU* presents sexual abuse as an individual pathology and not the result of structural vulnerabilities. The monstrous mother becomes the nodal figure through which sexual violence can be managed.

In other storylines, mothers' injuries against children are often related directly to disordered caregiving, through actions such as manipulation, withholding of food, and failure to nurture. In 'Retro' (8: 5), a white mother fails to treat her infant child's AIDS with traditional medicine, while in 'Fight' (9: 8), a drug addicted black mother works against the interests of her twin sons. In 'Responsible' (8: 18) a white mother, who wants to be a friend rather than a parent to her teenage daughter, sleeps with high school boys, serves alcohol to her daughter and peers, and is ultimately responsible for the death by alcohol poisoning of one of her daughter's friends. In each of these instances, mothers across races are depicted as incapable of distinguishing between prudent mothering and criminal behavior. As we have already indicated, mothers of criminals are also more often implicated in their children's actions than are fathers of criminals, although a few episodes do draw an explicit connection between paternal abuse and child criminality. The misogynist feminism these narratives tap into helps to present bad mothering as a more substantial threat to the social order than is bad fathering. Furthermore, it is precisely through parenting that female criminals pose the most significant threat to the social order. As we document in the following, the criminal insanity of female characters is often signaled through their failure to function as mothers or nurturing caregivers. Meanwhile, the father's role is repeatedly construed in traditionalist terms: fathers are distant figures whose crimes of sexual predation against their children exist in the distant past and only occasionally create lasting psychological effects that reverberate through the social realm. Because their parental role is understood as less psychologically significant, their abuses only infrequently cause serious damage to their children or reach further to create problems in the larger social order. Children's criminality is most often linked to maternal neglect, such as in 'Locum' (12: 1) and 'Wet' (12: 5), with problems in the mother–child relationship offered as the central explanation for children's criminality. The transgression of mothers who harm their children is presented as more problematic than harmful fathering. Mothers seem to be held to a higher standard than fathers, and their failures are more dramatically presented.

As previously indicated, the monstrous maternal is one of the clearest figures through which we can identify *SVU*'s misogynist feminism. Several narratives feature criminal failures of maternal care as well as crimes of selfishness. In 'Sacrifice' (3: 7), a porn star abandons her chronically ill child and frames her husband for murder in order to pursue her acting career. The mother is depicted as narcissistic, greedy, and egocentric. In contrast, the porn-star father is portrayed sympathetically as someone willing to sacrifice everything for his child's well-being. 'Shattered' (11: 24) features an anthropologist mother who is over-committed to raising her son in a non-patriarchal manner. In a vindictive custody battle, she stages her son's kidnapping, which inadvertently results in his death. Toward the end of the episode, in an emotionally distraught state, she shoots her husband as well as Stabler, injuring both of them. A mother's misguided political commitments are also to blame in 'Home Invasion' (13: 14), in which a queer activist fails to protect her daughter from the father's sexual assaults. In each of these instances, initially the narratives depict both parents as culpable, but by episodes' end only the mother is indicted for her actions. Many episodes feature surrogate mother figures including grandmothers ('Care' 3: 9; 'Privilege' 4: 17; 'Sick' 5: 19; 'Wet' 12: 5), wives ('Beef' 11: 20), or sisters ('Disabled' 11: 17). In these stories, mothering, even if undertaken by a surrogate, becomes dangerous and even fatal for children who are not receiving proper care. 'Sick' features a grandmother who has poisoned her granddaughter with mercury in order to gain attention and sympathy. In 'Care' a foster grandmother beats a to death a five-year-old child in her family's care. 'Disabled' is about a sister who angrily beats the wheelchair bound adult sister with whose care she is tasked. In each of these storylines, documenting the breach of a primary social contract, the adult women's greed, selfishness, and jealousy override their responsibilities toward those for whom they should care. It is the helplessness of the victims that accentuates the criminality of these caregivers. These storylines feature a key feminist insight that abuse is about power yet they also present women as the perpetuators of the abuse.

Not only is mothering a frequent cause of social and personal problems, but in *SVU* maternal themes may be attached to stories that did not originally involve motherhood, or may emphasize disordered mothering as the form of crime at play. In 'Chameleon' (4: 1), the facts of the highly publicized story of serial-killer Aileen Wuornos are transformed into a tale of twisted maternal devotion, in contrast to that of the childless lesbian of the original case. Maternity is not only grafted onto the story, but becomes a central motivation for serial murder.[12] The episode opens with a police raid on a brothel and the gruesome discovery of a prostitute victim of rape and murder. After a second rape-murder, detectives trace the suspect to a hotel room, where they discover a murder scene: apparently a third would-be victim (Maggie Peterson) has shot and killed the rapist in self-defense. Viewers (along with the detectives) see a bloody Maggie, clutching her dress and crying, while claiming rape. The SVU squad is convinced of Maggie's innocence and plan to drop all charges. But technicians discover forensic evidence suggesting that Maggie lured her victim with the intention to kill him. 'Chameleon' begins with the SVU detectives pursuing a rapist-murderer, but the storyline is transformed into a case involving a female serial killer. In the process, the storyline elaborates on Maggie's monstrous maternal personality: she murders her victims, steals their credit cards, and then purchases lavish hotel rooms and amenities for herself and expensive toys for her two-year-old son. During her trial, Maggie asserts 'I do what I can to make a life for myself and my son … When I thought about him, [murder] was the only thing I could do.' Maggie's misdirected maternalism is developed further when the detectives uncover evidence that she had murdered a young mother and kidnapped the dead woman's baby, whom she has raised as her own son. It is Maggie's believability as a victim that is so frustrating for detectives and prosecutors: although guilty, lying, manipulative, and sociopathic, she is convincing as the scared rape victim, devoted mother, and proud prostitute. 'Chameleon' depicts Maggie as manipulating feminist perspectives on rape as well as social stereotypes about the maternal instinct not only to commit crimes undetected, but also to protect herself from justice. 'Chameleon' places the onus of a potential miscarriage of justice on a general willingness to believe women's claims of victimization. This episode exemplifies the deleterious misogynist feminism central to family-centered *SVU* storylines.

An episode entitled 'Design' (7: 2) also combines the elements of dangerous motherhood and false rape accusation. In this episode, Benson is called to the scene where April Troost, claiming to be pregnant from a rape, threatens to jump to her death from a rooftop. After Benson talks April down, the SVU detective sees herself as a savior to the sobbing woman, who recounts the details of her date rape by prominent investor Barclay Pallister. When DNA evidence confirms Pallister's paternity, it seems like a clear-cut case. However, Pallister does not rely on a claim of consensual sex; he asserts there was no sexual contact at all between the two. As the SVU squad discover details of Troost's effort to extort money from Pallister in exchange for dropping the legal case against him, her rape claim unravels. Using an electrical device to shock the men through the anus and produce an involuntary erection (while the men are drugged with 'roofies' administered in their drinks), April collected sperm from numerous wealthy men in order to later impregnate herself, falsely accuse the men of rape, and collect on out-of-court legal settlements. This episode creates a complete role reversal of a typical real-world scenario, undermining feminist work in exposing and educating young would-be female victims about the use of date rape drugs. Whereas the use of 'roofies' is usually known for enabling date rape of unsuspecting women by deliberate male predators who place the drugs in their drinks, here the same drug is used to subdue men who are then raped by their female assailant.

When April's mother Lorraine (played by Linda Carter) appears, the storyline makes explicit that April's criminal behaviors are the product of Lorraine's poor mothering. The defense attorney claims that 'April was raised without any moral values whatever … like a suicide bomber …

she lives her life by the lies her mother told her.' It is striking that poor mothering is equated with terrorism, a concern that recurs only in storylines about the global other. The victims in this episode are April's father (whose wife, Lorraine, abandoned him and stole his child), Barclay Pallister and the other famous men April roofied and raped, and April's baby. The baby is saved from her mother and grandmother by her biological father. Lorraine's poor mothering of April has created a heartless and manipulative criminal with no feelings, even for her own newborn child. Although extreme, this episode combines the elements of false accusation (in the form of deliberate framing of the biological father by the mother), victimization and exoneration of an apparent male criminal, and explicit blaming of two generations of mothers not only for causing severe damage to their children, but also for potential damage to the larger social order. This is one of the instances on *SVU* where wealthy white men are victims of women's reproductive rapaciousness.

Working at reproductive concerns from a different angle, 'Birthright' (6: 1) examines the issues of rape and criminality in relation to maternity and maternal harm to children. The episode opens with a little girl, Anna, running away from an attempted kidnapping. Detectives soon discover that the kidnappers were hired by Michelle Branson, a woman who claims (and later proves) to be Anna's biological mother, although the mother who is raising the girl gave birth to her. Because a doctor, committing what is described as 'genetic rape,' impregnated one woman with another's fertilized eggs, Anna is Michelle's biological daughter. This episode introduces the concepts of genetic and gestational mothers, but does not elaborate on these categorical confusions or consider them fully. Instead the episode returns to the theme of parentification and presents Michelle as a woman distraught after the death of her husband and child. She has Anna kidnapped and places herself at risk of criminal conviction in order to be reunited with the child she considers her own. By episode's end, unlike other monstrous maternal figures, Michelle understands that her actions are harming Anna, she renounces her claims, and leaves the pre-existing family intact. The episode ends with the SVU squad's discovery that Michelle has several additional biological children born to other women who were impregnated with her eggs, unbeknownst to all of them. In this narrative, Michelle is at first a criminal who believes that she must gain custody of Anna even through illegal means.

Criminality and bad mothering are equated. By the end, Michelle's criminality is cured simultaneously with her renunciation of her claim to Anna and her assumption of the appropriate maternal attitude of self-sacrifice for the good of the child. Significantly, this episode expands the definition of rape to include what would otherwise be considered medical malpractice and unethical behavior. The storyline does not pause to ponder the concept of genetic rape, but in the context of the misogynist feminism the storyline promotes, we consider the introduction of this term significant. It helps link maternal desire with a series of crimes (those of the doctor and of Michelle).

The repeated trope of the monstrous maternal does not destabilize *SVU*'s investments in the heterosexual family. Rather these storylines invoke a nuclear family that rests on the careful monitoring of the mother figure. In *SVU* storylines, fathers tend to err in the direction of overprotectiveness, as in 'Chat' (8: 2), in which a father is misguided in his overzealous protection of his adult daughter who suffers from Turner Syndrome. Passionate and overprotective fathering is modeled in *SVU* by Detective Stabler, who is depicted repeatedly as envisioning his own children in the victimized positions of those whose cases he investigates. Stabler's frequent rages, which lead increasingly to official sanctions related to his problematic work style, are usually connected to his emotional projections of his children in this way, or to his emotional bonding with the parents of victims. Hannah Hamad has characterized the tendency for popular culture to emphasize protectionist fathering in the post 9/11 era as a key trope of postfeminist masculinity.[13] A hands-on emotionally involved mode of fatherhood has become a prerequisite for the attainment of mature, ideal masculinity in postfeminist media culture. On *SVU*, however, overprotective fathering is generally depicted as problematic, but not as harmful to the children themselves. The differences in *SVU*'s representations of abusive mothers and fathers merit underlining. As noted already, a number of storylines connect women's criminality with disordered mothering and highlight the damaging effects that can be caused by mothers on both their children and on the larger society.[14] In general, abusive fathers tend to be vulnerable, misunderstood, pathetic, falsely accused, absent, or reformed. Criminal fathers are most often marginalized, exonerated, or pitied, and often depicted as powerless. These contrasting representations of abusive parenting compound the series' misogynist feminist sensibility.

Strikingly, the male SVU detectives offer a contrasting model of positive fatherhood; Fin, Amaro, and Stabler are each shown as flawed but good fathers. However, there is no analogous model of motherhood available on the series. Since season 16 Benson has been depicted as a nurturing mother, but the series has not developed this aspect in a manner that would ameliorate the negative traits associated with the monstrous maternal we have outlined. In the absence of alternative maternal figures, *SVU* narratives about monstrous maternal figures echo a much larger cultural anxiety about women's power within the domestic sphere.

The Absent Abusive Father

If *SVU* focuses clearly on monstrous maternal figures who commit easily detectable crimes consisting of misdirections of nurturance in the immediate present, the crimes of its abusive fathers are much more difficult to observe. In cases for which they cannot be explained away or reframed as false, father's crimes, as discussed in this section, are limited primarily to acts of sexual predation and nearly always locked in the distant past. Thus, while mothers and their criminality often become the focal points in these narratives, abusive fathers are found at the margins of their stories and are often not present at all: either they are not visually depicted or their crimes were committed at such a historical remove that they are aged and often pathetic by the time their abuse is detected. In cases when fathers are guilty, another device involves a shifting narrative that includes maternal crimes that are ultimately worse than those of the father figure.

Not only does abuse by fathers tend to have taken place in the distant past ('A Single Life' 1: 2), but claims or beliefs that father–daughter incest has occurred sometimes turn out to be false. 'Repression' (3: 1) is an extreme example, with an innocent father falsely accused through the recovered memories of his daughter. In the end, a female psychologist, who used sodium pentathol to induce the false memories, is to blame. 'Mask' (12: 13) rehearses a similar argument. In this storyline, a therapist father believes he raped his daughter in the past, when he was an alcoholic and sex addict. However, the real possible victim was his daughter's best friend, who eventually claims that the encounter was consensual, further exonerating the therapist.[15] In this episode, the emotionally tortured therapist/

father, estranged from his daughter for 20 years, struggles to do the right thing throughout the episode: protecting patient privacy, reconnecting with his daughter, and finally teaming up with Stabler to catch a serial rapist. In other cases, either the abuser or his victim have been killed before the episode's narrative begins, so that dialogue between abusive fathers and their daughter-victims is almost non-existent, and the abuse is not the crime at the center of the investigation ('Home Invasions' 13: 14).

A rare instance featuring father–daughter incest in which a daughter actually confronts her abusive father is 'A Single Life' (1: 3). Here detectives investigate a suicide (by jumping from an apartment building), which for most of the episode appears to be a rape-homicide. Eventually detectives discover evidence of incest decades earlier and learn that the victim's father has a new family and a young daughter. An adult sister agrees to confront the father in order to save the little girl from what the older sisters went through. In an emotional scene, the adult daughter (who appears to be in her late 40s) reads out loud to their father the obituary her dead sister wrote for herself before committing suicide, indicting him for destroying his daughter's childhood, self-esteem, and hope for a happy life. The father repeatedly says that these things were in the past and that they should not be discussed any longer. By the end of the scene, the remaining daughter hysterically grabs her father, lashing out in anger and grief for the pain he has caused her and her sister. The emotional scene is rare in conveying some of the lasting devastation to victims of incest. While the primary victim is dead at the story's beginning, the suicide victim's sister, also a victim of the father, is able to give voice to some of her pain. The father's actual crimes against the daughters are also named. Although the father is weak and pathetic at the time his daughter confronts him, this episode is notable for the naming of the father's crimes of incest, confrontation of the parent, and the articulation of damage to children through father–daughter incest. Aired early in season 1, it stands out as a rare example including these elements. In this instance, *SVU* taps into a feminist understanding of sexual assault and its causes as stemming from power imbalances.

The feminist attention to sexual abuse within the family is re-articulated in 'Justice' (3: 19). This storyline centers on a case of father–daughter sexual abuse, although the abuser is a stepfather rather than biological relative of the victim. Here, the abuse is situated in the more recent past, as the victim (discovered dead at episode's start) is still a teenager. In the convoluted storyline, SVU detectives initially believe they are investigating a rape-murder but soon discover that the teenager, Patricia, had consensual sex with an ex-convict prior to her murder. The sexual assault, however, occurred in the past and the judge was the assailant. The stepfather judge is cast as a morally dubious character. He is a rapist who impregnated his stepdaughter. He also misused his authority by committing Patricia to a 'kiddie prison' when she was 12 to get rid of evidence of her pregnancy. But in the exculpatory trend we have identified, the storyline does not depict him as evil. Instead as he lies in a hospital bed he querulously explains to the SVU captain '[d]on't ask me for an explanation. I've searched the depths of my soul and I can't for the life of me find one.'

Until this point, the narrative is unusual for its naming of paternal sexual abuse of a (step)daughter. However, Patricia, the dead rape victim, is cast in a more disturbing manner. She befriended convicts who were sent to prison by her stepfather. She seduced one of them and convinced him to kill the judge for her. The judge thus is depicted as a victim of his stepdaughter, while his own abuse is located in the past. Similarly, Patricia's mother fares no better. She refuses to believe her daughter's accusations and in a fit of rage hits Patricia with a beer bottle which causes the teenager's death. The mother's guilty statement provides the chilling end to the episode: 'she gave me this look like I was the one who had betrayed her.' Thus, a mother who did not believe her daughter when she should have, but instead attacked her, is the real cause of the daughter's death. Abuse by the stepfather, though an important part of the trail of evidence, is not directly related to the crime under investigation. Rather, the crime at hand is a mother's murder of her biological daughter. In another extreme example, 'Confession' (10: 2), the mother is presented as the bad parent although it is the stepfather who beats the son to death.

In other instances, the storyline no longer taps into elements of misogynist feminism but instead can only be characterized as promoting an anti-feminist understanding of sexual assault. 'Repression' (3: 1) features a young adult woman, Megan, who appears at the precinct claiming that her father followed her home and raped her, and that this was merely the extension of a pattern of abuse carried over from her childhood. Megan claims that her father repeatedly raped her from the age of 12 (she is now 18) and that he is also abusing her two younger sisters, ages fifteen and seven. Based on forensic evidence and testimony the SVU detectives are convinced that the seven-year-old sister is being raped. Confronted with physical evidence of abuse, the mother finally turns against her husband and declares '[h]e should burn in hell for what he did to my daughters.'[16]

However, the incest case soon begins to crumble and Megan, the initial rape claimant, becomes the object of police scrutiny. By narrative's end the abuse claims are proven to be false. In an even more damaging move, Megan and her teenage sister appear to have murdered their father. The SVU detectives shift their attention to Megan's therapist, who planted the repressed memory in Megan. The bereaved mother laments, '[m]y husband is dead, killed by my own child's hand and my willingness to believe he was a monster. How awful it must have been for my husband to know that the people he loved most had turned against him.' Here again the mother holds the real power within the family by being the one who decides who is telling the truth and who should be blamed. By making the wrong decision and doubting her husband, she becomes the problematic parent. In 'Repression' and 'Justice,' the mother's actions and feelings toward her children become more central to both the story and the criminal investigation than those of the father. While in 'Justice' the mother refuses to believe the actual victimization of her daughter and kills her in a moment of rage, in 'Repression' the mother makes a different fatal mistake in judgment, believing a daughter's false claim of paternal abuse. Megan, the daughter, has not only falsely accused her father of years of horrific sexual abuse (while believing her claims are true), but has also fabricated evidence framing her father and turned his other children and wife against him. The father is depicted as an innocent victim and, as such, has more screen time, scenes, and lines than the guilty fathers in 'A Single Life' and 'Justice.' The anti-feminism and reversal of gendered dynamics of power within the family in this episode extends to hostility toward psychotherapy, proof of false accusation, and a father's victimization by his daughters.

A similar narrative of deceptive daughter structures 'Alternate' (9: 1). SVU detectives believe that a father's horrific abuse has resulted in the murderous rage of both of his daughters, who conspire to kill their parents. Notably, the sisters direct their anger almost equally at their mother for her failure to protect them from their father and for her tacit participation through silently watching some of his acts of brutality against them. The sisters develop a complicated plot to murder their parents: the older sister, played by celebrity guest star Cynthia Nixon, pretends to have a multiple personality disorder so that she can successfully plead insanity in the murder case. The SVU detectives discover the scheme but are unable to prevent the murders. The detectives realize that although the father was abusive, the daughters conspired to commit premeditated murder.

Although paternal incest is admitted and described in this episode, a number of mitigating elements are worth noting. First, the father's abuse took place in the distant and unspecified past, apparently 20–30 years before the detectives became involved in the case. The representation of his years of sexual abuse of his two daughters is limited to 1–2 minutes of dialogue in which the daughters describe it. By episode's end, the daughters are still claiming that they murdered their parents because of abuse, but it is not clear which details they have previously narrated are to be believed, and which were part of their scheme to get away with murder. The episode thus presents the brutal shotgun murder of the parents as worse than the crimes of their father. And, the sisters' decision to treat their mother the same as their father implicates the mother equally in the crimes of the past.[17] In these narratives, the father–daughter incest plot functions as an alibi for the series to entangle with misogynist and anti-feminist understandings of sexual assault. Contrastingly, episodes featuring father–son abuse are very rare.

'Web' (7: 21) starts as a rape-murder investigation but soon the SVU detectives discover a paternal abuse subplot. Once again the father's abuse of his son is locked away in the distant past. Near the end of the episode, Stabler tells the victim/older son (who has sexually abused his younger brother), 'your dad screwed up your head so bad you don't even know what you've done.' However, the actual depiction of the father as a character is quite sympathetic. The father is afforded scant screen time, during which his lines focus on his remorse and on the ways in which his past crime is ruining his current life; he is 'a grown man who lives with his sister' and has no freedom. In this episode the mother condemns her former husband in no uncertain terms. She is equally forceful in asserting that her sons deserve love and protection. Still it is the father of the past who is the criminal, and not the contrite and sympathetic one who concretely appears in the episode.[18] Even this episode, unusually critical of the damage caused by paternal abuse, deflects attention away from the abuse.[19]

Similarly in 'Hardwired' (11: 5) a stepfather's sexual abuse shocks and horrifies the boy's incredulous mother (played by Rosie Perez). The stepfather is partly exonerated by providing the police with information about members of a man–boy love group called 'Our Special Love,' who believe that love between adult men and young boys (children) is acceptable and 'special.'[20] Here both the stepfather and a pedophile-rights leader are convicted, but the stepfather's crimes are greatly overshadowed by those of the so-called pedophile ring. As with 'Web,' paternal sexual abuse (occurring in the domestic sphere) is dwarfed and minimized in comparison to other more monstrous predators in the public realm. Unlike the misogynist feminism that predominates in family-based episodes these narratives reiterate foundational feminist understandings of sexual assault. But this understanding comes at a cost. Repeatedly in episodes featuring paternal criminality, the narrative focus is seldom on sexual abuse but rather on the ways in which the father-figure is ultimately victimized.[21]

Exoneration of Fathers

A number of *SVU* narratives feature men who take on a paternal role in some form, although they have no biological relation to the child they are parenting. While surrogate mothers participate in some of the same elements of monstrous maternalism as do actual *SVU* mothers, paternal figures who are criminals tend to be false fathers. In 'Father Dearest' (13: 20), a man poses as the biological father of several teenage girls, claiming that he was a sperm donor. He uses the claim of a genetic connection to lure the girls into a sexual relationship. Meanwhile, the real sperm donor-genetic father convinces detectives that he has never attempted to meet with his biological offspring. As was the case with 'Birthright,' this storyline too does not explore the theme of genetic versus social parenting but uses it simply as a narrative device for a new form of criminality.

The exoneration of a father figure, combined with the element of the monstrous maternal, is reprised in 'Haystack' (8: 15), which centers on the kidnapping of a year-old baby from his crib. The mother accuses the baby's estranged father and SVU detectives arrest him in an emotional scene in which viewers, along with Stabler, believe that they are watching the infant son being thrown into the Hudson River in a duffle bag. Stabler dives in and recovers a bag that contains 8 kilos of cocaine rather than a dead baby. As the story unfolds, this scene serves as a summary of the action: this father, while a criminal, is not a child abuser. In the end it turns out that this cocaine-dealer is also not biologically related to the child. After the baby's mother commits suicide (because detectives and the press believe she is the kidnapper), it turns out that his biological father snatched him because his own mother 'would give me no peace' until she 'got' the baby. The grandmother bribed her son with a new car and the offer of full-time childcare. Thus, the father's crime is limited to kidnapping and the baby is unharmed. The mastermind of the kidnapping plot, who also provides the motive, is the grandmother, who wants to raise the baby for herself. Thus, she is implicated in the mother's death as well as in the baby's kidnapping. The baby's father, though unsavory and unethical, is merely a pawn in his mother's scheme, and the episode does not involve sexual abuse. Finally, the de facto father, the one who sympathetically claims he 'has been raising' Kendall in the belief that he was the baby's biological father, is awarded custody after a court battle in which the grandmother's scheme is revealed. Thus, in this episode, two criminal fathers are effectively exonerated while the theme of the monstrous mother is reprised.

In contrast to the narratives that exonerate criminal fathers, 'Shaken' (5: 10) depicts a mother who is convicted and sent to prison after she accidentally shakes her baby to death. The episode ends with Stabler confessing to Cragen that he once physically harmed his oldest daughter Maureen, who was a baby at the time, and that he has always realized that he could have unintentionally killed her at that moment. Although this scene partially exonerates the young mother for the murder of her daughter through Stabler's confession, the story nonetheless ends with conviction and prison for her crime. Stabler, meanwhile, is not only innocent (he did not in fact murder his daughter), but also plays the role of the good, repentant father in the final scene, confessing to having been over-emotional and crossing a boundary even though the actual harm was minimal. Themes of repentant fathers, and fathers' ability to acknowledge the harms they have caused to their children, are echoed in other episodes including 'Quickie' (11: 11), in which a grandfather cries, 'I should have raised him better,' and

'Merchandise' (12: 4), in which a father sells two of his children as farm laborers in order to care for his other two children. His disbelief at the abusive situation they have entered into, and his remorse for his actions, are a major focus of the episode.

The issues of contested paternity found in 'Haystack' are echoed in other *SVU* narratives, which also sometimes couple questions about paternity with crimes involving child abuse ('Outcry' 6:5). In these, as in 'Haystack,' fathers are exonerated. In 'Paternity' (9: 9), a traumatized boy is found with someone else's blood on his clothes. Detectives first suspect that the boy's father, Jake Keegan, has murdered his wife, but they soon discover that the murder victim is instead the boy's nanny Jody, and that Jake's wife is merely missing. In a storyline reminiscent of 'Haystack,' it turns out that Jake is not the boy's biological father. The episode ends with the non-biological and marginally adequate father (here instead of a drug dealer the putative father is a workaholic) reunited with his son and looking toward a brighter future together without either biological father or mother. In these episodes, paternal rights are granted to men willing to fulfill the duties of a father, rather than being reserved for those with biological connections to their children. These men exemplify the postfeminist masculinity we discussed earlier.

Criminal False Fathers

While some non-biological fathers are exonerated and even recuperated as honorable after being falsely read as abusive, in other episodes false fathers also serve as some of the most unsympathetic and visually present father figures. 'Underbelly' (8: 7) centers on a pimp, who portrays himself as a father to his 'girls' and treats them with an apparent kindness they have not experienced in their families of origin. However, when the 'girls' refuse to bring in profits at a suitable rate, or step out of line, he murders them. The pimp enacts abusive, criminal, manipulative, and self-interested paternalism. However, he is not the girls' actual father, only someone who exploits their need for paternal love. The episode veers away from the pimp's role to focus on a murdered girl's biological mother. The mother is uninterested in her daughter's murder but sees this as an opportunity to sue Child Protection Services for neglect. This mother violates cultural dictates that mandate she should love and care for her daughter. She is vilified by the narrative as the criminal. 'Underbelly' is unusual in its focus on black family structures, but the narrative taps into popular stereotypes about the indifferent black mother and the pathology of the black family. Along with other episodes featuring dangerous surrogate 'fathers,' 'Underbelly' exemplifies how the worst paternal abusers of children are criminals first and only erstwhile fathers.

In another twist, 'Monogamy' (3: 11), an episode starring John Ritter, a husband fearing he was cuckolded attacks his pregnant wife and kills the fetus she is carrying. The husband, to his horror, discovers he was mistaken and he has accidentally caused the death of his own unborn child. Here a father commits murder only because he thinks the victim is not his child. This is the inverse of *SVU*'s most criminally dangerous mothers, who are mothers first and, through (or because of) their mothering, commit their most heinous offenses. Through a range of innovative narrative devices, connections between fathering and harm to children are marginalized, omitted, deflected, overshadowed, or minimized. Rather than being vindicated, feminist critiques of patriarchal power and its proven dangers to innocent women and children are counteracted. It is in these gendered narrative maneuvers that one can discern the series' anti-feminism.

Another episode featuring a father who harms his children is 'Charisma' (6: 7), in which a cult leader and polygamist murders several of his biological children. While the cult leader, Abraham, does turn out to be the children's biological father, it seems at first that references to him as 'father' may be metaphorical, and much of the episode is spent trying to unravel the complex relationships among the cult members. The episode opens with a pregnant 12-year-old who refuses to give any information about her family except that the baby's father is also her husband. By episode's end it is clear that Abraham is insane and that he has fathered numerous children with many 'wives' including some who are also his own daughters. This episode comes the closest of any to mimicking the *SVU* treatment of criminal mothers in that this father harms his children so grievously that he creates a larger problem for the society at large, and in that his crimes are specifically explained by detectives as being related to a misguided/insane understanding of the appropriate parental role. In general, *SVU* narratives tend to combine representations of mothers with insanity and criminality, while fatherhood is bolstered and exonerated. Feminist insights about patriarchal power within the nuclear family are seldom emphasized.

Genetic Links

More typical of episodes featuring abuse of children by their own fathers is an emphasis on genetic dispositions toward crime passed from fathers to their children. The theme of genetic criminality can most clearly be seen in 'Inheritance' (3: 8), an episode in which a young man who is the product of a rape turns out to be a serial rapist himself.[22] In this episode, the father does not actually harm his son (he does not know of the son's existence). A better example in its focus on the father and his crimes toward children is 'Bad Blood' (1: 11), in which a father's sexual abuse of his sons becomes the subject of discussion. Like most *SVU* episodes, though, the father is not visually depicted and the dialogue about his crimes is quite minimal (the brother who has been denying the abuse finally admits that his father did 'do those things'). The episode does carry a clear focus on genetics and criminality. There is a 'bad' brother just released from prison and a 'good' younger brother who has always stayed out of trouble. DNA evidence from a (male-on-male) sexual assault surprisingly indicts the good brother (Jesse) for the crime, while the bad brother (Ray) gloats, happily taunting him with 'welcome to the family.' Eventually Jesse, the good brother, is exonerated when detectives discover that Ray drugged and baited him into committing the assault. However, the episode is more concerned with a possible genetic link than with learned criminal behavior/sexual assault passed from father to son. Like 'Web,' the episode combines and confuses father–son incest with homosexual sexual assault, as if the most monstrous and shocking perversions are cumulative and cannot really be distinguished from one another. In this way, father–son incest is treated differently from father–daughter incest: fathers' sexual abuse of sons tends to be portrayed in the context of sexual predation of boys and adult men outside the family. Father–daughter incest, when it is not simply a matter of false accusation, is limited to the confines of the family (or step-family) and is not connected with any general pattern of predation against women outside the family. Furthermore, the abuse of monstrous mothers is generally depicted simply as individual dysfunction and is usually not connected with any abuse that the mother herself may have experienced in the past. In short, narrative patterns that exonerate or shift blame away from abusive fathers are not found in episodes featuring abusive mothers. The cumulative implication of these various narrative patterns is anti-feminist: gendered structures of power are seldom implicated, and there is no focus on gendered relations of power within the family. Mothers are often more powerful as well as more damaging to their charges, as compared to fathers. Fathers, more often than mothers, are victimized by the false accusations of their own children. In some narratives, the play of gender and power within the family is reversed such that fathers are shown to be victims of their wives or daughters.

Both Parents as Abusers

In addition to the episodes in which a father is the abuser and his wife is implicated only through failure to intervene, a number of episodes feature mothers and fathers with more equally shared responsibility for abuse of their children. In most of these, it is the mother who carries the larger burden of blame for both the abuse and its effects on the children and society.

In 'Taboo' (7: 14), a father's incestuous relationship with his daughter is understood as an innocent mistake, whereas the mother's decision to deny all contact between the daughter and father are ultimately to blame for the crime the detectives investigate. The narrative focuses on a brilliant student at Manhattan Institute of Technology (MIT), who is believed to have killed her new-born baby. The detectives eventually discover that the student is a 'nutcase … serial baby killer.' The final minutes of the episode lead detectives to a city councilman who, it turns out, is both the girl's biological father and the father of her dead baby. The girl and her father confess that her babies were the product of father–daughter incest. Strikingly, the father's criminality and the psychological effects of his abuse are not the focus of the episode. Instead the narrative offers an apologia for this behavior. The father and daughter discovered their biological relationship after the daughter became an adult: her mother had cut her off from all contact with her father, leaving her with a desperate need to reconnect with him on an emotional level. Thus, the mother is once again implicated in the crimes of the father. The councilman is depicted consistently as morally questionable but not a criminal: his sex with his daughter was between consenting adults and he clearly loves and cares for her. The daughter on the other hand is depicted as the real criminal. She kills her babies to hide the evidence of the incestuous relationship, not because she feels victimized. Similarly, as we have indicated previously in 'Born Psychopath,' both parents are implicated, although mothering is given more weight and the mother has more screen time. Time and time again in family-centered narratives the mother or a mother-figure is held responsible for the crimes. The repeated invocation of the monstrous maternal, we contend, speaks to social anxieties about shifting gender roles and changing family structures.

Conclusion

Feminists have long provided detailed critiques of the play of power within the nuclear patriarchal family. Traditionally wielding most or all of the economic power within families, as well as being physically stronger and having socially sanctioned authority over other family members, fathers have been invested with several forms of power. The existence of such structural power has lent itself to paternal abuses in the forms of physical, sexual, and psychological mistreatment of wives and children. Historically, the assumption of paternal protection has also tended to shield abusive fathers from discovery. *SVU*'s examinations of power within the domestic sphere, however, in most instances not only fail to interrogate these forms of paternal power and privilege, but tend instead to steer clear of stories that place blame on fathers or share in feminist critiques of patriarchal power. Furthermore, stories that shift blame from father to mother, or feature men as physically vulnerable victims of predatory women, offer anti-feminist revisions of now-familiar themes. *SVU*'s narratives of parental abuse maintain an adherence to traditional gender roles and meanings as well as a commitment to the exoneration of paternal criminals. Abusive mothers are depicted as mothers first and criminals only in an ancillary way: their poor mothering spills over into criminal abuse. The worst of the abusive fathers often turn out to be imposter fathers or criminals who then become, or more likely pretend to be father figures. Most of *SVU*'s criminal women are mothers whose criminality victimizes their own children. While abusive mothers become central to the stories of their children's pain and suffering as well as the pain and suffering caused by their children, abusive fathers are most often found at the margins of their children's stories. Abusive fathers, whose crimes are locked away in the distant past and cannot be witnessed by either SVU detectives or its viewers, are frequently silenced or victimized. Their visual representation tends to depict them as contrite, pathetic, or aged, and often emphasizes their victimization. Exoneration and false accusation are common themes in stories touching on father–daughter incest. Thus, *SVU* narratives tend toward the recuperation of their paternal criminals, who through a variety of narrative strategies manage to escape blame for the harm they have done to their children. Criminal fathers often turn out to have little negative power over their children. Their power is often eclipsed by that of their children and partners. In narratives centering on real paternal abuse, some episodes at first appear to be based on feminist insight about familial power structures and vulnerability within the home. However, most often by episode's end, the focus has shifted either to an external threat, or the more serious criminality of another family member, often the mother. These shifting narrative elements, tending to focus attention away from paternal abuse of children in the nuclear family, and repeatedly placing blame on mothers, collectively present an anti-feminist understanding of violence within the family. *SVU* however does not offer a monolithic or static understanding of sexual violence. In the next chapter, we shift our angle of analysis to the series' representations of race and racial difference. These narratives, as we will see, offer a far more complex and complicated depiction of sexual assault and the ways in which race intersects with gender.

3

The Violence of Race

The politics of representing race and racialized characters on prime time television is a problematic and thorny concern. In a series that heralds its topical significance, avoiding the issue is not possible. Yet, given US society's complex and often contradictory responses to issues of race, addressing it is also a potential minefield. We contend that *SVU* tries to have it both ways, making race a hypervisible factor and simultaneously erasing the structural concerns of how racial difference negatively affects people of color who come under the purview of law and order institutions.[1] *SVU* repeatedly castigates and condemns racist attitudes and yet it does so by adopting a color-blind gaze that ignores racism in institutions and social structures. In a gesture emblematic of (neo)liberal societies, racism becomes the attitude of individuals; thus it is bad detectives or evil people who are racist. These narrative maneuvers ultimately help re-center whiteness, white sexualities, and white people as normative. These arguments about US television's racial representations are not new. Thus, in addition to unpacking the textual strategies of the series we also read it symptomatically to understand how the storylines with their depictions of race and racialized characters mobilize audience sentiments and secure their affective investments. Informed by Herman Gray's insights, in this chapter we address 'what sort of things – feelings, attachments, identities, sentiments, policy, violence – gather around the accounts of racism, race, and difference."[2]

Our focus is on *SVU*'s representation of race and we explore how these images conjure affect – be it identification, attachment, disgust, anger. We are interested in how particular sentiments are attached to particular characters and specific bodies and how meaning is organized around them. A central argument we make is that *SVU*'s representation of domestic/national race issues shapes how it contends with the global. In this chapter, we highlight how *SVU* tiptoes around issues of race and racial difference, highlighting existing stereotypes and disavowing them. This permits viewers to become aware of certain inequalities and also of how these racial logics continue. However, in its representation of global concerns *SVU* narratives display none of this rectitude, instead all of the existing stereotypes about people of color are transposed onto global subjects. It is by studying *SVU*'s international and national race episodes in juxtaposition that we can get a clearer understanding of the ways in which the narratives secure whiteness to the American experience. In this chapter we use the infelicitous term domestic/national race to underscore that American preoccupations with the color line are distinct from fears of the global other. Further, we highlight how the series helps engender a color-blind feminism, an understanding of sexual assault which foregrounds race and racializing processes all the while minimizing systemic structures of racism. Honing in on the series' representations of gender and women, in the previous chapter we underscored how the twin ideas of misogynist feminism and the monstrous maternal (and benign fatherhood) permitted a predominance of anti-feminist ideas. This chapter argues instead that episodes involving people of color have incorporated some key feminist insights about sexual assault but not those pertaining to the intersections of race and gender. Borrowing from the insights of a number of critical race theorists and feminist scholars we designate this sensibility as color-blind feminism.

In the decades since the passage of landmark civil rights legislation that were intended to mitigate against the historical legacies of centuries of racial exploitation and oppression, Americans have negotiated a prickly understanding of race relations. In the late 1990s when *SVU* first began, a slew of policy initiatives undermined some of the gains made through civil rights laws even as there was a growing consensus that racial disparities were widening. These attitudes towards race have solidified since the election of Barack Obama as the US President in 2008. Even as the media proclaimed the emergence of a post-racial America, whites have increasingly positioned themselves as victims of civil rights legislations, such as Affirmative Action, and racial inequalities continue to prevail.[3] Scholars such as Eduardo Bonilla-Silva have characterized this phenomenon as emerging from a sensibility of color-blind racism.[4] People proclaim a color-blind attitude, that they do not see color, even as racializing practices and racist institutions structure the material reality of everyday life for people of color. Color-blind racism involves the twin impulses of minimizing if not erasing entirely the issue of racism and of attributing social problems to the cultural deficiencies in people of color. This is a significant shift from past attitudes toward race, when exclusions and persistent inequalities were based on biological explanations. Strikingly the logic of color-blind racism rewrites civil rights initiatives not as redressing past wrongs but as helping to re-locate white people as victims. As we indicate repeatedly in the analysis that follows, *SVU* taps into this strain of thinking about race, identifying culture rather than structure as the central cause of racial inequalities. We contend that such an understanding of race shapes the ways in which the series defines sexual assault, its causes, and policy change.

Melodrama in White?

Despite being set in millennial New York, when the series first began it was strangely depopulated of people of color – there were enough of them as bystanders or in walk-on parts – with Detective Monique Jeffries the lone African American in the ensemble cast. Similarly, in the first two seasons, for a crime show that was ripped from the headlines, *SVU* seldom featured people of color as assailants or criminals (a sharp contrast to the overrepresentation of people of color in the incarcerated population). Thus a storyline echoing the pedophilia charges made against pop superstar Michael Jackson, 'Sick' (5:19), featured a white protagonist. The whitewashing of criminality is significant and we explore the consequences of such a narrative strategy.

In the early seasons, race was predominantly featured as a binary, black–white, concern. However over the long-term, the series has incorporated more people of color characters as recurring figures in the ensemble cast thereby complicating a simplistic understanding of racial difference in the US. Different members of the ensemble cast have become nodes of identification and certain traits and racial logics organize themselves around these individuals. In our analysis, we observe how the series makes members of communities visible and sentiments about their conditions palpable. But the storylines seldom present racial logics and racial feeling as a practice of inequality. Racism is instead presented as a matter of the heart. We elaborate below on how these mixed messages play out in the series. We outline as well how these representations and the affect they produce are gendered – how the male and female characters of color are differently represented – and look toward the cultivation of particular ideas about race, crime, and criminality.

In a weekly crime drama, characters who are not part of the ensemble cast tend to be the victim, suspect, or rapist.[5] The generic limits thus shape the limited images of people of color. Strikingly, *SVU* has tapped into the ranks of celebrities, such as athletes Chris Bosh, Carmelo Anthony, and Serena Williams, and rap stars such as Big Boi and Ludacris, to feature these people of color in bit roles (see Figure 3.1). As this brief listing reveals, men of color have been featured prominently on the list of celebrity appearances; we discuss below some of the reasons for this gender disparity.

Most prime time shows have drawn on the presence of celebrity guest stars to amplify their viewership during ratings weeks. *SVU*'s use of celebrity guest stars is of a different magnitude. Since the ensemble cast deals with the prosecution of sexual assaults, in any given week's episode the walk-on parts are assigned to guest stars. For the most part guest stars tend to be actors who have yet to make their name in the industry but in any given season *SVU* also draws on accomplished celebrities who bring their already established aura to the series (see Figure 3.2).[6] *SVU* episodes have included actors such as Cynthia Nixon, who brought to the series her *Sex and the City* fame along with the acclaim she has gained as theater actor, and Alec Baldwin, who drew on his *30 Rock* fame as well as media censure for his angry public outbursts. When the guests are people of color, the presence of readily recognized celebrities provides the series with a veneer of engaging more intensely

The Violence of Race

Figure 3.1: Tennis superstar Serena Williams appeared in 'Brotherhood' (5: 12) as Chloe Spears, a college basketball player. Screenshot of *Law & Order: SVU*, NBC, 2004.

with race than empirical data would support. In addition, as a media event the well-publicized presence of a rap star or a basketball superstar draws new audiences to the show. The celebrities offer a shorthand device with which *SVU* can press on its ripped from the headlines reputation, accenting its contemporaneity and drawing young viewers who may otherwise ignore a crime drama with few glossy features. As we discuss below the presence of guest stars populating the people of color roles in the show necessarily complicates the narratives of sexual assault the series offers.

Silent Witness

Women of color feature frequently in *SVU* narratives, but most often as victims who are already dead in the pre-credits portion of the episode. They are often mistaken for prostitutes until the SVU detectives set the record straight. Thus while the victimization of women of color may propel the activities of the unit, they are rarely given the opportunity to speak of their assaults like their white counterparts. 'Paranoia' (2: 14) featured the rape of Benson's mentor, a senior police officer, Sergeant Karen Smythe.

Figure 3.2: In 'Ballerina' (10: 16) renowned actor-comedian Carol Burnett appeared as a retired ballerina, Birdie Sulloway, whose husbands seem to die mysteriously. Screenshot of *Law & Order: SVU*, NBC, 2009.

However, even in this instance, the live black woman figures very minimally in the storyline as she withdraws her rape charge and the detectives focus on unraveling police corruption. It is important to note that the very presence of women of color as victims of sexual assault is an improvement over previous media representations. As Helen Benedict has so powerfully elaborated, media coverage in the US often depicted sexually active women, black women, or working class women as unrapable.[7] Given the US history of amnesia when it comes to the sexual exploitation of black women and women of color, *SVU*'s representations of women of color as legitimate victims, albeit most often dead, is a positive development. Thus, *SVU*'s representational practices are significant but they facilitate an insidious politics of multiculturalism.[8] The series invokes the feminist mantra of race, class, and gender, but does so on the most superficial terms. By presenting the majority of women of color as silent victims the series eschews engagement with the ways in which race and gender intersect to produce different experiences of sexual assault (and justice). It is also worth emphasizing that the *SVU* ensemble cast has had only one woman of color, Monique Jeffries, who left the series after the first season. The medical examiner, Melinda Warner, is a recurring figure but she is seldom accorded the screen time allocated to the detectives. Women of color are usually confined on the series to the limited roles of prostitute/sex workers or dead victims (we map out an exception later in this chapter). *SVU*'s color-blind feminism acknowledges racism and the presence of racist individuals but rarely acknowledges how the practices of inequality play out differently along the axis of gender.

Men of color have occupied different though equally limited roles on *SVU*. In the early seasons, men of color featured very rarely. When they appeared they were most often depicted sympathetically as victims of racial profiling or innocent bystanders (see 'Protection' 3: 12; 'Risk' 4: 12; and 'Rotten' 4: 13). We attribute these attenuated representations of men of color in the early seasons to the residual culture within the networks to censor programming. Although NBC had disbanded its Broadcast Standards and Practices office in 1988, the tendency to curtail its programming lest it offend audiences prevailed a decade later.[9] As several scholars have argued, prime time fictions from the 1980s and early 1990s are remarkable for their avoidance of race. Not willing to antagonize any segment of their audience by depicting so-called racist images, the networks opted to write out people of color. NBC seemed particularly reluctant to address issues pertaining to people of color, especially the depiction of men of color as fictional criminals. For instance, the original *Law & Order* series featured the 1992 intra-racial Mike Tyson rape case but with an all-white cast of characters ('Discord' 4: 3). On the rare occasions when people of color appeared in fictional programming it was almost exclusively as sympathetic, likeable characters; in sharp contrast was the news where they appeared primarily as criminals.

SVU narratives replicated and modified this prime time trend. For the most part, men of color were depicted as innocent even if they were initially suspected as criminals. For both men and women of color the limited roles offered to them ensured audience sympathy. Both were depicted as victims of systems beyond their control. These early narratives display the conundrum *SVU* faced as a result of its commitment to gritty realism. The series could not ignore people of color but it was also reluctant to alienate audiences by engaging with the topic fully.[10]

Three Strikes ...

In *SVU*'s formulaic narratives, once a crime has been committed the detectives tend to identify two or three potential suspects and bring them into the precinct for questioning before they arrest the 'real' culprit. In several early episodes men of color are brought into the precinct as suspects and questioned aggressively by the detectives. As part of the interrogation, the detectives verbally reenact the sexual assault and position the black man as assailant. Thus the series helps repeatedly reinscribe men of color as rapists, even if they are innocent of the crime being investigated. Typically a white, wealthy male is found to be the real rapist. These *SVU* episodes have it both ways; they demystify the black male rapist myth by finding men of color not responsible for sexual assaults. However, by repeatedly presenting them as suspects and verbally reenacting the crime with the black men as potential rapists, the storylines resuscitate the black male rapist myth. For instance, in 'Sophomore Jinx' (1: 6), the detectives are investigating the rape and death of a white college student. In the course of their investigations, Detectives Munch and Cassidy (Dean Winters) hone in on a star basketball player as their suspect. The black male student is quick to protest the interrogation, asserting 'when a white woman is killed, you round up all the black men first.'[11] Despite the absence of forensic evidence, he remains the object of investigation. The SVU squad eventually find the real criminal, a white male professor who speaks with a French accent and claims to enjoy sex with dead women. At the end of the episode, detectives Munch and Cassidy apologize to the black male student, but he has already lost his scholarship and athletic eligibility. Episodes such as this one depict sympathetically the cultural and social costs incurred by black men because of persistent racialized rape myths. They render visible the mechanisms through which people of color are criminalized but also exonerate the SVU detectives from culpability for these racist institutions. This episode permits viewers to identify with the black student's anger as well with the contrite detectives, who were simply doing their job. The episode alludes to institutional racism but simultaneously glosses over it. Angela Davis and other feminists have pointed out that the 1970s movement against sexual assaults often replicated this sensibility. In their desire to end the victimization of women, many feminists focused on criminalization policies and failed to consider how racist legacies continue to shape people of color's experiences of sexual assaults (both as victims and as the accused). Concurrently, the women's movement has been sensitive to historical intersections of race and gender, highlighting the ways in which the fear of white women's rape was central to Jim Crow policies.

SVU storylines' treatment of race became more complicated once rap star Ice-T became a regular cast member, playing the role of Detective Odafin Tutuola. As we have already discussed in Chapter 1 the decision to cast a rap singer, who became controversial for his hit-number Cop Killer, complicates *SVU*'s politics of representation. Unlike in his musical career, Ice-T's *SVU* personality vocally and vigorously denies the possibility of racism within the police force. Fin's past history working as an undercover officer in the narcotics unit permits him to play the native informant effectively. His knowledge of the drug trade as well as of the vernacular of street life, and more recently his racial identity, have become assets to the unit. Fin, though, is presented as a taciturn person.[12] The appeal of the figure lies in the visual realm; Fin's presence accentuates the reality of a cop-show set in New York City. In more recent seasons, his character has given voice to the complexities of being an African-American male in the NYPD.

Around the same time as his insertion as a full-time SVU detective the series lost some of its racial squeamishness and started to feature a few people of color as victimizers and assailants. For instance, 'Rooftop' (3: 4) is about a series of rapes in Harlem, an African-American neighborhood in which Fin grew up. Even as he laments the violence inflicted by local gangs on this community, Fin becomes the figure who tries to appease enraged residents protesting police negligence of black women's rapes. 'No matter what you say, Captain, you're not black and you're not from the hood,' Fin asserts as he takes on the task of addressing protesters. Viewers aware of Ice-T's history would note the irony of having his character deny charges of police racism. This is another instance of *SVU* having it both ways. Viewers unaware of Ice-T's persona could read Fin as a dedicated police officer, his appeasement of the protesters is tacit denial of racism within the NYPD. Viewers with intertextual memories note this moment as an ironic one that mocks NYPD claims of innocence.

In the early seasons, when *SVU* episodes feature a black male as guilty of rape he is cast as a monstrous figure and his victim is most often a person of color.[13] In 'Rooftop' one of the first suspects is an HIV positive black man who has unprotected sex with teenagers. While this ex-convict is technically charged with statutory rape, the real rapist inflicting terror on the Harlem neighborhood turns out to be a fake rap music mogul who lures young women with promises of a career in the music industry. Once he has raped them, he sets them afire. Not only is the black male rapist depicted as a monstrous figure, lest there by any mistake that this is a stereotypical representation of black people the narrative presents a confrontation between good black men, the neighbors protesting police neglect, and the rapist, an encounter facilitated by Ice-T's character. In this encounter, the black neighborhood condemns the aspiring rap mogul and casts him as a 'bad apple.' As we discuss in greater detail in Chapter 5, 'Inheritance' (3: 8) features an African-American serial rapist who targets Asian-American women. The convoluted storyline in this episode identifies the rapist's violence as genetic. In addition, his brutality is depicted as excessive. These representations of black men cast the rapist as an exceptional figure, an idea that feminists have long contested.

If in the early seasons men of color were rarely presented as assailants, by season 15 they are repeatedly figured as rapists ('American Tragedy' 15: 2; 'Betrayal's Climax' 15: 10; and 'Gridiron Soldier' 15: 15), sometimes of white women. They are rarely presented as monstrous figures. Instead, in narratives figuring a male of color as assailant, the rape becomes tangential to the storyline and the detectives focus on pursuing another crime. The black male assailant once identified is seldom the narrative focus or the figure whose arrest provides catharsis. The fleeting nature of black males' presence as rapists is symptomatic of *SVU*'s color-blind feminism; there is a refusal to engage thoughtfully with the ways in which sex, race, and violence intersect.

Race Thinking

When *SVU* narratives focus on a man of color assailant we witness a peculiar racial myopia that is central to the narrative conceit of the series. 'Grief' (4: 23) exemplifies this racial shortsightedness. The episode centers on a middle-class black father, Ray Bevins, who is grieving his teenage daughter's suicide, which occurs after being in an abusive relationship with a white man. Echoing the opening scenes of 'Hysteria' (1: 4), in this episode too the police who first find the dead woman assume she is a prostitute and dismiss the case as irrelevant. It is left to the SVU detectives to take the case seriously even though it does not include a sexual assault. In the process of figuring out the motivations of the suicide Stabler identifies with the father's anguish and sympathizes with Bevins as he grieves his daughter. Fearing that the white boyfriend will not be punished, the father shoots him and tries to commit suicide himself. Stabler has built a relationship with Bevins and manages to talk him out of committing suicide. By the end of the episode, Stabler agrees with ADA Cabot that justice is not served when individuals kill people. In this instance, Stabler approves of the father's actions initially because the two bond as parents and forge a sentimental alliance. The SVU detective is unable to recognize the alienation and disenfranchisement a black man may experience from the US criminal justice system.[14] Instead by narrative's end he reiterates the claim that justice is color-blind and that the unrepentant father deserves to go to jail. The interracial alliance the two men cultivate turns out be skin deep. This minimizing of racial difference is emblematic of color-blind racism; it is mobilized in this instance to offer a very sympathetic but glossed-over account of a black teenager's victimization. This twin capacity to deny racism and simultaneously use mainstream feminists' insights about sexual violence to understand black women's victimization is a characteristic feature of *SVU*'s color-blind feminism.

'Criminal' (5: 21) offers a poignant alternative. In this instance, a criminology professor, Javier Vega, is accused of raping and murdering a graduate student he has been dating. Despite the professor's protestations, Captain Cragen is convinced of his criminality because as a teenager Vega had been arrested for a similar crime. By episode's end, SVU detectives identify the real criminal, a jealous white male who had framed the professor. As was true with Stabler in 'Grief,' the SVU captain fails to recognize how racial myths shape his and the squad's actions. If in 'Grief' Stabler's identification with a grieving father allows him to whitewash a criminal of culpability, in 'Criminal' racial stereotypes work in the opposite direction. Despite all empirical evidence to the contrary, Captain Cragen is convinced of Vega's criminality. The SVU chief exhibits what Sherene Razack has described as race thinking. Developing insights from Hannah Arendt, Razack describes race thinking as a structure of thought that divides up the world between the deserving and the undeserving according to race.[15] By episode's end Captain Cragen apologizes to Vega.

Race becomes hypervisible and invisible in *SVU* storylines and mobilizes very different sets of emotions. In both of the above episodes, the black men are depicted sympathetically. The storylines, however, work to secure viewer identification with the SVU staff, who are depicted as abiding by the rules of their profession. While the white police officers have multivalent and complicated responses to their African-American suspects, Fin Tutuola is often the toughest on them.[16] His stance furthers audience identification with the detectives in these 'racial' encounters.

The representation of black masculinity in 'Venom' (7: 18) allegorizes the series' troubled accounting of racial difference and race relations. The episode showcases Fin's family and thematizes the alienation that is central to the millennial African-American experience. 'Venom' begins with Fin's son, Ken, a figure who has appeared in several storylines, being arrested for digging a hole in a Harlem parking lot. Ken does not reach out to his father but instead seeks Benson's help while Stabler remains vocally skeptical of his proclamations of innocence. As the storyline unravels it turns out that Ken is covering up for a crime committed by his cousin, Darius, played by rap star Ludacris. Fin is forced to recuse himself but continues to try and clear his son's name because he doesn't 'trust the system.'

In the extended trial segment that ensues, Darius reveals that he is not a cousin but a brother to Ken. Darius is the son of Fin's former wife, who gave birth to him after she was raped by her father. Darius uses the excuse of being abandoned by his mother as motivating his anger and criminality. The mother, on the other hand, is forced to take the stand and announce her plight as an incest victim who had to disavow a baby who would be a constant reminder of her rape. In a dramatic trial segment, Darius equates his mother's abandonment with the police treatment of black men, the city's stop-and-frisk policies, and systemic racial profiling. The storyline underscores these competing and radically gendered grievances, but does not present them as analogical modes of identity politics. The mother is depicted sympathetically but she is a bit-player and her victimization is glossed over in this narrative that centers on Darius.

A season later, the finale, 'Screwed' (8: 22), picks up on Darius at his trial for murder and rape. The defense lawyers call each of the SVU detectives to the witness stand to showcase how each of them had made mistakes or bent the rules but remained unscathed. In the court trial Darius emerges free and it is the SVU detectives who have to account for their actions. We contend that the narrative in 'Venom,' where Darius presents the denial of maternal love (by his biological mother and the motherland) as the cause for his criminal behavior, exemplifies *SVU*'s representation of racism. The discrimination experienced by African Americans is caused by individuals and not by structures of policing. Darius' sentimental evocation of maternal abandonment engenders audience sympathies even as his criminal actions invoke fear and vulnerability. Darius is limned as a reprehensible criminal and yet as someone with real grievances. His mother does not merit the same complex treatment for her experiences of incest. These gendered narratives haunt *SVU*'s representation of race, especially the ways in which black women's experiences are seldom foregrounded.

These two episodes reveal the ways in which the use of a celebrity rap star supplements the affect and emotion generated by the narrative. The celebrity persona of Ludacris becomes a mouthpiece for African-American disenfranchisement and alienation, themes echoed in rap music. He becomes a surrogate for a highly visible racialized masculinity. His persona in the two episodes links him to the forms of aggrieved nationalism espoused by early hip-hop practitioners.[17] The surplus symbolic value of his presence provides the series the ability to position itself as racially progressive, an ally of African-American grievances.

A Star Turn

More recently, *SVU* received a lot of negative publicity for its decision to cast former boxing champion and convicted rapist Mike Tyson as a murderer in season 14 (see Figure 3.3).[18] We contend that this episode reveals the problematic politics promoted by the series in its representation of sexual violence and racism, particularly its inability to address intersectionality.[19] Feminist legal scholar Kimberlé Crenshaw is credited with developing the concept of intersectionality to think through the multiple entanglements of gender, race, class, sexuality, and so on, in producing interconnected systems of disenfranchisement. Rather than prioritize the effects of one aspect of social identity, intersectionality demands a nuanced understanding of oppression as a matrix.[20] We contend that *SVU* narratives start to approach this concept in mapping out a character but by the time the storyline is resolved only one aspect of identity is prioritized.

'Monster's Legacy' (14: 13) centers on the Tyson character, Reggie Rhodes, a death-row inmate who was offered inadequate legal representation in

Figure 3.3: Former boxing champion and convicted rapist Mike Tyson appeared as a guest actor in 'Monster's Legacy' (14: 13). The episode generated vigorous online protest campaigns. Screenshot of *Law & Order: SVU*, NBC, 2013.

the trial that resulted in his conviction. The episode borrows generously from Tyson's biography (without attribution). It starts in the Catskills, where SVU detectives are investigating the manager of a boys' summer camp for sexual assaults.[21] SVU detectives presume that Reggie Rhodes too was sexually abused as a child while at the camp and also later in Ohio. In a curious turn, the plot concerning the serial assailant is set aside and the episode's focus shifts entirely to Rhodes. Benson solicits the services of the African-American defense lawyer Bayard Ellis (Andre Braugher), whom she has gradually befriended over several episodes, to investigate prosecutorial misconduct in the trial that originally sentenced Rhodes to death. The two New Yorkers work in Ohio and successfully secure a stay of execution once they are able to establish that Rhodes himself is a rape victim suffering from PTSD. The storyline does not contest the death-row inmate's status as a murderer, but by bringing to bear the history of assault and trauma Benson helps to reposition Rhode's culpability in the crimes he committed. The episode ends with Benson and Ellis hugging Rhodes exultantly.

The stunt casting in this instance is very problematic because of the way the storyline merges biographical and fictional elements. The episode gives voice to cases of prosecutorial misconduct and miscarriages of justice that have been publicized by the media; it also elaborates on the manner in which the judicial system tends to be weighted against people of color. By folding in aspects of Tyson's 'real' life experiences in the Catskills with this fictional account of murder, the episode offers a tepid critique of the carceral state/prison nation. It achieves a lot more though for Tyson's public narrative. That a series devoted to exploring the 'especially heinous crime' of sexual assault ends with an SVU detective hugging a (real-life) convicted rapist with a beaming smile is significant. The casting choice and the decision to end in an ebullient hug were no doubt designed to draw audiences through controversy (although protesters believed the episode was designed to sanitize Mike Tyson's image).[22] But given that the Bayard Ellis character has appeared repeatedly in seasons 13 and 14 to highlight police excess or the racist actions of the police or judiciary, intertextually the hug takes on more salience. Similarly, Benson has been presented in the series as a passionate, sometimes overzealous, officer who is determined to make rapists accountable for their crimes.[23] Having these two characters hug Tyson's character seems to almost exonerate the boxer of his conviction for rape.[24] Given the boxer's celebrity status it is impossible to read this narrative as simply asserting Rhodes status as a victim of the law and order system. *SVU*'s decision to cast the convicted Tyson in this role suggests that the storyline was devised to suggestively blur the lines between real and fictional. If 'Venom' is an allegory for *SVU*'s brand of race-thinking, 'Monster's Legacy' offers a revisionist account of sexual assault. Perhaps this narrative is about *SVU*'s new commitment to rehabilitation over retribution, but as we explain in Chapter 5 this does not hold true in other storylines. Unlike other storylines we analyze in this chapter, this one episode mitigates against carceral feminism. But to the extent that its critique of existing judicial processes skirts the issue of race and instead centers on the continued neglect of rape trauma (PTSD), this episode too works within the logic of color-blind feminism we have identified.

Re-writing Racism

Unlike 'Monster's Legacy,' in most episodes featuring men of color assailants, the storylines perform acrobatic feats to redirect the narrative focus elsewhere. 'Storm' (7: 10) initially centers on a black man who abducted three girls from a Katrina-ravaged New Orleans and raped one of them. The SVU detectives track down the rapist early in the storyline and devote most of the episode to the more monstrous crime of anthrax poisoning and bioterrorism featuring a white suspect. Narratives such as this one showcase a liberal colorblindness that is aware of racism but refuses to confront how central racism is to the institutions of the police and judiciary. This episode taps into a complicated understanding of feminism, wherein the narrative underscores power as the central cause of familial abuse but avoids examining the contours of racialized femininity.

The gendered disparities in *SVU*'s depiction of people of color must be underscored. As is true with 'Grief' (4: 23) and 'Hysteria' (1: 4) black victims may trigger the actions of the SVU detectives but they are rarely given an opportunity to speak; their corpses instead are the fetish objects for whom the police force acts. 'Disabled' (11: 17) is a rare episode where a victimized black woman is featured in a central role. However, as a paraplegic she is literally consigned to a role of silence and her victimizer turns out to be her jealous sister (railing against the mammy role she is expected to fulfill).

'Funny Valentine' (14: 16) offers an equally poignant but different account of intimate partner violence as it plays out in the klieg light of celebrity culture. Drawing on aspects of the well-publicized 2009 Rihanna–Chris Brown assault case, 'Funny Valentine' limns stereotypical understandings of racialized femininity and masculinity. The episode begins with a home video of an endearing girl singing a song which dissolves into the adult Micha Green, an aspiring R&B singer, recording the same song in a studio with her celebrity boyfriend, rap star Caleb Bryant. Through a few concise gestures the series establishes Micha's desire to succeed in the music industry. Unlike most *SVU* episodes 'Funny Valentine' features the assault on screen and viewers see Caleb hitting Micha after an altercation.

At the hospital a bleeding and bruised Micha reluctantly identifies her assailant and tells Benson about the people who witnessed the attack. However all of the witnesses deny seeing an attack, privileging their career interests over the assaulted singer's well being. This culture of silence is presented as symptomatic of African Americans and the bruised Micha is visually represented in the familiar iconographies of other celebrity victims: Rihanna, Whitney Houston, Tina Turner, to name a few. By threading together these different 'real' accounts the episode suggests the seeming inevitability of black women's violation and the resilience of violent black masculinity, especially that of 'gangsta' masculinity.

In its portrayal of Caleb 'Funny Valentine' makes explicit reference to several African-American celebrities – basketball superstar Kobe Bryant and rappers Tupac Shakur and Biggie Smalls – who have received extensive media coverage.[25] The repeated references to these men draw on viewers' intertextual memory to help naturalize the idea of violent black masculinity. Within the diegetic space of the episode Caleb's lawyer accuses the SVU squad of racism asserting that if Caleb were a singer at the Metropolitan opera he would not have been charged with assault. This storyline draws viewers' attention to prevailing stereotypes about violent black masculinity, which could limit the lives of African-American men. However, since viewers witnessed the assault they can reframe these appeals as a cynical deployment of the race card.[26] 'Funny Valentine' participates in what Karen Fields and Barbara Fields have identified as racecraft, a process akin to witchcraft wherein racism becomes race, the structural transmuted into the cultural.[27]

Micha is depicted as a far more sympathetic if conflicted personality. She files charges against Caleb and withdraws them several times during the episode, either to protect her newly emerging singing career, or because she is convinced of Caleb's love for her and believes that the assault was anomalous behavior. Even when Caleb shoots and kills her mentor, Micha can only see her boyfriend as the victim of a racist NYPD. Unable to convince the assaulted woman of the resources that are available for her safety and protection, the SVU squad are resigned to what Benson terms as the 'inevitable.'

'Funny Valentine' ends with the two reconciled singers vacationing on a yacht and having an altercation. The final shot of the episode has a television news anchor reporting on Micha's death in Bermuda and Caleb's arrest. This episode uses the didactic mode to highlight the cycles of domestic violence. It also encourages sympathy for the assaulted woman. However, the repeated named references to violent black men and the visual linkages asserted with a series of assaulted black women permit a binarized view of victimized femininity and brutal masculinity.[28] The Micha character is depicted as foolhardy for not following police advice and following her desires. This episode echoes the themes of misogynist feminism we have identified in the previous chapter. At the same time its depiction of the protagonists taps into themes of color-blind racism as well, one where violence is located in African-American music culture. The simultaneous avowal of feminism and disavowal of racism is a structuring trait of *SVU*'s color-blind feminism.

Civil Dis-ease

While African Americans are depicted in limiting roles, civil rights history fares no better. 'Reparation' (12: 21) is striking for the flexible ways in which *SVU* deals with recent US history. The storyline begins with a white woman, Catherine Harrison, charging a black man with her rape. The original suspect, Kevin Wright, is on the sex offender registry. As the SVU detectives pursue the case they discover that the bipolar, claustrophobic Kevin had been falsely accused in this instance as well as in the past when an overzealous police officer lazily misinterpreted photographs to connote pornography. This subplot underscores the problems with the sex offender registry, how easy it is for people to be assigned to the list and the difficulty getting off of it.[29]

'Reparation' nevertheless features a black man, Dwight Talcott, who did consider assaulting Catherine but decided not to follow through. However in the narrative veering trend we have previously noted, the episode shifts directions first to highlight that Catherine had fabricated the assault charges and second to foreground white supremacist attitudes. In the extended trial segment SVU detectives discover that Catherine brought rape charges on the advice of her grandfather, a Klansman. Apart from the false rape charge, they also discover that during the 1960s the grandfather had raped Dwight's aunt, an SNCC worker. This narrative turn, wherein a white Klansman's family feels entitled to make false rape charges while a dignified black woman cannot call the gang rape an assault, allows *SVU* to showcase systemic racism in the US. By locating this event in the past the series resituates and relegitimizes the SVU detectives; they can help undo past wrongs even though the law and order institutions themselves are shown to be implicated in this issue. In this and other instances *SVU* storylines thematize who can and who cannot be a rape claimant; the episodes skillfully indicate the salience of race in claiming victim status. Nevertheless by presenting the heroic SVU detectives as rescuers, the series undoes the systemic critique it has the potential to offer. By presenting the white rapist as a Klansman and his victim as a dignified Civil Rights activist, the storyline deftly aligns viewer sympathies along the good/evil axis instead of race. Further, both Dwight and Catharine are sentenced to prison, the black man for attempted rape and the white woman for filing a false rape claim. With this sleight of hand set of equivalences, the storyline reinstates the judiciary as color-blind (and just). This episode lays bare the series' commitment to carceral feminism even as it is willing to foreground the actions of racist individuals.

In addition, in the most recent seasons white women are depicted several times as falsely accusing black men as their rapists ('True Believers' 13: 6; 'Beautiful Frame' 14: 11; 'Wonderland Story' 15: 4). This trend culminates in a poorly scripted season 15 episode, 'American Tragedy' (15: 3), which blends together the storylines of the Trayvon Martin murder in Florida with celebrity chef Paula Deen's racist tirades. In the *SVU* version of these narratives, a celebrity chef murders a black teenager in a hoodie out of fear that he was about to rape her. Several other white women identify different, innocent black men as their rapists while the real rapist is not apprehended until much later. More significantly the narrative underscores Fin's desire to reclassify the murder of the black teenager as a hate crime, not just because he was in the wrong place at the wrong time but because he was the 'wrong skin color.' However, in the trial segment of the episode the chef's lawyer convincingly equates her actions with the racist underpinnings of New York City's stop-and-frisk policies, in which the black detective himself participates. Acknowledging the NYPD's tarnished reputation allows the series to maintain its aura of gritty realism. Simultaneously the defense attorney is presented as crass and audience sympathies are geared toward the familiar Fin.

In each of these episodes where white rape claimants falsely identify black men as their assailants *SVU* betrays its inability to adopt an intersectional approach. The repeated narrative device of white women incapable of distinguishing between black men and falsely accusing them of rape brings back to the forefront early twentieth century ideologies that resulted in the lynching of black men.[30] *SVU* narratives do not crassly castigate these rape claimants but by foregrounding the fragility of their testimonies, the series makes white women's rapes the fulcrum from which the series can espouse its liberal, color-blind, anti-racist politics. In 'True Believers' (13: 6) the defense lawyer Bayard Ellis successfully defends a black man against charges of rape by highlighting SVU detectives' procedural violations. He points out, 'the NYPD declared war on men of color a long time ago,' raising the specter of racial profiling. In defending the accused black man Ellis also highlights that the rape claimant had previously had consensual sex with a black man. The accused rapist, who claims his mother always asked him 'to stay away from white women,' is not convicted. The episode resuscitates a number of rape myths but a post-trial conversation between Ellis and Benson helps articulate concerns about the carceral state and the overrepresentation of men of color in prison populations. Justifying his defense against the 'war on men of color' Ellis points out that '84 percent of the young men in New York jails are black and Latino.' He also adds that if other detectives did their jobs as well as Benson he would retire. In this brief aside Ellis is able to outline some aspects of what Michelle Alexander has characterized as the 'new Jim Crow' society: police incompetence, violations of civil liberties, racial profiling, and the prison state.[31] This particular storyline manages to cohere identifications around both the SVU detectives as well as systemic racialized injustices through the figure of Bayard Ellis. The defense attorney's character allows *SVU* to articulate the vulnerabilities and fears men of color experience in the criminal justice system, even as it shores up the police as the best available remedy to combat sexual assault. The woman's rape, which motivated the storyline, remains unsolved in the background.

Similarly, 'Unstable' (11: 1) centers on the wrongful conviction of an innocent black man and arrives at a similar indictment of police procedures but with very different effects. In this earlier episode, Stabler realizes mid-way through the storyline that he may have helped wrongfully convict an innocent man. He takes it as a personal challenge to secure the innocent man's freedom but by narrative's end is unable to do so. This unsatisfactory resolution helps shift the blame to judicial procedures and bureaucracies rather than policing practices that resulted in the false conviction. Highlighting Stabler's guilt and anguish permits the storyline to mobilize sympathies for the police rather than against policing practices. In a throwaway line Fin points out that if after a 'fair trial' an innocent man is convicted, the whole system failed, not just Stabler. Similarly the 'real' rapist in this storyline mocks the police for not knowing how many times they catch the wrong man. But these insights of systemic failure are not pursued in this or other episodes.

Working in a different register 'Dissonant Voices' (15: 6) articulates poignantly the costs incurred by black men when they are falsely accused of rape. A charismatic, gay black music teacher, Jackie Walker, is falsely set up as a pedophile.[32] Prophetically, Detective Rollins objects to the arrest pointing out that he is an openly gay music teacher and that the costs of a mistaken accusation would be high: 'He's a celebrity. He gets accused of pedophilia? I mean, the charges may go away but the stain won't.' The other SVU detectives insist on arresting the teacher. By foregrounding different perspectives within the squad the storyline parts ways with the good cop–bad cop formula and instead permits an understanding of how dominant ideologies could shape detectives' insights. Most of the SVU squad relies on available forensic evidence to condemn Walker, while Rollins foregrounds the very limited social space hegemonic society accords to black gay men. Within the squad Rollins is the only one who is willing to look beyond the materiality of the forensic evidence to tease out inconsistencies in witness testimonials. Amaro and Benson can see the gay black music teacher as an always-already pedophile and predator; they are also blinded by their faith in forensics (we elaborate on this aspect in Chapter 5).

After several narrative twists and turns the SVU detectives discover that all of the incriminating evidence was planted by two vindictive white teenagers, former students who feel rejected by their teacher. The two teenagers are painted within the broad-brush strokes of misogynist feminism we highlighted in the previous chapter. They are part of a vindictive, mean girl culture, which trades on femininity to promote their self interest. Walker is acquitted in court, but the storyline foregrounds his bleak future, without a job, a home, or a livelihood, while the two white women culprits are asked to conduct community service for a year. This storyline touches upon the differential outcomes whites and blacks can expect from the judicial system but deflects blame from the judicial system to individual SVU detectives' overzealousness in charging the music teacher in the first place. It nevertheless mobilizes sympathy for the SVU detectives as well because of their inability to read accurately upper-class white women's actions: mothers as well as angry teenagers. Visually, 'Dissonant

Voices' engenders identification with the (falsely accused) black man and his plight; none of the characters draws attention to his race although his sexuality is repeatedly highlighted. This storyline betrays again *SVU*'s inability to address intersectionality. It exemplifies instead a commitment to a theory of 'competing marginalities,' unable to simultaneously address how his blackness and his gay identity contribute to the conundrum.[33]

Expanding the Rainbow

SVU's casting choices best reflect the series' concerns with racial difference and the idea of competing marginalities. As we have noted in Chapter 1, *SVU*'s shifting cast of core characters serves as a paean to visual multiculturalism. These racialized figures nevertheless play an important role in containing the ideological capaciousness of the series' understanding of sexual assault. Within individual storylines recurring cast members play a central role in facilitating the series' color-blind attention to racism ('Secrets Exhumed' 14: 14; 'Funny Valentine' 14: 16), which we have outlined above. Fin and Dr. Huang often have to perform as cultural translators, even as they protest the roles assigned to them by colleagues. In more recent seasons Detective Amaro and ADA Barba have become representatives of the Latino population. Between 2002 and 2006 the series included the recurring figure of forensic technician Ruben Morales (Joel de la Fuente) whose technical expertise further complicated a simplistic understanding of Latino masculinity.[34]

The presence of this diverse police force is reflected in the practice of detection and the unique cultural skills each of them brings to the job. Amaro has embraced his Spanish fluency unproblematically to be a more effective detective. He often speaks to suspects and victims in Dominican slang to elicit information. This is in striking contrast to Dr. Huang who protested his colleagues' assumption that he must speak 'Chinese' (see 'Debt' 6: 2).[35] He mocked the SVU squad's stereotypical belief that English is a second language for all people of color. Overall, Dr. Huang occupies a narratively productive liminal space within *SVU* storylines. His visual presence and his repeated assertions of psychological insights, even while marginalized, expand the narrative horizons of the series. Dr. Huang's sexuality is not asserted except for a passing reference he makes when he returns to the series as a guest actor in season 13. This narrative silence allows the series to avoid trafficking in stereotypes of Oriental sexualities. Viewers may also draw on a broader cultural archive to recognize that the forensic psychiatrist is played by the Tony award-winning B. D. Wong, who is closely associated with his role in the Broadway production *M. Butterfly*, which offers a trenchant critique of Western stereotypes about Asian femininities.

ADA Barba is more akin to Dr. Huang in his reluctance to disclose private information or assert his racialized identity within the work sphere. Nevertheless in 'October Surprise' (15: 5), ADA Barba's childhood in the Bronx is central to understanding and solving the crime at hand. When the ADA speaks Spanish it is with his childhood friends in this episode or in his antagonistic relationship with Amaro, where they code switch to express their wrath with each other.

SVU sets the stage for the presentation of these variegated racialized masculinities by earlier casting choices that broaden the series' invocation of multiculturalism. In season 9 (2007–2008), Canadian actor Adam Beach joined the cast as Fin's partner, Chester Lake. Over several episodes viewers gathered that Lake, whose family had lived in New York City for generations, identifies as a member of the Mohawk nation. Television critics have identified Beach as the first Native American cast member in a prime time crime drama. His recurring presence on *SVU* enriched understandings of multiculturalism and the operations of race in the US. Within the diegetic space of the series, Lake often voiced critiques about imprisonment as the solution to violence. In 'Fight' (9: 8), he persuaded his colleagues that imprisoning two African-American teenagers, who were themselves victims of gang activity, would not help reduce crime. Unlike Fin or later Amaro, he gave voice to some of the arguments made by prison abolitionists, which we have outlined in Chapter 1. His voice functioned as an antidote to the carceral feminism privileged by the series, attitudes that are reprised by the guest character of Bayard Ellis, which we analyzed earlier in this chapter. Nevertheless his portrayal as an angry detective who remained unconvinced about the police as a solution to social problems perched him on the precarious stereotype of the sensitive, noble Indian. Beach remained on the series for one season, exiting after he killed a rapist police officer who had escaped prosecution. Viewer responses to Beach's character were largely negative and this may account for his departure. His presence reveals the show's efforts to broaden the category of race beyond the black–white binary. The series was more successful in this effort of expanding the racial horizon in its inclusion of Latino characters within the ensemble cast.

Once Stabler left the series at the end of season 12, *SVU* both expanded and shrank its horizons of visual multiculturalism. Amaro was introduced in season 13 as a replacement for the white Stabler and as Benson's new partner. Dr. Huang left the ensemble cast after season 12 and appears subsequently as a guest star, but the visual presence of Asian Americans has been considerably attenuated. ADA Barba was introduced in season 14 as a prosecutor for SVU cases and became a regular cast member in the following season.

When Amaro was first introduced as a replacement for Stabler, he was presented as a bookish, cerebral detective. Gradually these intellectual traits have been minimized, and instead, the working-class, married Catholic detective has echoed many of his predecessor's traits. Within the space of two seasons Amaro's character started to display the same anger-management issues Stabler had. He goes through a divorce and his grief over losing custody of his daughter spills over into the workplace.

Like Fin, Amaro too often acts as a cultural translator. In the pursuit of criminals, he willingly deploys his fluency in Spanish and his knowledge of Catholicism ('Presumed Guilty' 14: 10). His past experiences in narcotics also help the SVU squad make inroads in cases involving Dominican gangs. Above all it is Amaro's experiences as an Iraq war veteran that help him recognize PTSD symptoms in a suspect and successfully arrest the real criminals ('Traumatic Wound' 14: 21). However, like Stabler, Amaro is overinvested in cases involving children. The tacit subtext is that his experiences as a father shape his responses. Thus 'Spring Awakening' (15: 24) depicts Amaro in a very sympathetic light as he assaults a man, Simon Wilkes, whom the SVU squad had unsuccessfully tried to prosecute as a pedophile. In the season 15 finale, Amaro sees Wilkes taking photos of children at a playground and he is unable to control his rage. The episode and the season end with Amaro in jail; he is eventually demoted and transferred to patrol duty in Queens. As we write this chapter, midway through season 16, Amaro has been reinstated in the SVU squad at Benson's request.

In sharp contrast, ADA Barba is presented as a suave, reserved, Harvard-educated lawyer.[36] In the courtroom, Barba is a tenacious prosecutor who zealously protects his professional reputation. He refuses to be swayed by SVU detectives who try to persuade him to pursue cases on sentimental grounds, yet he is also principled. In 'October Surprise' (15: 5), he is depicted as loyal to his childhood friends. He is still willing to pursue a case against his erstwhile best friend and aspiring mayoral candidate. Over the course of his two seasons at *SVU*, Barba cultivates a close friendship with Benson as she takes charge of the squad.

The presence of two recurring Latino men, who are different in temperament and career trajectory, helps *SVU* offer a nuanced understanding of Latino masculinities, or what Jennifer Rudolph has described as masculatinidad.[37] Their fluency in Spanish becomes a shorthand device to underscore their difference from the rest of the squad. The antagonistic and complicated relationship between the two Latino characters helps offer a more nuanced depiction of non-hegemonic masculinities, although these threads have so far been less developed.

Before season 13, when the two Latino men joined the regular cast of characters, few episodes featured Latino/as in positions of power. 'Name' (7: 7) features the rare instance when a recurring forensic technician Millie Vizcarando motivates Stabler to undertake a cold case featuring four missing Puerto Rican boys, arguing that the case would have never been neglected if the victims were white. Similarly, in later seasons Fin becomes the mouthpiece for the racial double standards of policing. In a storyline about an abducted child ('Vigil' 14: 5) Fin argues with his colleagues that if the child abducted a decade earlier had been white the police would have devoted more resources to finding him. In 'Born Psychopath' (14: 18), Fin ventriloquizes the critical perspective that if their suspect were not a white child from a wealthy upper east side family he would have been under state supervision a lot earlier. His remonstrations of double standards or the gently chiding Huang help maintain the currency and urgency of the series but neither of them is able to alter significantly the operations of the unit.

These voices help secure identification with the squad, which seems to have internal 'checks and balances' against police malpractice.

Overall, the representations of Latino criminality are similar to those of black men that we have outlined earlier. However as we depict in the following chapter, Latino men become the node where the global and the domestic intersect when they are depicted as drug dealers or traffickers. As is true for black women, Latino women figure most often as sex workers or victims. Asian Americans feature in a handful of narratives and in the binarized roles allocated to other people of color: victim or gang members, both of which are rigidly gendered.

The narrative (lack of) attention paid to women of color is also reflected in *SVU*'s casting choices, which have remained deeply gendered. The women of *SVU* remain white; Benson has been supplemented by Amanda Rollins, a southern, white woman. When Benson becomes the head of the SVU squad, Rollins and Amaro become partners, offering an echo of the Benson–Stabler coupling. As we discuss in Chapter 5, medical examiner Melinda Warner adds some color to this group but she has mostly been limited to a bit part in the series. These casting changes illuminate the limits of the crime drama genre and its limited ability to incorporate issues of diversity in a nuanced manner. They also facilitate the color-blind feminism we have identified throughout this chapter.

Labile Whiteness

So far we have isolated how *SVU* narratives engage with questions of race and racial difference through an examination of the portrayal of people of color. We end this chapter with a few examples that illustrate the storylines' capacity to recenter whiteness. Juxtaposing the representations of people of color with the ways in which white characters represent the normative helps us underscore the cultural work conducted by the show. In these narratives we see the hidden logic of color-blind racism, that whites are the real victims in post-racial America.

Most storylines highlight white women as rape claimants and they are easily accorded the role of the victimized. In a few instances some of the detectives question these claims but these are often rhetorical devices that help the series challenge rape myths. There are a few exceptions though.

As discussed in Chapter 2, 'Design' (7: 2) is about a pregnant white woman who claims to have been raped by a wealthy scientist. In the process of securing evidence, SVU detectives find out that she was a false claimant who had been stalking and extorting wealthy men. None of the detectives initially question the credibility of the rape claimant or her claims of victimization. This stands in stark contrast to the presumption that dead black women must have been prostitutes and hence are unrapable, at least in the eyes of officers who are not part of the unit. When confronted with evidence that the pregnant woman in 'Design' had lied, Benson takes it as a personal affront that the rape claimant had abused her trust. The series thus underscores white women's purity and credible claims to sexual assault. Similarly, 'Merchandise' (12: 4) features a dead white 15-year-old who had recently given birth to a child. Stabler and Benson are horrified when they find out the teenager had been kidnapped to serve as a farm hand and that she was raped. The same sense of shock is absent in 'Perfect' (4: 24), which starts with the body of a dead black teenager, whom a doctor had tried to impregnate. The presumption of white women's sexual purity and the shock at their violation echoes nineteenth century ideologies of racialized gender norms, which the series as a whole dismantles. But these moments of shock are worth noting for the presumptions underlying them. Femininity is the shaky identity *SVU* is unable to disentangle and articulate in a nuanced manner; the same is not true for the series' representations of masculinity, which continues to be the invisible category in depictions of sexual violence. We single out an exception to this trend below; even when masculinity comes into visibility *SVU* manages to separate the linkages between masculinity and violence.

Angry White Men

'Ripped' (7: 4) showcases a range of white masculinities and does not valorize any of them. The episode is about a seemingly charming, physically abusive white male high school athlete. When Stabler arrives at the school to investigate the case he discovers that the athlete, Luke, is his former partner's son. Both father and son are steroid users, which causes their aggressive behavior. In effect the episode presents aggressive white masculinity and criminality as a product of steroid use. By highlighting the medical concerns the storyline detracts attention from social structures and existing gender roles. In its depiction of the father–son pairing, the storyline seems to be on the verge of addressing the violence central to both athletic masculinity and police masculinities (or the masculinity of the security state). However, by redirecting viewers to the effects of steroid use the storyline loses the opportunity to highlight the centrality of violence in definitions of hegemonic masculinity.

The majority of this episode is devoted to Stabler's conversations with his therapist. He reluctantly turns to the therapist after he beat his former partner to a bloody pulp. During an extended session designed to unravel the cause for his aggression, Stabler reluctantly describes the abuse he suffered as a child from his authoritative father. He also comes to recognize that many of his actions as an adult are still motivated by the desire to please a demanding (deceased) father. The episode taps into feminist insights about violent masculinity as learned behavior. At the same time as the storyline centers on a key protagonist and his sense of infantile helplessness, the series manages to paper over his violent masculine traits and to underscore his vulnerabilities without destabilizing the hegemonic white masculinity valorized by the series. Stabler is provided the space to articulate a victimized masculinity without having to forego his aggression, even though he has come to recognize that his violent behaviors need to be curtailed. Earlier in this chapter, we discussed Mike Tyson's depiction of the figure of the accused murderer, Reggie Rhodes. We pause here to unpack the differences in the representations of victimized masculinity in these two instances. 'Monster's Legacy' unravels the issue of PTSD to highlight injustices in prevalent law and order systems. Rhodes' victimization is presented as evidence of mitigating circumstances for his criminality, which could result in a sentence less than the death penalty. Stabler's violence in 'Ripped' and other episodes is not depicted as criminal in the first place. Instead the therapy session where he narrates his childhood experiences serves to enrich audience understandings of this recurring figure, who has been repeatedly depicted as a passionate, if overzealous, police officer. The childhood abuse functions as an explanatory frame for a complex and complicated persona; the therapy session is not designed to help Stabler become less violent. 'Ripped' offers no repudiation of violence, instead it offers different explanations for violent actions.

In his assessment of neoliberal gendered formations, Hamilton Carroll argues that white masculinity co-opts the impulses of multicultural discourse by claiming for white heterosexual men a semi-minority status: 'White masculinity has responded to calls for both redistribution and recognition by citing itself as the most needy and most worthy recipient of what it denies it already has.'[38] In his conversation with the therapist and the elaboration of his childhood, Stabler succinctly replicates this idea of a besieged white, aggrieved subject (much like the father–son pair in the episode). Stabler and by extension white masculinity moves through, between, and around the discourse of sexual violence to recenter themselves as the hegemonic subject. This repackaging and reconfiguration of white masculinity is what Carroll identifies as exemplifying its lability. *SVU* takes the idea of labile masculinity a step further. In recent seasons, the storyline has depicted Amaro much like Stabler. The Latino detective is able to comfortably occupy the role of victimized masculinity that was initially extended to Stabler. Our point here is not to argue that Amaro becomes white but that the notion of victimized masculinity extends to male figures who can remain pugnacious even as they discuss their vulnerabilities. As was true for Stabler, Amaro does not have to repudiate his violent tendencies. Instead he offers an explanation for his actions. As we have already argued the inclusion of two Latino men in the series has allowed *SVU* to offer a complex and complicated portrayal of racialized masculinity. The series' depiction of labile masculinity works in counterpoint to the misogynist feminism we highlighted in the previous chapter: the male detectives' vulnerabilities as well as hypermasculine traits are presented as integral to their complex personas, however vulnerabilities displayed by female characters are presented more problematically.

When the original *Law & Order* series started, NBC officials chided Dick Wolf into expanding the cast beyond a white male enclave. In contrast, *SVU* has offered a visual multiculturalism wherein racial suffering has been the pathway to inclusion. The series has thus affirmed a politics of identity grounded in injury. But this remains a highly gendered narrative, one that echoes the black feminist lament, 'all the women are white, all the blacks are men.'[39] *SVU*'s color-blind feminism results in a racial shortsightedness. The series is attentive to men of color's victimization by the police and is quite effective at drawing attention to racializing processes. But the series is unable to expend equal energy on depicting women of color's experiences of violation. Nevertheless when narratives center on people of color, the series promotes feminist ideas about violence and sexual assault even as it disavows racial inequality as a material reality. As we highlight in the next chapter, the series' engagement with race makes more sense when juxtaposed with its depiction of foreigners.

4

A Foreign Affair

The Global Turn to Gaze at the Self

SVU has been erratic in its approach to the globe and issues of sexual crimes that emanate from other parts of the world. When we first encountered the series we lauded it for its attention to international instances of sexual assault, notwithstanding its flaws.[1] In the seasons since its pilot episode *SVU* storylines have deployed the global arena as a stage to reposition and articulate American anxieties about both the world and sexual assaults. The global narratives illustrate how gender and violence intersect with an American understanding of the nation and its citizens. Whether the episodes engage carefully or cursorily with a foreign instance of sexual assault, they nevertheless illuminate how prime time fiction narrates American insecurities and vulnerabilities. In all of the storylines we analyze in this chapter, the foreign or the global turn serves as a circuit through which *SVU* redirects our attention to the American self. As a result of this narcissistic turn, these episodes are more revealing about the US as imagined community, who belongs and who does not, than they are about the world. Despite its international veneer *SVU* permits a cultural citizenship that remains inherently parochial; it is a prime time program in global drag. *SVU* is not flat and uniform in its depiction of the foreign, but as the analysis illustrates the storylines mobilize the globe in dramatically different ways to produce diverse effects. In her assessment of US feminist activism

Kristin Bumiller concludes that within the contours of the nation, sexual violence is understood as a crime control issue, but elsewhere it is rewritten as a human rights violation.[2] Our chapter offers insights into such acts of translation, especially how an American inflected human rights discourse is mobilized. We contend that this transformative act is highly gendered, such that the foreign man and woman are not represented in analogous fashion. Instead gender is a key factor in determining whether a person should be protected or should be cast as a threat. Scholars such as Susan Jeffords and Judith Steihm have elaborated on how the protection scenario is repeatedly invoked in discourses of nationalism and nation-building.[3] The protection scenario is a rhetorical device that helps classify people into one of three interconnected categories: threat (villain), protected (victim), and protector. Jeffords cautions that the categories are interdependent, constantly in tension, and are not stable, fixed identities. Further, these roles are inhabited and not acquired. For instance, protectors have to constantly reiterate the validity and viability of the need for protection. If the protectors do their job too well there will be no need for protection; thus they must locate 'continuous threats and continuing victims.' In the protection scenario, Jeffords argues, rape becomes a metaphor that stands for a threat to the community at large. We use these insights to think through how *SVU* narratives articulate a protection scenario and how roles are assigned to the various foreign characters. In what follows we highlight how the gendered nature of these roles is refracted through a global lens.

We are designating as foreign those episodes wherein the sexual violence is identified in the narrative as emerging from a place outside the United States, either through an immigrant or through the travels of a US citizen. In all of these instances, the global enters the field of the visible through a limited range of narrative devices, each of which reassert the sense that New York is a global city, simultaneously both exceptional and representative of the US. The storylines present New York as an immigrant city par excellence, and nevertheless the quintessential American city, a space that people from different parts of the world inhabit, blending into the fabric of the city and asserting their distinctive differences. The foreign presence – be it a person, culture, economic mode, sexual practice, or technology – renders New York a vibrant, dynamic, and constantly modernizing terrain. The city inadvertently becomes a crucible for new iterations of sexual violence. The brutalities articulated through these crimes render New York unique and distinctively different from the rest of the nation. Simultaneously, the SVU detectives' ability to pursue new crimes and criminality serves as a testament to the enduring stability of American ideas of justice. In this thread, the city is positioned as representative of the American state. It is in this narrative dialectic, wherein episodes highlight tensions between the new and the enduring, that we trace the cultural work conducted by *SVU*'s foreign turn.

Given the geopolitical relationship between the US and the rest of the world, there is no innocent or transparent way for *SVU* storylines to engage with the non-American, as place, space, or person. Instead we underscore how the generic limits of the series – witnessing and solving of a (sex) crime – inevitably reproduce a rigid gendered identity that is easily transposed onto American/non-American, first world/third world, East/West dyads. We also highlight how the concept of sexual violence is recalibrated through American eyes.

In general, *SVU* establishes its cosmopolitan credentials and inscribes New York's global status through a few shorthand devices.[4] Often taxi drivers are portrayed as South Asians or Africans whose sartorial choices visibly mark them as foreigners. These foreigners speak in heavily accented English and perform racial difference through what Shilpa Davé has termed as brown voice ('Vigil' 14: 5 and 'Payback' 1: 1).[5] The foreign is also invoked in ways that are more reminiscent of Orientalist discourses, which depict the non-West as simultaneously exotic and dangerous, as is done with the invocation of a Hindu motif in 'Mask' (12: 13) and 'Theatre Tricks' (13: 13). When the detectives encounter these traces of the foreign they are not fazed, displaying their cosmopolitan credentials and their ability to thrive in these global currents. In this chapter, though, we are interested in *SVU*'s engagement with foreign concerns at a deeper level.

A long-term trend is noteworthy: Between 1999 and 2004, *SVU* storylines repeatedly thematized sex crimes that are based outside the US. Strikingly, in two-thirds of the seasons we examined, even as American investments abroad became more weighted, the globe receded from visibility. In later episodes, when the world outside is invoked it is only as a stage to rework domestic concerns. In the early seasons *SVU* could be characterized as facilitating an Orientalist cosmopolitanism, that revalorizes the

US while denigrating the foreign other. In the more recent seasons, the global storylines facilitate a looking inward with the globe becoming the circuit through which a parochial perspective is reiterated. The securing of national borders and preserving the security of the nation (as culture if not as state) are reiterated in these episodes.

Orientalist Cosmopolitanism

The earlier episodes (seasons 1–6) stage the American encounter with the global and the foreign in a complicated manner. Many of the storylines bring into visibility 'exotic' cultural phenomena which are designated in the US as sex crimes, such as polygamy and honor killings. The translation of the foreign normal into the US criminal is revealing of the American self. Informed by Edward Said's *Orientalism* and a Kantian definition of cosmopolitanism as a universal hospitality, our term Oriental cosmopolitanism signals how *SVU* produces cultural discourses that simultaneously assert an incommensurable difference from the foreign other and an American capacity to flourish in these sites of difference. There is concomitantly in these episodes a racial conundrum that we underscore. In the immediate aftermath of 9/11, the presence of foreign characters and foreign venues became sites of racial displacement. In the last chapter, we enumerated that in the early seasons *SVU* narratives tiptoed around the topic of race and racial difference. People of color were seldom depicted as assailants, although they were repeatedly apprehended as suspects. Reading these early race episodes in tandem with the global episodes we analyze in this chapter, we observe that anxieties about race and racial difference were displaced onto the foreign characters. Foreign criminals, almost always male, function as a narrative cipher through which local fears about race and racial difference are enacted. In later seasons, as *SVU*'s depiction of race and racial difference become more complicated, there are fewer episodes with a foreign focus.[6] The victims of foreign crimes, like women of color, are always depicted as feminine and in need of protection from the SVU detectives (and in a larger sense by the American state). In the previous chapter, we highlighted the hypervictimization of women of color, often either dead or otherwise silenced. There is a similar tendency prevalent in *SVU*'s representations of foreign women.

In the following analysis, we outline two predominant visual grammars the series has developed in representing sex crimes in a global context: the haremic gaze and the policing gaze. These representational practices overlap in some episodes but they each mobilize different sets of emotions and sentiments in the viewer. The haremic gaze highlights the foreign victim and espouses a narrow brand of feminism that rehearses Orientalist stereotypes. The woman is placed within the protection scenario as requiring rescue by the SVU detectives. The policing gaze underscores the fears and vulnerabilities the foreign person poses to the stability of the American state. These storylines, which dominated the later seasons, normalize practices of surveillance and regulation as the foreign is presented as an imminent and dangerous threat. The US and Americans arrogate to themselves the role of disciplining the disorderly globe; they are the protectors against the foreign threat. The disciplinary and regulatory impulses of the two gazes are analogous but they are distinct. The haremic gaze has a libidinal charge and is directed at rescuing the imperiled foreign woman. The policing gaze is a more muscular response directed at those who threaten the body politic. Both gazes could be characterized as serving as a proxy for xenophobia but we have isolated them to identify the very different modes through which they appeal to audience sentiments and emotional investments in the series. We also believe that *SVU* narratives are far more subtle in their invocation and disavowal of the foreign than the charge of xenophobia can accommodate.

Over its many seasons, *SVU* has engaged with foreign topics that we have clustered into three categories. In the first instance, the storylines focus entirely on a non-American culture as the root cause of sex-based crimes. These episodes tend to focus on the victimizer and consequently depictions of the foreign assailant betray attitudes that are shaped equally by Orientalism and American exceptionalism.[7] In a related but different node, storylines tap into news from distant lands and bring them to bear in New York City. These episodes often foreground atrocities outside the US and reposition the city not only as a welcoming space but often as a refuge and haven which can help heal the victimized. In this instance the storylines tend to focus on the victimized/survivors and reiterate a universalizing feminism, one that reiterates the logic that sisterhood is global. The haremic gaze dominates in these two clusters of episodes. The third cluster we have identified involves storylines that address the world outside the US but the globe becomes a stage for discussing local anxieties. In this instance, the policing gaze dominates. Trafficking (drug, sex, child) has been a recurrent concern in *SVU* episodes and constitutes the third set of storylines we analyze. These episodes present the victim and victimizer in rigidly gendered terms; the trafficker is the male threat while the victim is a feminized self in need of protection. Cumulatively, these episodes highlight the particular ways in which New York City is at the crossroads of transnational flows. The city is buffeted by global flows – people, money, products – transforming New York; but simultaneously core 'American' values of justice and liberty are restored repeatedly. In the rest of the chapter, we begin with an analysis of episodes that focus on the foreign criminal and the policing gaze that ensues. In the latter part of the chapter, we focus on victim-centered episodes that epitomize the haremic gaze.

The Narco-monstrous

Michel Foucault has theorized the gaze characteristic of modern society in a couple of different contexts. In *Discipline and Punish*, he elaborates on the concept of the panopticon as being central to modern forms of governmentality. The original panopticon was an architectural innovation to supervise prisoners; the authority figures remained invisible while prisoners felt they were permanently observed and modified their behaviors to avoid punishment. Foucault believed that like the prison structure, modern European societies rendered individuals docile through invisible structures of surveillance.[8] Our use of the policing gaze is informed by these elaborations on the optics of modernity. *SVU* naturalizes the police as the beholder of the disciplinary gaze. In the foreign-themed episodes the policing gaze helps underscore the threat posed by disorderly migrants to the body politic. Thereby these storylines justify the surveillance practices that increasingly regulate and govern American and non-American lives. In the following section, we explore episodes engaged with trafficking to highlight the mechanisms through which they naturalize the policing gaze. These narratives normalize existing surveillance mechanisms. Indeed, their representations of the foreign criminals argue for a more systematic and rigorous mechanism through which we can distinguish those in need of protection from those who threaten victims.

Drugs and drug cartels are one of the most repetitive narrative devices through which foreign elements are inserted in *SVU* narratives. In these storylines, racial difference is magnified and the culprits are depicted as unfathomably evil, the narco-monstrous. In her analysis of the burgeoning genre of the prime time drug dealer, Deborah Jaramillo has pointed out that 'organized illegal activity in the US' opens the space for foreigners in 'narratives driven by white characters.'[9] *SVU* proves to be no exception. Foreigners emerge as the villains and the criminals in narratives about drugs and trafficking. These storylines are also highly gendered. In a manner akin to the gendered representations of people of color, the foreign woman appears primarily as victim and as lacking agency while the foreign man is brutal and misogynistic. We offer a few examples of how the series produces the narco-monstrous, which legitimizes the policing gaze.

SVU detectives' actions in 'Loss' (5: 4) are propelled by the rape and murder of an undercover police officer. During the course of their investigations they arrest a member of a Colombian drug cartel, Rafael Zapata. The Colombian is depicted as arrogant, short-tempered, and violent; during an interrogation he calls Assistant District Attorney Alexandra Cabot a 'bitch' and does not hide his misogyny. Apart from these traits and his accented English there are no visual cues to distinguish him as a foreigner. He could be any of a number of men of color suspects SVU detectives bring to the precinct for questioning. He could also be one of the Latino drug dealers *SVU* narratives have featured. Zapata is however presented as more lethal and his connections to the Colombian drug cartel render him more dangerous than the people the detectives normally deal with. These differences are clarified through his accented English and his actions. Zapata's narco-power is so extensive that even from prison he manages to set up a shooting to kill ADA Cabot, who ends up in a witness protection program unbeknownst to her colleagues.[10] This storyline normalizes the need for the 'war on drugs.' More significantly for our analysis, by visually depicting the foreign criminal as just like us, at least within the parameters of multicultural New York City, *SVU* leaches audience emotions away from police excesses to the brutality of the foreigner. It is only by exceeding the law that the American body politic can be kept safe. 'Loss' helps underscore the vital importance of the policing gaze in protecting law-abiding subjects such as ADA Cabot. By making an ADA the target, the narrative literalizes the threat posed to the key American principle of justice.[11]

ADA Cabot returns alive in 'Ghost' (6: 16) as a prime witness to testify against an assassin for the Colombian drug cartel. Like 'Loss' this storyline too sets up the Colombian drug cartel as a ruthless threat to American citizens. In this instance, a young boy is left to testify against his parents' murderers, including a mercenary from Northern Ireland who has found a job with the Colombian drug cartel when peace descends on the English territory. ADA Cabot leaves witness protection to join the brave orphan's testimony. The fortitude of the child and the woman are highlighted to underscore the cartel's callousness. Episodes such as this one set up the drug cartel as a ruthless threat to American citizens. Whether cartel members are South Americans or mercenaries from other parts of the world, they are distinguished by their accents from the other New Yorkers who appear on screen.[12] They may look like New Yorkers, but their voices and their criminality locate them as other. The surveillance and regulation of all foreigners is thereby justified. Within the policing gaze a traditional gendered binary is recapitulated: men are the locus of criminality (i.e., the threat) and women are victims in need of protection.

In more recent seasons, the war on drugs on *SVU* has shifted from Colombia to Mexico. Although the sites of the drug cartels are new, the representations of the narco-monstrous and the gendered dimensions of the threat posed to American values remain constant. 'Spooked' (11: 6) features a Mexican drug cartel with agents operating in New York City and begins with the rape and death of a young couple. In this instance the prime suspect, Manuel Rojas, takes Benson hostage and kills another police officer on duty. Like Zapata, Rojas too is rude and misogynistic, calling Benson a 'bitch.' His brutality, ruthlessness, and accent contribute to his non-Americanness, as does his willingness to transform everyday objects such as a cell phone into a deadly weapon, or to use a teddy bear and breast implants to transport drugs. Unlike the drug dealers in *Breaking Bad* (AMC, 2008–13) or *Weeds* (Showtime, 2005–12), two lauded cable contemporaries, *SVU*'s drug dealers and cartel heads are depicted as brutal and muscular threats to the nation. 'Spooked' includes several gory murders which shore up audience sympathies for the police actions against the narco-monstrous foreigner. The policing gaze is thus no longer perceived as a threat to individual freedoms but is recast as mandatory for civic order. The monitoring and surveillance of ordinary citizens that has become central to the post 9/11 US culture of security is underscored and naturalized by these storylines.

The Lure of Sex

Child and sex trafficking have offered an equally productive avenue for *SVU* narratives to address the world outside the US. Lawmakers and feminists have addressed these issues as well. In the new millennium, the US Congress has passed a number of laws to prevent trafficking. Often these have been folded into the Violence Against Women Act (VAWA), which has been renewed several times since it was first introduced in 1994. Under the aegis of VAWA, several NGOs have started to address sex trafficking as modern-day slavery and have established shelters and resources to assist trafficked people.[13] By foregrounding the loss of freedom and the abject conditions of those who are trafficked NGOs, such as the Coalition Against Trafficking in Women (CATW), have characterized sex trafficking as extolling un-American values and as a throwback to the past. Some feminists have tapped into this new interest in trafficking to establish robust rescue and rehabilitation projects.[14]

SVU episodes have collapsed the long-standing war on drugs onto this newly formed war on the sex trade. As we discuss below increasingly *SVU* episodes have rehearsed central arguments about the rescue and rehabilitation campaigns. Over the seasons, *SVU* has also addressed this issue with varying levels of nuance and complexity. All of the storylines nevertheless highlight New York as a global city where people from across the world live, either legally or otherwise. These global citizens who inhabit the city become the fulcrum for the enactment of crime, as victims and victimizers. Foreign men and women occupy key positions in the protection scenario mobilized by these narratives.

In the early seasons when *SVU* narratives engaged with 'foreign' subjects, the storylines tended to be didactic, spelling out the issues for viewers.[15] However in more recent seasons, the storylines are more reticent in providing information about these foreign phenomena, expecting audiences to be familiar with some of the primary concerns based on their past engagement with the series. Thus, 'Slaves' (1: 22) elaborated very carefully on the phenomenon of sex trafficking and also why an East European country such as Romania with its white-like population is such a vital hub for this crime. As is true of the narco-monstrous, the episode underlined the foreign elements. 'Slaves' begins with a heavily accented older man, filing a report at the police precinct and unable to provide a clear crime or victim for the detectives to pursue. He clarifies for the detectives that he is from Romania, not Hungary, and that when he gets upset he lapses into his native tongue. The last time this happened, he was accosted by a woman who told him in Romanian that she was being kept captive and that she was being abused. He is unable to provide any other information. Captain Cragen succinctly sums up the inauspicious task before the detectives, 'Okay, let me see if I got this straight. Some girl is being sexually abused by some guy somewhere in Manhattan.' From this flimsy beginning, the detectives are able to track down Ilena, the Romanian who was supposed to attend college in the city and was brought to the US by an American businessman she met at a Bucharest discotheque. Once in the city, she was held in captivity, chained in a closet for six months, and then tortured routinely until she became compliant. Two years after her arrival in the US, she was permitted to go out of the house acting as the couple's nanny. Ilena is the subject of both sex and labor trafficking.

'Slaves' exemplifies *SVU*'s investment in the slogan 'the local is global' and reveals the intertwined and interconnected nature of lives in contemporary conditions of globality. By narrative's end the SVU detectives rescue Ilena from a coffin-like structure in which she was imprisoned in a wealthy, upper west side house.[16] As the Romanian woman is accorded very little screen time, the storyline highlights the perpetrator, his desires, and his need for control. The rich, white, heterosexual male banker is depicted as domineering, demanding, and abusive. If the drug cartel leaders looked just like New Yorkers but their actions were evil, the sex trafficker is figured as the archetypal successful New Yorker. The storyline locates the source of criminality in the heart of the city, the financial sector, and thereby shores up viewers' affective investments in the detectives' actions, especially their policing gaze. Such a storyline reiterates the need for the police to be able to monitor and survey the activities of all New Yorkers, not just foreigners.

The episode thus naturalizes and reiterates the surveillance practices characteristic of millennial global cities.

A season later 'Parasites' (2: 19) returns to Romania as a hub for sex trafficking but this storyline places the blame on Romanians living in the city. The storyline centers on a modified mail-order bride scheme, which results in the legal entry of Romanian women into the US. While the American men who marry these women are featured, the central problem the show uncovers is what happens to the brides who are 'returned' by their husbands as being 'unsatisfactory' wives. Through a convoluted storyline featuring identical twins, 'Parasites' once again features a powerful, domineering man who works in the Romanian consulate as the root of the problem. In 'Slaves' the abusive banker was portrayed as a stickler for details while in 'Parasites' the diplomat is depicted as a finicky man who obsesses over his orchids. Both storylines reference these seemingly normal men's capacity for evil by lingering on these character traits. Strikingly neither of these storylines highlights how the whiteness of the Romanian girls may contribute to their popularity in the sex-trafficking routes between the US and East Europe.[17] The invisibility accorded to whiteness in these storylines is striking. As we enumerated in the previous chapter, in storylines featuring people of color, culture, such as 'gangsta' masculinity, becomes the primary explanation for criminality. In striking contrast, the whiteness of the criminals and victims remains unremarked in the abovementioned global narratives. In these and other narratives, such as 'Night' (6: 20), white men are the criminals. They use their social and cultural capital to prey on women who are either in the US without legal documents or are unaware of the laws that protect them. The foreign women become the backdrop against which white men's predatory proclivities are played out. These narratives produce a universal, rapacious masculinity, which is reminiscent of the rapist figure in early feminist writings about sexual assault. But whiteness itself as a social category is not explored. There are aspects of the haremic gaze prevalent here but for the most part these stories emphasize the difficult task of the SVU squad. These storylines argue tacitly for better surveillance mechanisms that would make the tasks for the detectives easier. The storylines thereby emphasize the policing gaze central to carceral feminism.

'Debt' (6: 2) offers a change in setting, with the locus of criminality centered in Chinatown. The episode focuses on Chinese women who are trafficked into the US as part of a tightly controlled sex ring. This storyline makes a brief detour into sweatshop industries, another prime site of trafficked labor. While in the other episodes discussed in this chapter SVU detectives are able to communicate with the main suspects, in this instance they turn to Dr. Huang to go undercover and catch the accused. The detectives assume that the Asian-American psychiatrist must be fluent in Chinese and expect him to serve as their translator and intermediary. This is also one of the few instances where Asian and Asian-American men figure as the culprits and are depicted as being ruthless.[18] Some of the stereotypical ways in which these men are presented are reminiscent of the 'yellow peril' arguments Gina Marchetti has singled out as core to Hollywood depictions of Asian Americans.[19] Chinatown and its inhabitants are presented as mysterious and dangerous, radically different from the rest of the city. These differences are emphasized through visual and aural cues. *SVU* does not assuage anxieties but fosters viewers' fears and insecurities about Chinese and Chinese Americans. Dr. Huang, as a regular cast member, escapes these stereotypes and the anxieties surrounding Asian Americans.

By seasons 13 and 14, *SVU* narratives represent sex trafficking almost as a banality and all of the didactic elements from previous seasons are absent. Storylines repeatedly engage with the presence of invisible but palpable sex trafficking webs within the city. The season 13 finale, 'Rhodium Nights' (13: 23), outlines the far-reaching power of the sex trade industry while the following season's first episode, 'Lost Reputation' (14: 1), details the elaborate maneuvers SVU detectives have to undertake to arrest the key actors in this industry. Significantly, the storylines reference sex workers of different nationalities but do not identify the crime as sex trafficking. The refusal to name the practice as sex trafficking is noteworthy. While the narrative focus on political and police corruption may justify this practice, it is also likely that since the series has dealt with the topic of trafficking repeatedly, viewers are expected to be familiar with the contours of this phenomenon without having to spell it out.[20]

Similarly in 'Acceptable Loss' (14: 4) sex trafficking becomes the hook for the detectives to investigate a terrorism plot and the emergence of terror cells in the city. In this instance, SVU detectives are called to a car accident because one of the passengers is a young Colombian woman, Pilar, with a bar code tattooed on her neck. Unable to prove any criminal activity or to make arrests, the detectives go undercover to find the place where the sex workers are housed. Before they are able to arrest the Bosnian men guarding the trafficked women, the Department of Homeland Security intervenes, claiming that the sex trafficking ring is connected with an Al Qaeda subgroup. With the threat of an imminent attack on the city, SVU detectives work to nab the terrorist, a young Pakistani woman, Sofia.[21] SVU detectives are able to distinguish her from the other women in the sex-trafficking industry because her bar code is erasable. Benson announces to her colleagues that a Muslim woman would never get a tattoo. The assertion of difference through a religious turn helps set up a narrative conundrum wherein Sofia is simultaneously a terrorist and a victim. The depiction of a woman as a threat destabilizes the gendered aspects of the protection scenario. But since this episode is a rare exception, the protection scenario itself remains the dominant framework in *SVU* storylines.

The interrogation that follows highlights the inadequacy of binarized understandings of East/West, Muslim/American, foreign woman/foreign man. Once Sofia is in the precinct, the SVU detectives are eager to bring the Pakistani woman into the fold of global sisterhood; they highlight the plight of the other foreign victims, the enslaved and raped trafficked women. Sofia, however, compels the detectives to confront a different kind of violence enacted on vulnerable foreigners by asserting that her actions were propelled by the US military. She turned to terrorism because US drone attacks killed her father, who as a doctor had gone out to help people injured in other drone attacks. Sofia tries to convince her American interlocutors that she is in the US because this is 'where the drones come from.' Since Sofia is accorded very little screen time the reference to US foreign policy and military actions is a throwaway line that is not elaborated. The statement appeals to American ideals of justice but also serves as a narrative fulcrum to assert an ineluctable cultural difference. Analyzing the limited ways in which Western feminists understand Palestinian women bombers, Amal Amireh has pointed out that they are always seen as dupes of Muslim culture who need to be rescued.[22] 'Acceptable Loss' maps out how SVU detectives undertake a similar maneuver. They are unable to see Sofia as a politically motivated actor; they are eager to position her as someone to rescue. However, Sofia evinces no sympathy for the innocent, trafficked women and rebuffs attempts at rescue and rehabilitation. Thereafter, the narrative repositions her as someone who has failed to understand the basic tenet of feminism, that sisterhood is global. Instead Sofia is depicted as a masculinized threat to the nation, the Muslim terrorist.

Each of these episodes underscores the need for the vigilant gaze of the SVU detectives who are able to sniff out a crime even in the absence of a complaint. Apart from offering ballast to the policing gaze, these storylines reposition the detectives as 'freedom fighters' on behalf of foreign women. They offer fodder for arguments supporting surveillance practices already in place by the state.

Save the (Brown) Children

Racial difference appears parenthetically when *SVU* narratives engage with the topic of child trafficking, which inevitably leaks into sex trafficking. 'Angels' (4: 6) features boys from Guatemala who are in the US for an education but find themselves traded as sex slaves (rehearsing ideas developed in 'Slaves' but towards different ends). The detectives identify the dead pedophile who owns the boys as a wealthy Wall Street lawyer (he claimed to have adopted the boys, but detectives discover that he circulated them among his friends). The dead lawyer was not just a homosexual; the storyline also depicts him as a pederast, someone interested in the North American Man–Boy Love Association.[23] While the criminal white men in the two previous cases we have discussed, 'Slaves' and 'Parasite,' were depicted as despicable and controlling, the perpetrator in 'Angels' is represented as evil in a different register. Stabler declares him to be 'an utterly worthless human.' As the detectives unravel the ring of wealthy, educated men who undertake 'sex tours' in Central America, one of the suspects proclaims the futility of the arrest since there are no state laws prohibiting sex tours and federal laws demand a complaining witness. The unrelenting detectives are able to disband the pedophile ring of 17 wealthy men and arrest them through some legal maneuvers. What is striking about this storyline is the manner in which white men's refusal of heteronormativity is depicted; pedophiles are depicted as unable to comprehend the concept of statutory rape, which is the crime they are accused of committing for having sex with minors. The anger the detectives heap on these men, with Stabler declaring them to be 'sick bastards,' is qualitatively different than in '911' which involves nine-year-old Maria from Honduras who is trapped in a child pornography circuit. The white man who is identified as the child pornographer is depicted as vile, but in '911' the focus remains on Maria and her travails rather than on her victimizer. In both of these instances the narratives do not remark upon race or racial difference, but the economic plight of Central American countries is repeatedly underscored, serving as an explanation for why the children may have falsely assumed that the US would be a haven for them. By highlighting the vulnerability of innocent, immigrant children, *SVU* storylines promote the need for surveillance practices. Maria and other immigrant children are presented as in need of protection from predators, who must be evicted from the body politic. In these narratives sexuality and erotic desires, not nationality, become the primary axis of difference as well as threat to the nation.

Like the other storylines that focus on trafficking, 'Ritual' (5: 20) maps the contours of this global concern, pointing out that the trade in children is the 'third largest money maker for organized crime in the US.' The episode contains two overlapping criminal stories, a whodunit concerning the grisly murder of a Nigerian child and a subplot concerning the hoary global trade in child labor. Within the child trafficking subplot the episode outlines how children from third world countries are brought to the US for domestic labor as well as sex and marks both these practices as equally problematic.

'Ritual' begins with some grounds staff in Central Park finding a dismembered and decapitated child's body. Near the corpse they find some objects: bowls of blood and a candle, arranged carefully, indicating a ritual practice. By tracing the origins of the candle, SVU detectives are convinced that the murder was part of a Santeria ritual, a religion practiced in some parts of the Caribbean, Latin America, and Africa. In a didactic aside characteristic of the series at that point, Fin explains Santeria to his colleagues and cautions that human sacrifices have been banned for over a century. Nevertheless, true to the *SVU* formula of tracking down false suspects, the first suspect in the case is the director of the Center for the Study of Santeria. Stabler is particularly abrasive in questioning the Center's Director who argues ineffectually that Santeria is no more violent than Christianity.

SVU viewers are inured to seeing Stabler become invested in crimes dealing with children; his status as a father serves as the unarticulated explanatory subtext for his actions. When the director refuses to divulge his membership list as constitutionally protected information Benson reminds him, 'your religion has a history of human sacrifice.' In contrast to the crass tactics of the two detectives, the Santeria director is calm and dignified. Similarly, a judge cautions ADA Casey Novak and the SVU detectives against racial profiling. The insertion of these cautionary voices into the storyline draws attention to the SVU detectives' excesses but these failings are designed only to increase identification with the recurring cast of characters. The detectives' actions are always depicted as propelled by forensic evidence; if they harass innocent people this is presented as a small price to pay for securing the real criminal.

Through methodical police work SVU detectives discover that the murdered boy was trafficked into the US from Nigeria with his sister, Na'imeh, who is employed as a domestic servant in an upper east side house. In the whodunit section of the episode, after harassing the Santeria center and making several other detours, the detectives track down a white art history professor for the murder of the Nigerian child. He had secretly purchased the boy as a sex slave but when his wife unexpectedly cut short her visit abroad he killed the boy and, drawing on his art history knowledge, staged a Santeria ritual in the park. 'Ritual,' however, does not end with the apprehension and prosecution of the murderer. The art history professor's criminality is reduced to a venal individual's sexual predilections, overshadowed by the much larger global problem of child trafficking. In this episode, catharsis pivots on the prosecution of the foreign trafficker.

Fin takes the lead in the child trafficking plot and is enraged at the robust 'modern day slavery' that exists in the city. His anger at the rich, white woman who seems oblivious to the humanity of the child she has purchased secures viewer identification with the detective. Similarly his indignation at the inhuman conditions in which the Nigerian children are held before being sold mobilizes audiences' affective investments with the squad. By having an African American take the lead role in unraveling a crime that resembles the historical trafficking of slavery, the episode blurs the public–private divide, underscoring the idea that for Fin the issue is not an abstract one. This personal angle also predisposes audiences to condone any excesses in his actions.

In their quest to entrap the Nigerian trafficker, the SVU detectives enlist the services of a consular officer, who speaks fluent but heavily accented English. Fin and the consular agent meet the trafficker masquerading as a Nigerian couple looking for a domestic servant.[24] The trafficker, Martin Bosuh, is arrested only after Fin assaults him physically. Like the narco-monsters, Bosuh is depicted as a corrupt misogynist, who does not see the criminality of his activity. He asks the consular agent, 'What can a woman do? Claw my eyes out?' Bosuh's bravado and brashness disappear and he becomes more contrite once he discovers that she has the power to revoke his passport and deport him to Nigeria. Bosuh divulges information about his trafficking project, recognizing that the US would offer him a different form of justice than the one that awaits him in Nigeria. With this simple assertion of the US being more just, the series legitimizes American claims to exceptionalism. This narrative turn permits viewers to overlook the fact that minutes earlier Bosuh had pointed out that he was beaten by a police officer, 'another African man brutalized by a vicious cop.' *SVU* thereby helps bolster the idea that the American policing and judicial systems are just even though a passionate police officer may break the rules. By relocating the faults in the policing system onto an individual, the episode permits viewers to ignore the ways in which people of color are systematically disenfranchised by existing law and justice systems. The storyline nevertheless justifies once again the use of surveillance mechanisms and the need for the policing gaze to protect the innocent.

In 'Ritual', wealthy US citizens who buy children as domestic servants are oblivious to their complicity in the sustenance of 'modern day slavery.' Instead, they are convinced that they are humane because the meager salary they offer is significantly more than the children would earn in their home countries. Similarly, those who purchase children for sex are equally blind to the criminality of their actions. The Nigerian parents, on the other hand, are depicted as naïve for sending their children to the US to obtain a better education without confirming the validity of these arrangements. Bypassing the deeper structural issues that sustain child trafficking, the episode instead hones in on individual culprits that viewers are directed to despise. *SVU* offers thus a simplified representation of the current global crisis: foreign masculinity, which is discernible on an aural level, is the threat to the nation.

If we were to examine 'Ritual' through the protection scenario we described earlier in the chapter – the Nigerian trafficker is the threat, Nigerian children and in a more generalized sense the US social order those in need of protection, and the SVU officers and the American state the protectors – we can see how the episode reiterates and recapitulates a foundational national narrative of the state as the protector. 'Ritual' and storylines featuring the Colombian drug lord or the Chinese sweatshop owner present the threat to the nation and its citizens as from within the nation state. They help produce a new physiology of criminality, with foreign men as potential criminals, and their presence in the US shows how the nation is under threat both from within and without.

'Ritual' ends with SVU detectives rescuing the latest batch of Nigerian children brought illegally to a New York City warehouse with Fin urging children's services, 'take good care of them, they are a long way from home.' With this ending, the narrative repositions the SVU team into the fold of the caring and compassionate police force and not as one given to violent outbursts that reveal the soft underbelly of US law enforcement agencies. *SVU* unerringly reinscribes the police as the protector of the vulnerable rather than as generating a state sanctioned violence. Fin's final injunction also reiterates the policing gaze and the need for better surveillance mechanisms to protect the innocent.

Re-visioning the Harem

The discourses that have dominated *SVU*'s portrayal of foreigners and foreign spaces have a distinctly gendered dimension that we characterize as constituting a haremic gaze. Elaborating on art historian John Berger's insights, feminist scholars have developed the concept of the male gaze, arguing that the objectification and 'to-be-looked-at-ness' qualities of women are structured into the sinews of Western visual culture.[25] Similarly, adding a gendered dimension to Edward Said's elaboration of Orientalism, feminist scholars have highlighted how an imperialist gaze infantilizes and eroticizes non-Western women.[26] In a manner akin to the male gaze's objectification of women, the imperial gaze apprehends non-Western cultures only through Western eyes. In particular, the non-Western woman is often reduced to the trope of the haremic subject, as someone oppressed and contained by her culture, simultaneously exotic, erotic, and dangerously different. Our concept of the haremic gaze combines the generative potential of the male gaze and the imperial gaze to think through how a contemporary prime time series mobilizes the energies of these concepts in the depiction of the radical other, the Muslim woman. A few *SVU* storylines focus on a singular foreign cultural practice such as honor killing, polygamy or female genital cutting. Examining these hot-button issues through Western eyes, *SVU* episodes insidiously produce gendered violence as the product of foreign traditions, often emanating from Muslim societies. Aspects of the haremic gaze are also visible in the trafficking narratives that focus on the trafficked victim, which we have discussed previously.

'Honor' (2: 2) throws into sharp relief the central components of *SVU*'s haremic gaze and some of these elements are reiterated 10 seasons later in 'Snitch' (9: 10) and in throwaway lines in other episodes. Like so many other *SVU* episodes, 'Honor' begins with the police discovery of an unconscious woman in Central Park; she has been stabbed repeatedly, seemingly raped, and left for dead. While the episode is about the phenomenon of honor killings, the narrative makes an interesting detour drawing rhetorical equivalences between Muslim culture and urban (i.e., African American) youth culture. Benson and Stabler wonder at the scene of the crime whether wilding is back in vogue even as they declare their hatred of the term.[27] This throwaway term as well as reference to 'wolfpack type activity' taps into a rich cultural node of anxieties late-twentieth century New Yorkers have experienced with respect to Central Park. Wilding is a shorthand term to signal that the woman was gang raped and beaten with rocks. The Crime Scene Unit technician comments, when he finds a bloody rock, that the victim was subjected to a 'good old fashioned New York stoning.' In the first few minutes of the episode, the storyline has already established the severity of the crime and the heinousness of the criminals, and has tapped as well into local and global archives of cultural memory (the Central Park jogger case for those who recall it and the more contemporary use of stoning in Taliban-controlled Afghanistan). The detectives soon identify the victim, Nafeesa, as the daughter of an Afghan diplomat who is enrolled in a local university. In the course of their investigations, the detectives give voice to a number of prevalent stereotypes about Islam, the status of

Muslim women, and the then prevailing Taliban regime in Afghanistan. Exemplifying the didactic mode we have previously identified, a professor of Middle East Studies explains to the detectives that 'Afghan women cannot leave their homes on their own' while a friend explains that Nafeesa would change out of her 'robes' when she got to school and that she hated wearing them.

'Honor' was first aired in 2000, months before knowledge of the Taliban's repressive regime became commonplace in the US. Revisiting the episode in 2014 it is striking to observe how much nuance and complexity the storyline tries to introduce in its depiction of the Koran and Muslims. Nevertheless the episode harbors a haremic gaze and we unpack below the constituent elements of this mode of representation, because it enables a narrow vision of feminism.

When the detectives finally question Nafeesa's parents in their well-appointed apartment, the father speaks exclusively to Stabler. Clad in a Western suit, he looks modern, but his accent and traits betray him as a foreigner. He refuses to interact with Benson. His burqa-clad wife, whose eyes are the only visible part of her body, remains silent throughout this interaction. She becomes the visible signifier of the foreign other. The father disavows his daughter saying, 'she is dead to us' because she rejected tradition. Even when the detectives describe the violence inflicted on Nafeesa, the father remains impassive and describes his daughter's actions as constituting *zina* (shame). This narrative strategy permits a disidentification from the Afghan parents who do not display the sets of emotions associated with a family that has lost a child. The father becomes the embodiment of Afghani patriarchy.

The narrative heightens the sense of an encounter with an alien culture through a series of expository asides about the Taliban, each of which reduce Afghanistan to the fundamentalist regime. Benson explains to her colleagues that Nafeesa 'brought shame and dishonor to her family. They behead women for that where she comes from.' Nafeesa's Afghan boyfriend reiterates this perspective on Afghan culture by pointing out that he wanted her 'to stop acting like she is from some primitive tribe.' The Middle East Studies professor clarifies that in Afghanistan 'having a job, going to school, or leaving the house alone or without every inch of her body covered, she would be scorned as a vicemonger.' To live as 'a modern woman' Nafeesa had to leave her parents' home. If she had attempted this in Afghanistan she would have been murdered, he cautions. Similarly the boyfriend underscores Nafeesa's plight in an oppressive culture by noting that, 'she wanted to be more than a factory for producing sons.' These repetitious characterizations of the Taliban produce it as a vile, monstrous, misogynist culture. It is axiomatic that Afghan women should be rescued from such a culture. While it is not explicitly stated, the central assumption of this storyline is that Afghan women should be saved into Western culture and Western modes of living. A precondition for their emancipation would be that Afghan women reject their cultures.

Once the detectives have established that Nafeesa's brother killed her to restore the family honor, the storyline primarily focuses on the legal possibility of charging a diplomat's son.[28] The most significant aspect of the trial is that the brother, clad in traditional Afghani clothes, makes a compelling argument that he was programmed by Afghan culture and the Koran to kill.[29] To contest this compelling nurture argument and ensure a victory in the courtroom, Benson urges having Nafeesa's mother on the stand to rehumanize the murdered daughter and to underscore the gendered dimensions of foreign criminality. Both Captain Cragen and Fin object to the strategy, pointing out that the mother would be sentencing herself to death. The next scene shows the mother clad in a white burqa condemning her husband's actions on the witness stand.[30]

The Afghani mother is seemingly presented with a choice and exercises her agency by opting to testify. This narrative turn of the once silenced woman offering testimony against Afghan culture in an American court allegorizes the constitutive elements of Western liberal feminism. Scholars have clarified that liberal feminism tends to focus on the individual and developing her skills and capabilities rather than on enabling social change. Liberal feminism's refusal to analyze power relationships that structure individual lives is exacerbated in the international context where the US role in enabling unequal geopolitical structures is unquestioned. Similarly, 'Honor' shows the unnamed Afghani mother becoming a resistant subject under the guidance of white women. Two years after this episode first aired, anthropologist Lila Abu-Lughod posed the searing question, 'Do Muslim Women Really Need Saving?' after the US government decided to liberate and save Afghani women by waging war.[31] Abu-Lughod questions the West's obsession with the plight of Muslim women and condemns liberal feminist desire to rescue and rehabilitate Afghani women from their oppressive culture. The storyline in 'Honor' treads this rescue path, offering Nafeesa's mother freedom from her oppressive culture by giving her the opportunity to testify in public. However, by narrative's end, the mother has been murdered by her husband. This bloody ending offers a cautionary note against proclaiming a universal feminism where Benson and ADA Cabot can join in sisterhood with an Afghani woman.

In more contemporary *SVU* episodes, foreign culture or foreign practices serve as a hook from which the narrative takes a detour to examine local American practices/criminal acts. For instance, 'Snitch' (9: 10) starts as though it were about female genital cutting with both Benson and Stabler offering brief accounts of why this practice is harmful.[32] However, the storyline quickly veers to polygamy in the Nigerian immigrant community and settles on the more mundane internecine gang violence against informants. Similarly 'Retro' (10: 5) starts with traditional healing practices in Gambia that are used to address HIV, but quickly shifts into a narrative about the criminality of not receiving proper medical treatment in the US. In both of these instances and in 'Honor,' *SVU* storylines present 'foreign' culture or religion as the primary determinant of sexual violence. The storylines assert that the foreigners are not like us, they are traditional and not modern. By linking gender insubordination with cultural differences these episodes perpetuate what legal scholar Dicle Kogacioglu terms as the 'tradition effect.'[33] The foreign criminal is represented as the importer of disorderly difference. The women, survivors and victims, shed their cultures as a precondition to emancipation (even if that act results in their death). These storylines produce foreign culture and feminism as locked in a zero-sum game, wherein women are presumed to be emancipated when they have abandoned their culture.[34] In each of these instances, sartorial choices such as the veil for Muslim women or the agbada for African men serve as additional markers of difference. There is simultaneously an assertion of sameness and difference which helps serve the calls for a universal feminism. As Bumiller has noted, in these instances sexual violence is presented as a human rights violation.

War Crimes

We end this chapter with the pilot episode, 'Payback' (1: 1). As we have noted previously, the series paid more attention to sexual assaults enacted in the international arena during its early seasons than it has in more recent years. In 'Payback' the externalized gaze is structured to promote viewers' identification with a cosmopolitan identity. This particular episode includes the haremic gaze (exemplified in 'Honor') as well as the policing gaze that arrogates to the US the role of protector in the rescue/protection scenario we described earlier in the chapter.

The episode opens with Detectives Stabler and Benson arriving at a murder scene late on a rainy night. A cab driver has been stabbed 37 times and castrated posthumously. As the storyline unwinds, the cab driver is found to have been using a false license and there are no clues to his real identity. Nevertheless, the detectives are able to track down his pregnant wife and five-year-old child and break the news to them. It is only half way through the episode that the storyline introduces rape, as the murder victim turns out to have been a wanted international criminal. The detectives discover that the dead cab driver, Stefan Tanzic, was a Serbian indicted for war crimes: the rape of 67 women and ethnic cleansing. Fifteen of the rape victims survived and five of them live in the city. Detectives devote the rest of the episode to narrowing the field of suspects from among these five women.

It is important to note that although the storyline identifies the male as a Serbian it does not offer the ethnicity of the rape victims. This is significant because in the civil wars that followed the breakup of Yugoslavia in 1992 women of every community, Bosnians, Serbs, Croatians, were raped as were some men and boys.[35] The International Criminal Tribunal for the former Yugoslavia (ICTY), working under the aegis of the United Nations, has held hearings since 1993. The ICTY declared wartime sexual violence as a crime against humanity and has indicted numerous officers. While this aspect was covered in the news, by returning to the topic in 1999, *SVU* in effect updated viewers on the process, although there was no mention of the ICTY. Nor does the storyline mention that in the international realm, sexual violence is framed as a violation of human rights and a war crime. Instead, as we describe, the episode represents rape survivors as having no recourse.[36] This naturalizes the protector role the SVU detectives adopt.

During the course of their investigation, Benson and Stabler visit the home of one of the five rape survivors living in the city. Along with the detectives, viewers are introduced to Ileana, who is blind and has a thoroughly disfigured face. Ileana is presented as the 'ultimate rape victim';[37] her blindness and scars are revealed simultaneously to the detectives and viewers, with the two officers modeling the shock and horror viewers are expected to feel. When Ileana hears that her rapist (and the man who disfigured her) is dead she weeps and chants *Allah-o-Akbar*. This chant in itself is remarkable today because it is done to both underscore the woman's Muslim identity and to mark her as a sympathetic, religious person; such a gesture would be radical in the post 9/11 television landscape. As in 'Honor,' this episode too presents Muslim femininity as vulnerable and in need of protection. This sets the stage for the rescue narrative, wherein the US and the West are configured as havens from crimes and injustices committed outside the national boundaries.

By highlighting the depravity of Tanzic's crimes, the episode marshals support from its viewers. The episode spends a considerable amount of time depicting the other two survivors (and murder suspects) in an equally sympathetic manner, although their religious identity is not marked visually. Both women are shown as traumatized and scarred by the war and gang rape, and the storyline underscores the reasons rape victims are transformed into murderers. The first suspect is a young architect who recounts stoically how Tanzic raped her continuously for 23 days, 'sometimes he was too drunk so he did it with whatever was there, a wrench, a pistol, a broom handle …' The second suspect is an older restaurant owner who omits her personal experiences of rape to tell the detectives about Tanzic's murder of her husband and grandson. The graphic details of these crimes elicit audience sympathies and Benson, the neophyte SVU detective, reflects these emotions, crying visibly and vomiting after speaking to one of the women. The restaurant owner commits suicide so she can be with her family, and by narrative's end the District Attorney's office agrees to sentence the architect to 18 months in a psychiatric ward.

This episode is adept at showing the difference between justice enabled through legal channels and the rape revenge that some survivors desire.

While Stabler is initially insistent that the murder suspects be treated like all other criminals, by the end of the storyline he tacitly agrees with Benson that imprisoning the lone surviving culprit would not serve the larger goal of justice.[38]

At the most basic level the narrative highlights the porosity of national borders, how the trauma of rapes committed elsewhere leaks into New York City. This representation of survivors of crimes committed elsewhere makes viewers aware of a global problem and offers a survivor-centred perspective of the crime of rape. However, this notion of the global village is explored only with regard to criminality. We have no similar sense of accountability on a larger scale. The storyline also makes a local–global parallel by featuring Benson having dinner with her mother, a rape survivor, and discussing the case with her. The mother sympathizes with her European counterparts but refuses to condone the revenge murder. This subplot helps establish the contours of the American mode of justice, wherein the responses are not always cathartic or satisfactory emotionally but the rule of law is always upheld.

SVU storylines have reprised the theme of rape in conflict zones in subsequent seasons such as in 'Hell' (10: 17) featuring the Ugandan civil war and the Lord's Resistance Army and 'Witness' (11: 16), which centers on the Congolese civil war.[39] Unlike in 'Payback' in these two later episodes the storylines make reference to the United Nations (even featuring the building) and international policies that make rape in conflict zones a war crime.[40] Both episodes also refer to the US refusal to participate in the International Criminal Court and to sign CEDAW (the convention on the elimination of all forms of discrimination against women). In both of the episodes, the ideas of rescuing and saving vulnerable African womanhood is repeated. Nevertheless these storylines also pay heed to the presence of laws and not just the benevolence of good detectives.

With these three episodes one could argue that the series has lived up to its producer's wish to be educational. In many interviews, Dick Wolf has stated that while many episodes might be painful to watch, *SVU* will educate the public. 'Honor,' 'Payback,' and other episodes clearly make us aware of a problem and open our eyes to events around the world. However, at the same time the storylines rehearse the familiar scenario Gayatri Spivak has called brown women waiting to be rescued from brown men by white men (and women).[41] A haremic gaze shapes these episodes; contemporary concerns are rerouted through an Orientalist lens.

Trauma on the Homefront

There is a fourth cluster of storylines that center on the wars in Iraq and Afghanistan and articulate how these distant conflicts shape the lives of people in the city. These episodes radically rewrite commonplace understandings of rape in war. They also radically rewrite the gendered nature of the protection scenario we have outlined so far.

As illustrated, *SVU* narratives are adept at blurring the divide between the global and local, even as they emphasize the two as separate but intertwined entities. Storylines help highlight as well how the public and private spheres are intimately interconnected. The blurring of these lines is thematized in a small cluster of war narratives that underscore the local effects of the wars in Iraq and Afghanistan.

'Hate' (5: 13) reveals how the wars in Asia may serve as an alibi for an individual's pathologies. The episode begins with the murder of three Arabs by a white man, Sean Webster, who claims to have a genetic predisposition to hate Arabs.[42] As the storyline unfolds, viewers find out that the Sean's father did not die in the 1991 war, Desert Storm. Rather, the father moved to Detroit after marrying an Arab woman he met in Kuwait. The detectives eventually discover that Sean's murderous rage is about a personal, familial betrayal rather than being propelled by larger geopolitics or genetics. The investigation of Arab American deaths, though, opens the space for some stereotypes to be aired. For instance, the medical examiner can identify a woman because the henna pattern on her foot is a 'Muslim' design.[43] While not an insidious stereotype, this bit of information taps into a rich vein of Orientalism that continues to shape American knowledge about the Middle East and Muslims. It is noteworthy that the SVU detectives reposition Sean's actions as a hate crime, a rare instance where this legislation is invoked. Sean is convicted of the murders but the hate crime aspects are dropped in court.

'Traumatic Wound' (14: 21) features a veteran suffering from PTSD who is arrested for participating in the gang rape of a teenager at a concert. Detective Amaro notices the veteran exhibiting traits of PTSD and the storyline showcases the ways in which trauma affects people long after they have left war zones. Similarly 'Goliath' (6: 23) is about two Afghan war veterans who kill their wives. In this instance it is not trauma but the anti-malaria medication they both took in Afghanistan that induces their violent behavior. In each of these instances the aggressive actions of white men are recast as the expression of victimized masculinity; we highlighted this process in the previous chapter in discussing Stabler's persona.

'Official Story' (13: 12) and 'Harm' (9: 5) center on private military contractors working in war zones. Both episodes feature rapes in war zones but their effects are presented in New York City. This cluster of war-related storylines effectively shows that combat effects transcend space and New York City is not immune from the damages incurred by 'wars over there.' But in terms of sexual assault these storylines offer war as an alibi for violent behavior even as they hold the military accountable for the acts of individual soldiers. By prioritizing the effects of war on US combatants these storylines offer a different twist on the growing international consensus that sexual violence in conflict zones constitutes a crime against humanity. Significantly these storylines modify the gendered narrative of the protection scenario: soldiers and veterans, male and female, are presented as the victims who need protection and the threat is the US military. This cluster of storylines promotes the need for surveillance and regulation, characteristic features of the policing gaze.

Updating the Protection Scenario

> How is it that in a society where women have no authority, she has so much power?

ADA Cabot poses this question in 'Honor' (2: 2) about the murdered Nafeesa's capacity to bring shame on a family. This statement probing the paradoxes of non-Western femininity is central to understanding *SVU*'s representation of the foreign woman. In *SVU*'s worldview, non-Western women are abject and oppressed. They lack American freedoms and liberties; they are denigrated by their cultures as weak and vulnerable and yet the men in these societies devote a lot of energy to controlling women, who are seen as uncontrollable. Rather than understand that this paradoxical perception of women as all-powerful and repugnant is central to patriarchy, *SVU* narratives present this as alien. By making the oppression of women a product of an idiosyncratic culture *SVU* undercuts the central premise animating the series, that sexual assault is not an exceptional phenomenon but an expression of power. Foreign men, on the other hand, are presented as legibly uni-dimensional: they are criminal and a threat to the body politic. In the last chapter we detailed *SVU*'s color-blind feminism, which similarly depicts the victimization of women of color as a product of culture. Strikingly the majority of those narratives did not seek to rescue and protect women of color. In *SVU*'s narratives the protection scenario is limited to foreign women and children, not women of color.

Despite the length of this chapter, it is worth underscoring that *SVU* narratives have downplayed the global angle. Fewer than 10 percent of all episodes engage with the global even at a cursory level. The quest for novelty may propel the series' international optic but the depiction of foreign crime, criminality, and victimization serves as a reassertion of the American self. One could characterize *SVU*'s depiction of the foreign as ethnography-lite. The storylines help describe the lives of people other than Americans, but unlike an anthropologist who observes foreign cultures first-hand, these narratives fetishize the exotic.

In an era of wars abroad and terrorist attacks, the presence of the foreign criminal helps *SVU* maintain its ripped-from-the-headlines aura. In its depiction of the foreign criminal, *SVU* in effect racializes the global arena. The world beyond the US often enters prime time as a space for sublimation and displacement of racial anxieties. In the early episodes that are globalized viewers witness a melodramatic spectacle that helps reassert US moral and cultural superiority. From re-centering the US in a neocolonial global order, the later episodes instrumentally use the specter of sexual assault as a narrative device, offering the moral grounds for US anti-terrorist policing. Rape becomes a metaphor for the threats experienced by the US.

These storylines point out poignantly how the concept of citizenship, as Etienne Balibar has argued, can be universal only in the abstract, because the concept of citizenship must have someone against whom it is defined.[44] Citizens are those who do or could hold the position of protection: non-citizens are those who are declared threats and those who are designated as in need of protection. In *SVU* storylines, the presence of non-citizen assailants or at least the detectives' constant invocation of their presence among us helps rewrite constantly what it means to be American in the post 9/11 era; in a country that is under threat from non-white males, white Americans have to vigilantly protect the unprotected.

It is worth emphasizing that *SVU*'s global turn should be read in conjunction with its representation of race. The universal feminism exhibited by *SVU* personnel works only in the context of foreign women; domestic women of color are not hailed to be part of the global sisterhood. As we have argued in the previous chapter, women of color and their experiences of violation are present but seldom explored. *SVU* episodes rarely give voice to the particularities of women of color's experiences. Equally significantly, seldom do SVU staff seek to rescue and protect women of color the way they do with foreign women. In the *SVU* worldview, US women of color are excluded from the protection scenario, effectively excised from narratives of citizenship and belonging. Men of color are increasingly being represented as complex and complicated characters in their domestic avatars. However in their foreign version they appear almost exclusively as venal and monstrous. In these instances, *SVU* helps enunciate the contours of a carceral feminism, where punishment is the solution for violence. In the global storylines, culture and tradition are often mobilized as explanatory factors for the violence enacted by foreign men. Not surprisingly these topics are largely absent in storylines dealing with domestic race concerns. Most significantly the global storylines help normalize and draw audience support for today's cultures of security.

In this and preceding chapters, we have analyzed *SVU* episodes through a unique entry point. In the rest of the book we examine how the changing transmedia context and technological advances have shaped the forms of feminisms *SVU* narratives showcase. In addition, we spell out the ways in which the series engenders paratextual discourses among feminists. It is from within this multiplicity of perspectives that the series forges a millennial theory of sexual violence.

5

Images of Truth

The Science of Detection

In the new millennium, crime dramas have become a fertile source for the presentation of images of science. Glossy, color-saturated computer generated images (CGI) and forensic technologies have been mobilized as difference-making devices. For instance, the *CSI* franchise distinguished itself from its *Law & Order* counterparts through the central role it assigned to forensic technologies in the storylines. On *CSI*, fantastical images of electronically magnified fibers and particulates vie with medical technologies such as brain scans to help redraw the boundaries between the visible and the invisible. In effect, science and technology occupy center-stage in today's narratives of crime and punishment. The scientific analysis of forensic evidence drives the narratives with the scientists and technicians (rather than detectives) positioned as the protagonists; the lab rather than the squad room is the site of action. Consequently, the magnified images of bodies and forensic evidence have become key nodes that generate affect and emotion. Critics concur that these visual conceits have revitalized the crime drama genre, infusing it with new energy and transporting aesthetic devices from Hollywood to television screens.

Cultural critics contend that the proliferation of forensic technologies in prime time programming has radically altered our understandings of the concepts of law and justice.[1] Some scholars have characterized the primacy given to visual evidence and visual arguments in establishing truth-claims as constituting the *CSI* effect.[2] They point out that juries now expect all criminal procedures to be substantiated with scientific evidence. These crime dramas tap into what Richard Sherwin has described as baroque visuality. Like the earlier baroque era, contemporary popular culture is a site for the proliferation of images that celebrate the act of seeing even as there is doubt about the image's capacity to represent the truth.[3] Today's crime dramas participate in this science-inflected visual spectacle. The ways in which they mobilize science and technology help repackage our understandings of crime, criminality, gender, and race behind a glossy façade.

Unlike its counterparts, the *Law & Order* franchise with its commitments to the gritty police procedural has remained decidedly stodgy and old-fashioned in its mobilization of images of science as well as forensic technologies. The detectives' truth seeking skills are supplemented by technology and science, but seldom do the scientists and technicians become protagonists. Almost every storyline includes the medical examiner or a technician using a range of forensic evidence to establish the truth about a victim or a criminal. Viewers, however, are seldom offered a technologically simulated re-enactment of the crime or the wounds inflicted by acts of violence. Still, as we describe, the series shores up science as an indubitable practice of accessing truth. Science's capacity to speak the truth is established by characters viewers have come to associate with authority. *SVU* taps into a limited repertoire of images to index scientific truth, as we detail below.

One of the dominant effects of such modes of visualization and storytelling is that *SVU* helps produce new truth claims about sexual assault and gendered difference. In this chapter, we explore three different facets of the series' mobilization of science and technology. In the first section, we offer an overview of how the storylines have integrated the use of technologically mediated ways of seeing or what some scholars have called the visual sublime.[4] We map out how crime and criminality are redefined within this scientific optic. Marking the paradigmatic shift entailed by the technology of the camera, Walter Benjamin has theorized that it made possible a new optic. The camera's ability to zoom in and out, to enlarge, the use of slow motion and other technical capabilities allow the viewer to see images that escape natural vision. This optic makes visible a new structural formation of the subject, one that captures the particularities of the condition of modernity.[5] We modify this insight to argue that *SVU*'s deployment of science and technology helps produce a new regime of visuality, one that we term as facilitating a scientific optic. We chart the ways in which this particular optic re-packages our understandings of sexual assault, the assailants, and victims. We tease out how the scientific turn locates the causes of crime and criminality differently than feminist theories of rape have done. The second section of the chapter unpacks the cultural work conducted by the scientific optic. Specifically, we explore how *SVU*'s scientific turn helps formulate a narrow understanding of sex and gender. In the final section we explore how these technologies of gender help shape *SVU*'s engagement with sexuality in episodes with explicitly gay themes. We highlight how trans identities are fixed and unglued by a reliance on scientific evidence of sex features (chromosomal, genetic, cerebral configurations) whereas queer subjectivity is unmoored from reliance on any pernicious account of gay science. The series' strategic deployment of science is consequential to the understandings of sexual assault; we map out the contours of this contradictory and cross-cutting televisual landscape.

Scientific Optic

The changing technological environment in the US has shaped the nature of the crimes SVU detectives investigate. It is easy to overlook the fact that *SVU* has more or less tracked the rapid explosion of internet technology and the more recent social media revolution.[6] Given the ripped-from-the-headlines nature of the episodes, *SVU* has elaborated on the uses and abuses of new social media, new technologies, and the new forms of criminality they have engendered. We first provide a brief overview of how the storylines have integrated the use of technologically mediated ways of seeing. Later, we focus on how the storylines have deployed scientific knowledge to trouble our understandings of crime and criminality. In particular we argue that *SVU*'s scientific optic helps undermine feminist understandings of sexual assault. Through the scientific turn the series develops a subtle redefinition of crime and criminality, almost resuscitating biology as destiny.

In the quest for equality the women's movement in the US has contested the idea that 'biology is destiny.' During the 1970s and 1980s feminists challenged the ways in which science and scientific ideas were used to fix gender differences and naturalize social inequality. Concurrently, though feminist scientists started to alter the ways in which scientific truth is apprehended. Scholars such as Donna Haraway did not abandon scientific practice but instead redrew the ways in which we consider scientific objectivity and knowledge production. Feminist scientists and science studies scholars have not only highlighted sexist underpinnings of science but have also transformed foundational ideas in many of the sciences. *SVU* taps into some of these ideas in narrating sexual assault but seldom does its scientific optic include the transformative ideas about neurobiology that feminists have inspired. As the following analysis indicates, *SVU*'s commitment to scientific truth is at a remove from feminist commitments to science and knowledge production.

As mentioned previously, *SVU* establishes scientific truth claims not through spectacular visuals but by the authority associated with particular characters. A medical examiner, Melinda Warner, has been a recurring figure in the storylines.[7] She is often confined to the morgue or her lab, and interacts with the detectives from these spaces, which are sterile and marked by the presence of microscopes and computer screens. Warner proffers medical/scientific information, which helps the detectives track down the criminal (or victim). The medical examiner's authority is established through her white lab coat and her use of technical language to describe her findings (see Figure 5.1); the detectives act as translators who transform medical knowledge into everyday language. In addition, to authenticate the reliability of her findings the medical examiner often deploys a limited set of scientific images: DNA sequences, fingerprints, x-rays of broken bones, dental records, toxicology reports, and on rare occasion brain scans. In some storylines, such as in 'Crush' (10: 20) the medical examiner is able to identify violence inflicted on a woman, even though the putative victim denies it. In the face of two competing truths, the presence of x-rays testifying to broken bones verifies the medical examiner's assessment. In storylines such as this one the medical examiner through science is able to identify invisible signs of assault. These narrative strategies present the medical examiner as an expert and objective observer of

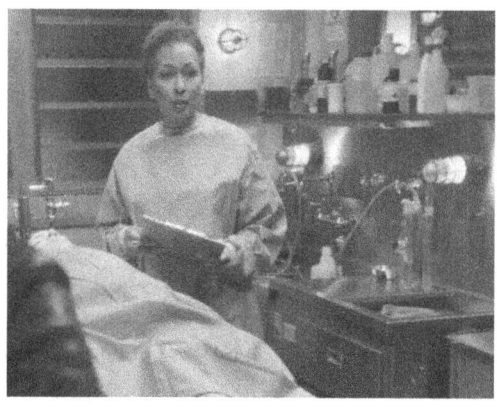

Figure 5.1: Medical Examiner Melinda Warner often provides scientific backing to the detectives' hunches. Screenshot of *Law & Order: SVU*, NBC, 2013.

data; her evidence trumps the victim's own testimony. The resident psychiatrist, Dr. Huang, often supplements these claims; we discuss his role at greater length below. In other instances the medical examiner is able to identify the nationality of a victim by examining her dental work ('Lunacy' 10: 4; 'Ritual' 5: 14) or the oxygen levels in her hair ('Hothouse' 10: 12). The medical examiner helps render the body transparent, but this knowledge is produced to assist the detectives.[8]

The series also showcases forensic technologies by often including a technician clad in a white lab coat from the Technical Assistance Response Unit (TARU). *SVU* deploys these technicians as bit-players who offer empirical data to bolster the detectives' hunches.[9] The technicians work in a dingy room crowded with a bank of monitors, on which they analyze surveillance footage or audiotapes (which are visualized as graphs on computer screens). In the early seasons, the technicians' work was limited to tracking bank and credit card use, monitoring cell phones, unraveling metro card use, and conducting fiber analysis. The most frequent forensic visual was that of fingerprints being collected at a crime scene and later being analyzed. The reliability of this technology is asserted through a visual of an array of fingerprints flashing by on a computer screen until a match is found in the national database.[10] Immediately a person's photo and identifying information pops up on the screen to help the detectives track their suspect (or in the rare instance identify a dead victim).[11] This televisual technique minimizes, if not erases, the interpretive aspects central to forensic technology and instead helps assert an optical empiricism.[12] In his historical account of detective fiction Roland Thomas notes that the rise of this genre in the late nineteenth century occurred at the same time as the evolution of fingerprint technology, forensic profiling, and crime photography.[13] This intertwined history is revealed repeatedly on *SVU*. Visually underscoring its reliance on fingerprint technology and profiling helps the series establish its fidelity to the detective fiction genre.

SVU's reliance on DNA technology is a product of more recent innovations but it is visually cued identically. Most often, the medical examiner shows the detectives two transparencies of DNA sequences, which are displayed as a series of band patterns, posted on a light board. Highlighting the visual match, the medical examiner physically moves one image over the other to display the correspondences. These storytelling strategies focus on evidence collection and systematic processing, offering a specious set of equivalencies and asserting that the outcome of such detailed activity must be the truth.[14] Unlike forensic dramas which foreground vision and visuality, *SVU* resolutely focuses on the skills of detection. Forensic and medical technologies help mark and fix bodily identity to social identity, but it is the detectives who ultimately arrest criminals.[15]

At crime scenes, TARU technicians deploy instruments that offer spectacular visuals: luminol and UV lights to track the invisible presence of blood or other human secretions; heat detectors; and chemicals that reveal the presence of drugs. In more recent seasons TARU technicians have displayed how they track the digital spread of pornography ('Downloaded Child' 15: 19), identify web sites which allow users to fake their telephone numbers ('Crush' 10: 20), and, in general, how they break through digital mechanisms criminals have erected to hide their actions. For the most part, TARU technicians appear very briefly in any given storyline; the technical information they offer is complemented by computer screens and video monitors dense with visual data. The supplementary logic of these images is simple and uncomplicated; they help secure *SVU*'s generic credentials as a crime drama and assert a visual empiricism. In the rest of this section, though, we enumerate how the scientific optic has altered our understandings of sexual assault.

Criminal Intent

Over the course of the series, the kinds of crimes and criminals the detectives investigated have been altered by new technologies. As previously documented, in the early seasons technology was foregrounded primarily as a surveillance tool, one that required the expert knowledge of forensic technicians. The detectives' use of surveillance technologies was often restricted to phone tracking or unsealing library records. Both activities inevitably required a storyline detour to receive authorization from a judge. In a few instances, such as 'Surveillance' (3: 17) or 'Wet' (12: 5) the criminal deployed hidden cameras to stalk his victim(s). These storylines highlight the double-edged nature of new technologies: they can help track down criminals even as they can be used for illegal and criminal purposes. For instance in '911' (7: 3), Benson tries to track down a child pornographer by tracing a phone call made by nine-year-old Maria. The criminal used a virus to disrupt any surveillance of his phone line. In the absence of any confirmation that the Maria on the phone is really a trafficked child rather than a hoax perpetrated by a caller with voice changing equipment, Captain Cragen declares the case closed. Benson, however, remains convinced that Maria is a true victim and the detectives track down the pornographer as well as the child through tenacity, initiative, and other hallmarks of detective footwork. In another storyline, 'Lead' (10: 15) the detectives initially arrest the wrong man after heeding the DNA results compiled from the crime scene. 'Perverted' (11: 9) features a criminal who doctors DNA so the wrong person is implicated. These storylines present science and technology as malleable, used by criminals and also as supplements to conventional modes of detection.

Contemporary technology is depicted as a fecund site for criminality. In 'Choreographed' (8: 9), a husband who suspects his wife of infidelity implants a chip in her so he can more easily monitor her movements. 'Strange Beauty' (13: 22) features a criminal who amputates women. These 'extraordinary' criminals are in sharp contrast to the proliferation of storylines in recent seasons that feature smart phone apps and the internet as tools for criminal behavior ('Quickie' 11: 11; 'Spectacle' 12: 16). In addition, the internet has become a site on which the detectives observe a crime in commission. 'Wet' (12: 5) features a YouTube site for sex prowlers, while

'Intimidation Game' (16: 14) centers on the online gaming industry and subculture. In episodes such as 'October Surprise' (15: 5) and 'Crush' (10: 20) the storylines redefine as pornography the act of sending nude pictures in phone messages. Cumulatively these episodes register how new technologies expand the horizon of criminality as well as the taxonomy of sex crimes. These storylines help illustrate the capaciousness of the label sex crime under the twin impetus of the carceral state and neoliberal feminism. They also feature technology as the new frontier in criminality.

Several episodes caution against the visual empiricism central to *SVU*'s scientific optic. In 'Liberties' (10: 21) SVU detectives deduce from a range of evidence, including information posted on several dating websites, that a woman had made a false rape claim. The forensic evidence suggests she had participated in violent sex but there is no grounds for the sexual assault claim. Technical experts, however, are able to go beyond appearances to unpack a devious scheme where a jealous ex- used his expertise in computer technology to stage a rape. Both the man who is charged with rape and the raped woman are shown to be the real victims. A similar idea is developed in 'Theatre Tricks' (13: 11) where a jealous co-worker uses websites to elaborately choreograph a public rape of a rising star. In both instances, what the detectives initially consider to be false rape claims turn out to be accounts of real victimization. In other instances, new technologies are deployed to perform assaults. In 'Spectacle' (12: 16), SVU detectives are called in to investigate the live-streaming of a rape in progress. By narrative's end the rape is proven to be a hoax designed to draw the detectives' attention to a cold case. In 'Valentine's Day' (13: 18), a husband sitting in a Hong Kong airport lounge having a skype conversation with his wife becomes a witness to her brutal attack. The assault is once again a hoax enacted for the husband, who is unaware of his wife's affairs. In still other episodes, detectives misread images. In 'Traumatic Wound' (13: 21), a soldier is videotaped lying atop a naked woman. The detectives assume he had participated in a gang rape. By episode's end, the squad discovers that the soldier was shielding the teenager from her assailants and was not a rapist. In each of these instances *SVU* storylines enumerate Sherwin's concept of baroque visuality: the proliferation of images provokes doubt and suspicion in the axiom that seeing is believing. Paradoxically, the unreliability of images only serves to shore up science's credibility as a technology of truth.

In no other arena of social life has *SVU* more persistently explored technologically motivated criminality than those referencing women's fertility. Storylines have teased and challenged common-sense understandings of reproduction and rape. In 'Perfect' (4: 24), young girls are abducted and artificially inseminated by a monomaniacal doctor. The forced pregnancy however is not designated as rape because 'there was no penetration.' Despite the limits of legal definitions, SVU detectives are invested in ensuring justice for the young victims and pursue the case zealously. In 'Design' (7: 2) and 'Inconceivable' (9: 14), the theft of sperm and frozen embryos are showcased respectively. SVU detectives investigate these cases because, as Benson puts it, if embryos 'are not special victims, who is?' These storylines mark how new categories are added to the designation special victims. Equally significantly, reflecting some of the changes in society, the ideas of personhood and of whose rights count are pushed further and further in utero. These storylines highlighting the pathos of the unborn are emblematic of the series' ambivalent stance toward women's reproductive rights. Some episodes ('Persona' 10: 8; 'Rockabye' 7: 9) highlight how reproductive rights are being attenuated by new policies; these storylines tend to be critical of the policies. Yet in storylines featuring embryos or the fetus as 'special victims' ('Choice' 5: 7), the SVU squad tramples over the rights of adult women, especially those of pregnant women, in favor of the 'innocent victim.' These storylines tap into notions of personhood that are at a remove from feminist ideas about reproductive rights, thus their depiction of gender and women tend to be anti-feminist.

'Father Dearest' (13: 20) centers on a crime involving sperm donation and young girls seduced via email. The storyline does not demonize sperm donation, but neither does it endorse the use of artificial reproductive technologies. In 'Confrontation' (8: 5), a rapist, who desires to sire many children, tests his victims' urine to check their ovulation cycle. In fertility narratives, *SVU* highlights how the technological turn has enlarged the scope of criminality. Apart from a breezy statement that embryos are special victims, the series seldom probes how these fertility tales redefine feminist understandings of sexual assault. Too often in these storylines the scientific optic becomes a substitute for the exploration of 'the most heinous crime.' As we have explored in Chapter 2, these fertility storylines also figure in *SVU*'s redefinition of parents, family dynamics, and criminality.

Biology Recapitulates Truth

In its quest for newness *SVU* also showcases a number of little-known diseases as either causing criminal behavior or impelling criminality in others. Storylines have featured the murder of infants with Tay-Sachs disease ('Mercy' 4: 14), children who suffer from Pica ('Lead' 10: 15) or Williams Syndrome ('Savant' 9: 4), women who suffer from psychosomatic pregnancy ('Taboo' 7: 14) or Capgras Delusion ('Bullseye' 12: 1), as well as pedosexuals, people who are unable to control their sexual desires for young children ('Confession' 10: 2).

In 'Spiraling Down' (13: 10) the criminal, a former football superstar, suffers from chronic trauma encephalopathy. The SVU team speculates that as a result of repeated head injuries the football player is unable to control his actions. In each of these instances, in the didactic mode we have previously identified, Dr. Huang and the detectives describe in detail the nature of the disease and how it could produce criminality. In most instances, the diseases are broached to offer legal mitigation for the crime at hand. This explanation of diminished rationality is heightened by the use of medical images to explain the disease or impairment.[16] MRIs and PET scans are the visuals deployed most frequently to promote what Jeffrey Rosen has termed as neurolaw, a recalibration of the law to accommodate neurologically induced crimes.[17] These redefinitions of rationality with the help of scan images transform existing understandings of sexual assault. They suggest that brains commit assaults, not people.

'Head' (5: 25) offers a useful overview into the key ideas we wish to articulate about *SVU*'s use of brain scans and the politics of rape these visuals help encode. Two subplots propel this storyline. The first is about a man with a psychiatric condition who live-streams videos from toilets in public restrooms. All of the SVU detectives use this occasion to flaunt their punning skills about this unique kind of video voyeurism, a crime mediated by technology. The criminal in this 'spying' crime negotiates a lesser sentence by informing the detectives of a 'real' assault he had taped in a Central Park cafe bathroom. Through conventional detective work, the SVU staff figure out that the assailant was a school principal, Meredith Rice. The rest of the episode centers on this subplot focusing on the woman who assaulted 12-year-old Shane.[18] Upon arrest, Meredith is remorseful and cognizant that having sex with her students is wrong and immoral. But even as she is being questioned she turns sexually aggressive and attempts to seduce Stabler in the interrogation room. When Stabler pushes her away forcefully, she falls against a wall and into a seizure. In the remainder of the episode the hospital hallways, the doctor's office, and medical images help underscore the scientific authority with which a biological explanation for rape is secured.

SVU detectives discover that the school principal's seizure was not caused by Stabler but because she was suffering from a brain tumor the 'size of a baseball,' which had to be operated immediately. ADA Novak is next shown in a doctor's office demanding an opportunity to arraign the principal. When she discovers the nature of Meredith's crimes, the surgeon explains that 'frontal lobe damage can diminish impulse control.' The surgeon proceeds to illustrate this visually by displaying Meredith's brain scan on a light board. The camera hones in on a bright blue image of a brain with a huge red spot on the right front quarter. The surgeon explains that the red spot is the tumor 'in the right orbital frontal cortex' which controls behavior. With the brightly colored brain scan as evidence the doctor offers a medical explanation for Meredith's behavior: the tumor did not affect the principal's 'store of moral knowledge' so she knew assaulting a 12-year-old student was wrong but she was incapable of controlling herself. Even as the ADA chafes at the idea that a tumor is the cause of the assault, the surgeon points out that without the tumor the principal may no longer be a pedophile.[19] In a cutaway scene set in the squad room, Dr. Huang reiterates to the ADA that the principal lacked the '*mens rea*' and that the tumor 'disinhibited her.' This repetitive medical explanation for the assault from characters presented as authority figures helps secure this biological understanding of violence.

Shifting locations once again and reverting to medical authority, we next see Dr. Huang conversing with the surgeon in a hospital room. The space has the signature white tiles associated with hospitals, a few computer screens, and a sink. While the geographical space and authority of the hospital is established through a quick camera pan registering these iconic objects, the surgeon and Dr. Huang discuss the experiment they are about to conduct. Meredith is to be shown 'erotic' videos while undergoing a PET scan. The scene concludes with the surgeon averring that 'brain mapping is not an exact science yet.' The inconclusive nature of scientific truth claims is however undercut by the next scene occurring in the squad room where Stabler holds a multicolored brain scan and assumes that it reflects the brain of a pedophile. Dr. Huang contradicts him by pointing out an even more colorful brain scan posted on a board, which he asserts is that of an incarcerated pedophile. Beside it he pins the brain scan Stabler was waving and adds that 'Meredith's PET scan' reveals that she is no longer a threat to society. The scan is presented as a photograph, transparently rendering the brain's activity. This narrative strategy relies on the assumption of photographic realism and insists on the fact that the representation was a record of what was simply taking place in the mind, her thought process.[20] While the earlier scan the surgeon had pointed to was predominated by a red tumor, the scan Dr. Huang references is criss-crossed with blue, yellow, and red areas. Gesturing toward this visual evidence for confirmation, he explains that the principal 'showed no reaction to pedophilic stimuli.' According to Joseph Dumit, the presentation of pairs of images sets up a visual rhetoric that highlights difference. It provides proof that the difference between conditions is visible in the brain.[21] This storyline repeatedly underscores the indexical quality of images and this is reiterated by medical figures who proclaim this truth. It participates in what Stephen Morse terms as brain overclaim syndrome, the idea that the brain causes criminality.[22]

To further authenticate the veracity of this invisible truth, Dr. Huang next displays the principal's signature, which returned to normal once the tumor was excised. On-screen viewers are shown two signatures one below the other, an illegible scrawl above a neatly spelled out Meredith Rice. By juxtaposing an illegible scrawl with the neat signature, Dr. Huang is able to ascertain that although written by Meredith Rice they were actually not written by the same person: the scrawl was penned by a pedophile impelled by a brain tumor and the clear signature is that of a person who is not aroused by 'erotic videos.' Dr. Huang translates the knowledge encoded in the brain scans through another visual turn. The visible differences in the signatures help secure the 'expert' testimony offered by the brain scans. Similarly, in 'Ballerina' (10: 16) after examining a brain scan Dr. Huang promotes the idea of neurocriminality, that an ill mind produces criminality. The brain image reveals numerous cancer tumors and Dr. Huang instructs the detectives that 'the cancerous tumors may have secreted hormones' that may have driven a woman to murder. In this instance, the doctor's utterances are accompanied on screen by a close-up of a PET scan, making a cause–effect argument, that the cancerous tumors transformed an aging ballerina into a criminal. In each of these instances, the women are not mothers and their portrayal is in striking contrast to the series' depiction of the monstrous maternal we outlined in Chapter 2.

In a number of other storylines, brain images are used in an earnest indexical fashion; we are invited to see the scans as though they adhered to the conventions of photography. Scientists aver that an MRI presents a partial perspective of the internal part of the body, yet on *SVU* these images are repeatedly presented as offering the irrevocable truth about the body.[23] Through the MRI, *SVU* generates a clear and singular picture of the normal and the pathological. In addition, the scans reify the brain as a locus of control and the site for self-improvement. In these storylines, the victim/assailant is presented as a cerebral subject, as Sigrid Schmitz has characterized it, a person defined by their brain.[24] Episodes deploying brain scans and other medical images imply that people do not commit crimes, but rather that they are compelled to assaults by forces beyond their control. When this logic is extended to sexual assaults, it undoes the series' commitments to feminist definitions of rape.[25] *SVU* storylines do not adopt an essentialist perspective, but often fix the cause of violence in biology through a visual turn. Specifically, some storylines mobilize images of science to calcify the idea that sexual violence is caused by certain biological aberrations that are visible in brain scans. Inadvertently the cerebral turn transforms the criminal into a victim of a faulty body.

In other instances the biological basis for criminality is asserted through a genetic turn. 'Inheritance' (5: 4) is about a serial rapist who targets Asian-American women. Featuring Chinatown gangs, this is a rare storyline that goes beyond the black–white racial binary.[26] The episode unfolds to offer an explanation for criminality that resides not in the brain but in the genes. In this instance, DNA mapping technology allows the medical examiner to match the semen found at a rape scene with that of the criminal's relative. From this biological proximity, the detectives are able to track down an army veteran who had raped women while on tour in Vietnam. His estranged son is now raping Asian-American women in

Chinatown. A rapist is presented as begetting a rapist, suggesting that it is a criminality encoded at the genetic level. The storyline updates the myth of the black male rapist for the twenty-first century, making a genetic argument about criminality being hardwired. The conceit of this storyline is that any possible charges of racism that two men of color are presented as violent rapists is mitigated by the genetic turn. Critical race theorists have avowed that race has no biological basis and is instead a social construct. With the genetic turn, this episode reiterates a strand of scientific thought contending that race is a meaningful feature at the genetic level and genes themselves are deployed as rhetorical devices.[27]

In each of these storylines of neurocriminality or genetic criminality, *SVU* seemingly argues that sexual assault is not about the exercise of power as feminists have long proclaimed. Instead these narratives aver that such violence is encoded in our bodies, that biology is destiny. Such an understanding of sexual assault undoes decades of feminist effort to redefine the crime and can only be characterized as anti-feminist. It also runs counter to the feminist-inflected understandings of sexual assault the series elucidates in other episodes.

The Violent Unconscious

The scientific optic, which dismantles feminist understandings of rape, comes into sharp focus in the series' presentation of psychiatry and psychology. For the most part, psychiatry figures in the series as a discourse that offers an alternative to the retribution model of criminal justice associated with the carceral state. Since this runs counter to the raison d'être of *SVU*, the key protagonists maintain a prickly, often dismissive relationship with psychology and psychiatrists.[28] Stabler is consistently the most opposed to this mode of analysis and crime solving. Although the detectives come to realize that profilers and psychiatrists proffer useful information, they remain hostile to them. In the early seasons the storylines staged psychology and psychiatry as obstacles to conventional detective work. For instance, 'Repression' (3: 1) addresses the topic of repressed memories and Dr. Huang is a steadfast advocate of a woman who accuses her father of rape. The detectives are not just skeptical but contemptuous of the psychiatric processes through which such memories are accessed. By narrative's end the woman is depicted as laboring under a false memory, one that was induced by her psychiatrist. And in a staging of the triumph of the sciences we discussed previously, the medical examiner discovers through medical observations of an unbroken hymen that the rape claimant was a virgin. Psychiatric claims of accessing 'invisible' knowledge are repudiated in favor of an optical empiricism.

The dismissals of psychiatry and psychology are tempered once Dr. Huang becomes a regular cast member in season 3. Individual detectives cultivate friendships with him, but all of them, including the captain, are often skeptical of his assessments. Despite these reservations the radically different approaches to addressing criminality – retribution versus rehabilitation – are repeatedly thematized in *SVU* storylines. Since Dr. Huang left the series in season 13, conversations about rehabilitation have whittled away further even as storylines have pointed out weaknesses in the carceral model. The centrality of the retributive model of criminal justice over all other alternatives was underscored vividly in 'Mask' (12: 13) featuring academy award winner Jeremy Irons in the role of Cap Jackson, a renowned therapist. We single out this episode for analysis because it encapsulates how *SVU* has increasingly come to focus on a narrow vision of science, as one that is deployed through visually captivating forensic technologies. Psychology and psychiatry have been sidelined and increasingly dismissed as irrelevant to understanding criminality.[29] This shift in understanding crime and criminality has important consequences for how the series narrates and conceptualizes sexual assault.[30]

The episode begins with the on-screen assault (and rape) of a lesbian couple, one of whom is Cap Jackson's daughter. Jackson is a renowned sex therapist who had admitted to being a sex addict himself. In the storyline that ensues Dr. Huang is a star-struck admirer who explains the significance of Jackson's approach, which pivots on the rehabilitation model. The SVU detectives, however, are deeply skeptical of the therapist's prowess. While Dr. Jackson's daughter remains in a coma, the detectives figure out that the assailant is associated with the therapist's practice. The detectives urge the doctor to divulge information about his patients, a move he resists vigorously. The majority of the episode is constructed as a series of confrontational encounters between the therapist and Stabler. The two of them are presented as radically opposed in their visions of justice as well as in their divergent masculinities. Through the 12 seasons of his tenure on *SVU*, Stabler was presented as dismissive of psychological explanations of sex crimes; in 'Fault' (7:17) he dismisses psychotherapy as 'bull shit.' These attitudes reach their climax in 'Mask.'

From their very first meeting, Stabler exudes hostility toward the doctor for privileging his patients' right to privacy and confidentiality over the police needs to apprehend the rapist. Stabler positions the doctor's commitment to confidentiality as the sign of being a poor parent, a father who does not prioritize his victimized daughter's interests. Scoffing at Jackson's faith in the therapeutic model, Stabler repeats several times his belief that rapists cannot be cured. This theme is reiterated over a series of conversations wherein the two men confront each other with their radically different approaches to sexual assault.

Jackson: Listen, every day I treat people who are disturbed to the very core of their souls. Most of them were abused as children. Now, you call them sickos and send them to prison. But, my job is to listen to them and help them get better.
Stabler: People like that do not get better …
Jackson: … in prison certainly. My program, some do, if they can trust me.

Later in the episode the doctor reiterates this idea: 'it is too easy to say he is an animal and cage him'; instead he considers that all his patients are still human beings who deserve redemption and saving. Benson too shares Stabler's viewpoint, although she presents her ideas in a less abrasive manner.

The confrontations between the SVU detectives and the therapist come to a head after an interrogation session where Stabler pursues Jackson into a waiting elevator. Stabler repeatedly asks the doctor if in an alcoholic stupor he had raped his own daughter. Ultimately Jackson falls to his knees wailing that he cannot remember but he thinks he did. By bringing a renowned therapist literally to his knees and having him confess to the possible crime of incest, Stabler and his brand of justice appear to have prevailed. Viewers of the series are inured to the SVU detective's Manichean worldview, which is explained away as his zeal to 'put away' the bad guys. However, in this storyline Stabler violates medical and police protocols by going undercover as a recovering sex addict. The triumph of the retribution model is repeated at the conclusion of this convoluted storyline when the doctor abandons his earlier avowals of patient privacy and exclaims, 'Eliot you were right ... Let's go find the man who attacked my daughter.' And once the assailant is apprehended it is the doctor who proclaims, 'I hope they lock you up for life.' In a further blow to the validity of psychotherapy, Dr. Jackson realizes that he did not rape his daughter but had consensual sex with her friend. This narrative strand echoes ideas we have developed earlier in this chapter about the validity of repressed memories. Dr. Jackson is presented as harboring false memories about his own relationship with his daughter. Significantly too, while the women's movement sought to expand the horizons of sexual pleasure, the overarching argument in this episode re-centers monogamous heteronormativity.

At narrative's end, *SVU* has thoroughly disavowed the redemption model of criminal justice by having its most passionate advocate renounce it as well. The series' commitments to the carceral model are repeated in these and other storylines wherein any alternative to prison is evacuated from discussion. Further, the storyline repeatedly blurs the distinction between sexual assault and sex addiction, suggesting that rape is akin to all forms of non-monogamous sex. The storyline reiterates the myth of the rapist as a deviant individual. Although 'Mask' does not forward the scientific optic, its dismissal of psychology is a vindication for the visual model of truth. Ideas that the unconscious may propel a person's actions are dismissed and with them the idea of rehabilitation. Significantly, this shores up a hardwired model of rape, that some people are biologically coded to sexually assault.

In this section, we have offered a few of the paradoxical ways in which *SVU*'s scientific optic rewrites feminist understandings of sexual assault. Images of brain scans become a shorthand device to promote neuroscientific arguments, that the brain is the locus of our thoughts and actions. As we have illustrated, brain scans are used to argue for diminished rationality, which tends to imply that brains, not humans, commit crimes. In other episodes, genetic evidence is mobilized to forward arguments of hardwired behavior. In these storylines too the criminal is exonerated of their actions; instead their genes are to blame. In the following section we illustrate how images of brain scans as well as genetic science are used in a similarly contradictory fashion to shore up gender binaries.

Gender Outlaws

Adapting Foucault's insights to think through feminist strategies, Teresa de Lauretis uses the phrase technologies of gender to argue that gender, 'both as representation and self-representation, is the product of various social technologies, such as cinema, and of institutionalized discourses, epistemologies, and critical practices, and practices of daily life.'[31] *SVU* has never claimed to be a feminist series. Instead it spars with such a feminist conceptualization of gender. This is most clearly stated in episodes dealing with trans subjects, wherein the narrative spells out the limits of gender as a binary system as well as how individual actions are limited by institutions and structures which pivot on a dyadic structure.

Over its many seasons only a couple of episodes have featured trans characters as central figures; they do appear more frequently in walk-on parts where their presence solidifies New York City's status as a crucible for sexual diversity.[32] Although the trans characters in these episodes are played by guest actors they are not presented solely as victim or perpetrator. Instead in every instance trans characters are depicted as complex personalities, simultaneously victim and perpetrator. Each of the storylines encode attitudes that are skeptical of (if not hostile to) trans claims, even as several of the protagonists adopt a sympathetic if bewildered stance. The early storylines dealt with an all-white cast, although more recently the series has engaged with the entanglements of race as well. During this time frame, complex trans characters have started to inhabit the television landscape: Showtime's *The L Word* (2004–2009) included a trans character in its ensemble cast (he appears on *SVU* as we discuss below); *Glee* (Fox, 2009–present) featured a trans character for one season as did the teen drama *Degrassi* (MTV, 2001–present).[33] Netflix's *Orange is the New Black* (2013–present) and Amazon's *Transparent* (2014–present) have transformed the television ecology in this regard as has the presence of cable channel Logo TV (2005–present) which is geared toward LGBT audiences. As we enumerate below *SVU* does not adopt a monolithic perspective on trans claims. Much like the cacophony of feminisms the series permits, the trans storylines provide a venue for the airing of a multiplicity of positions towards trans subjects, the transphobia prevalent in society, as well as issues of legal standing. In what follows, though, we hone in on how the scientific optic is mobilized to legitimize trans claims even as the storylines help reiterate a very narrow understanding of gender and sex.

There are a few constants that are worth highlighting. From the debut episode 'Payback' (1: 1), Stabler has remained dismissive of trans subjects, calling them 'he/she' in each instance. Benson has served as the counterweight by being more sympathetic to trans claims and Dr. Huang, who is the mouthpiece for scientific claims, supports her position. The other recurring characters oscillate between skepticism and tolerance, while the ADAs have had to set aside their personal sympathies to abide by the legal claims to justice. Scholars have castigated the media for offering caricatures of transgendered people, which helps shore up conventional ideals of gender and heterosexuality.[34] *SVU* fares no better. Given the nature of the series, *SVU* storylines center on trans victimization or trans criminality, both of which lend themselves to sensational accounts. As we enumerate below, the series' balance tends to the sensational, with moving accounts of the stigma and shame trans people experience.

'Fallacy' (4: 21) features an MTF rape claimant, Cheryl, whose assailant Joe dies in the attack. The detectives initially believe that Joe's death resulted from an act of self-defense. Later they are convinced that Cheryl killed Joe once he had become aware of her MTF status and would have outed her. This shift in motives alters sharply Cheryl's legal status, from potentially defending herself in a manslaughter case to being a suspect in a murder case. When they first encounter Cheryl, Detectives Benson and Stabler are very sympathetic to her. Even in the absence of any corroborating evidence of her assault claims, the detectives establish Joe's criminal credentials by highlighting his use of crystal meth and his prior assault history. However once a forensic technician reveals that the blood samples from the crime scene feature only males, the detectives' attitude toward Cheryl shift, even as Dr. Huang declares her to be a 'pre-op transsexual.' As the storyline unfolds, Stabler subsequently calls Cheryl a liar, as a he/she who 'had us all fooled.' He has a visceral repulsion to her. ADA Cabot similarly presents Cheryl's undisclosed MTF status as an act of deception. This theme of duplicity is clichéd and perniciously undermines the very possibility of trans subjectivity, as scholars have argued.[35] Amid these lies, science helps clarify the truth about Cheryl.

Even though Benson remains consistently sympathetic, the most cogent arguments for trans claims are made by Cheryl's ambitious lawyer, who takes on her case to ensure broader civil rights change. The lawyer insists on calling Cheryl transgender rather than transsexual. He eloquently describes the prevalent transphobia and the forms of discrimination and oppression the trans community experiences. The SVU staff and Cabot, on the other hand, use the idea of a jury hostile to 'the transgendered' to secure Cheryl's arrest through a plea bargain. *SVU*'s investment in carceral feminism is reiterated in narratives such as this one. Cheryl rejects the plea bargain and opts for a trial. In the courtroom, Stabler remains hostile while Cabot becomes more sympathetic once she recognizes the depth of hatred and violence Cheryl has experienced. The complexities of the transgender experience are hinted at but never fully fleshed out.[36]

In a manner reminiscent of the hardwired arguments we have outlined previously, Cheryl explains her identity with a born-this-way argument. In a conversation with Dr. Huang she avers that since age seven she has known that she was different, 'every night I would go to bed dreaming about being a girl.' Even after being assaulted for her gender nonconformity she holds on to this identity. 'I mean it's me. It is how I feel. And I can't be anything else.' The hardwired argument, of being trapped in the wrong body, is corroborated in court by a doctor during Cheryl's murder trial. The unnamed doctor supplements his essentialist claims about gender with photos of brains. Clarifying the concept of gender identity dysphoria, the doctor brings three photos of brains to the trial. These photos are posted on a board and he points out one part of the brain in each photo as representing the *stria terminalis*. With help from Cheryl's lawyer the doctor avers that the *stria terminalis* is bigger in male brains than in female brains. He does not explain the significance of this brain part, but by posting the photos beside each other he is able to verify this claim and fix gender difference visually. A third photo on the board is that of a MTF transsexual whose *stria terminalis* is akin to that of the female brain. The photos seemingly offer visible evidence of gender difference. The doctor asserts that, for certain individuals, despite being born with male genitalia, a portion of the brain is identical to that of a female. The doctor and the lawyer claim that sex difference resides in the brain and is visible only to the expert. These assertions serve as ballast for Cheryl's claims of being in the wrong body. By presenting gender as a biological feature visible in the blood and in the brains and not a social construct, the narrative undermines key ideas of feminism.

In the 1970s, feminists often claimed that gender was a social construct best construed as a spectrum of behavioral traits. Sex, on the other hand, is a binary emanating from biology, the physiological body. 'Fallacy' partially voices these arguments. It ignores a vast body of feminist science studies scholarship from the 1990s that challenge the idea of sex as a binary category as well as arguments of neurosexism.[37] Nevertheless, the storyline highlights poignantly the systematic oppression trans subjects experience in contemporary society. Despite her protests, once Cheryl is found guilty of murder she is housed in a men's prison. Cabot avers that 'New York State determines a person's gender-based on their genitals' not their feelings. As she has not undertaken sex-reassignment surgery, Cheryl cannot be placed in a women's prison. After highlighting this conundrum, the episode ends on a melancholic note with Benson and Cabot discovering that Cheryl has been gang raped in Rikers. This episode adopts a paradoxical stance toward feminism, avowing feminist claims about the prevalence of transphobia even as it ignores feminist cautions about the overreliance on a binary sex/gender model.

A later episode, 'Identity' (6: 21), locates the truth about gender in blood and brains as well. This narrative is not about a trans subject but about a boy who was being raised as a girl after a botched up circumcision. In this storyline as well, the child, Lindsay, asserts the sense of being trapped in the wrong body, 'I never once felt right.' The therapist who treats her is loosely modeled on the sexologist John Money, renowned for the 'optimal gender of rearing' protocol he formulated for his trans patients. In this storyline the therapist offers a rudimentary feminist understanding of gender. He explains to the detectives that 'gender identity is determined by nurture not nature' and that Lindsay could be trained to be a girl. The weight of these feminist arguments are undercut by the storyline that presents the doctor as practicing 'monster ethics' and as someone who prioritizes his research interests over the well being of a child.[38] By narrative's end, Lindsay stops taking her estrogen pills, reverts to 'his true genetic gender' and adopts the name Luke.[39]

This storyline's depiction of Lindsay shares similarities with arguments promulgated by Cheryl Chase, a trans activist and the founder of the Intersex Society of North America.[40] Chase has argued that the medical management of intersex babies during infancy is akin to genital mutilation. While Lindsay's predicament resonates with Chase's arguments, *SVU* does not countenance gender fluidity. Rather it shuns the performative aspects of gender which the therapist espouses and instead uses Chase's arguments to reiterate the gender binary.

Coming Out as Trans

By season 10, when *SVU* returns to the topic of trans identity the narrative texture is significantly different. 'Transitions' (10: 21) does not offer any scientific evidence about gender, although Dr. Huang continues to assert that female brains are different from male brains. All of the SVU staff refers to Hailey as transgender (and not transsexual). Hailey is a 12-year-old who wants to transition to be a female even though her estranged father opposes the decision and continues to call her Henry. As he did in previous episodes, when Stabler first encounters Hailey he refers to her as a he/she. But in several aspects the storyline is significantly different. The narrative presents a child who feels beleaguered and stigmatized but is not alone. Hailey is presented as belonging to a trans collective that helps teenagers in their transition. Hailey is also depicted as having a supportive mother and guidance counselor, an African-American woman, Jackie Blaine.

The plotline centers on a murder attempt on Hailey's father, Mark. Hailey is initially considered a suspect, as are the other trans characters. The detectives finally hone in on the school counselor, Jackie, as the real assailant. In contrast to the other storylines where the truth of gender is averred through science, 'Transitions' offers a different avenue to access the truth of gender. Providing testimony in the courtroom Jackie enumerates the numerous ways in which Hailey has experienced transphobia in the school; she was teased, attacked, kicked, and so on. Jackie also characterizes the father's refusal to allow Hailey's use of hormone blockers as abuse, as being akin to a stab in the heart. In an attempt to rescue Hailey from her father, Jackie attacked Mark. Addressing the jury (and the TV audience), Jackie offers an eloquent account of Hailey being trapped in the wrong body. 'I had to save Hailey. I couldn't let her father kill the beautiful girl inside of her.' During the ensuing cross-examination Jackie uses the pronoun we to describe Hailey's plight and inadvertently 'outs' herself and the truth about her gender. The poised, elegant, and bejeweled counselor insists on speaking of her experience as MTF. She offers the jury a primer on growing up trans in America. 'I always knew I was a girl. But things were different back then. There were no pills, no counselors, no support groups. You had to live as a woman for three years before a doctor would even consider surgery.' With tears flowing down her face and her voice quavering with emotion, Jackie also narrates the violence and transphobia she experienced, which culminated with three men castrating her. Jackie is eventually sentenced to serve eight years in prison.

There are some noteworthy elements in this storyline. Jackie never references her race or how being black shaped her experience as gender non-conforming.[41] Nevertheless, although the narrative positions the guidance counselor as a sympathetic figure, in the final analysis she reiterates aspects of what Patricia Hill-Collins calls the mammy archetype.[42] Jackie Blaine is a compassionate, caring, nurturing figure willing to sacrifice her well being for the white child she is authorized to care for. In addition, Jackie becomes the inadvertent figure who heals the white, heteronormative family.[43]

In 'Fallacy' ADA Cabot worried that the transphobia of a 'jury of her peers' would work against Cheryl, but six seasons later the SVU prosecutor worried that the jury were persuaded by Jackie's narrative of the stigma and shame Hailey experienced. To secure a conviction against Jackie, the SVU detectives try to convince Hailey to testify against her counselor. If in 'Fallacy' photos of the brain helped fix the truth about gender, in this episode photos play a different but equally significant role. Stabler shows Hailey the photo her father carries in his wallet, a father–son photo from when Hailey was called Henry. Stabler manages to persuade Hailey that the presence of the photo in her father's wallet displays his abiding love, notwithstanding his refusal to accept her gender identity. The detective, who once characterized Hailey as a boy going through a dress-up phase, now hugs and consoles her as she agrees to testify.

Unlike in 'Fallacy' there is no mention in 'Transitions' of which prison Jackie will be assigned once she is arrested. Instead the episode ends with the camera lingering on Hailey with her reunited parents, declaring her desire to go home. This happy ending for the white family seals Jackie's role as the mammy figure. This storyline presents Jackie as a 'good transsexual' in Emily Skidmore's memorable phrase, but this acceptability is achieved by elaborating on archetypes of racialized femininity.[44] Strikingly in a narrative that offers tantalizing glimpses of alternative structures to the nuclear heterosexual family, the ending is disappointingly sentimental. The storyline though fleshes out de Lauretis' definition of the technology of gender; as images of trans characters proliferate in popular culture, the representations shift from ones of deviancy to sympathetic figures.

For the purposes of our argument about the scientific optic, it is worth noting that by season 10 *SVU* no longer needs images to bolster scientific truths about gender. Instead it suffices for Dr. Huang to explain that, 'for some children something happens in utero where the brain develops as one gender and the body as the other.' This fiction of transgender origins favors a biological explanation for accepting diversity without disrupting the gender binary or the ideas of gender as performativity or even the most rudimentary version of the five-sex model.[45] In their quest to determine the biological site of sex difference, what makes males different from females, biologists have realized that moving beyond the chromosomal level, sex can be best described as a spectrum rather than as a binary. In the early 1990s, taking into account gonadal and hormonal differences Anne Fausto-Sterling popularized the five-sex model, which included hermaphrodites, male pseudohermaphrodites, and female pseudohermaphrodites. She and other biologists have subsequently revised this model to a more expansive one. *SVU* storylines do not tap into this stream of knowledge production.

A later episode, 'Brief Interlude' (14: 23), features a male school principal who likes to dress in women's clothes. These 'unusual' sartorial choices elicit a range of negative comments from the SVU staff but the storyline does not engage with technologies of gender. Instead this storyline reverts to the 'psycho-killer-in-a-dress' cliché.[46] In general though, *SVU*'s limited representation of trans subjects stands out for not equating gender nonconformity with criminality. The reliance on a medical born-this-way explanation, which is supplemented with scientific images, is problematic. Suzanna Walters, among other feminist scholars, has argued that positioning the locus of queer identity in genes and biology feeds into a tolerance narrative rather than in altering ideas about gender or sex.[47] But such a perspective grounded in the biological reflects strands of feminist thought that support such genetic and neuroscientific claims about sexual difference. It is worth noting that in a series based on the exploration of sexual assaults, the rape claims that initially propel the trans narratives are set aside for a more elaborate discussion of the ontological status of the trans subject through a scientific optic. Curiously too the idea of hate crimes is never raised in these storylines even though the ADA in season 10 raised the prospect of redefining rape itself as a hate crime.

Policing Perversions

While *SVU* has been timid in addressing trans subjects and the technologies of gender this topic elicits, the series has been forthright in its representation of gay themes. In the following section we focus on storylines of same-sex rape. We do not single out a scientific optic since the series strikingly does not make any arguments about gay genes, gay brains, or gay neurocircuits as storylines have done about gender. We contend that gay-themed episodes provide a different angle of vision into the concept of technologies of gender. As is true of storylines engaging with trans subjects, episodes dealing with gay characters seldom present characters as perverse or deviant. Instead *SVU* has been consistent in offering sympathetic portrayals of gay subjects. In more recent seasons gay characters have become the pivot point from which to engage with the vexed topic of hate crimes.

In a nod to the shifting scholarly focus of sexual assault, from a topic that almost singularly concerned women to one that is now characterized as gender-based violence, *SVU* has repeatedly addressed the topic of same-sex rape as well as other crimes in LGB communities. In 2012, in its Uniform Crime Reports, the FBI, one of two agencies compiling rape statistics in the US, changed its definition of rape and sexual assault to accommodate charges of male rape as well as same-sex rape.[48] From the first season *SVU*, however, has challenged the heteronormativity of rape. In this regard the series has hewn close to feminist understandings of rape from the 1970s, which have consistently posited that rape is about power and that men could be raped. Until the 1990s though feminists set aside this topic to focus instead on female victimization. Given this background it is remarkable that *SVU* has repeatedly thematized the victimization of LGB communities, sometimes offering a sensational account.

In her analysis of 1970s cop show *Starsky and Hutch*, Amy Villarejo cautions against cultivating a teleological narrative of gay progress since the 1970s. Instead she argues for a more nuanced reading of the past and of television texts. For instance she has persuasively demonstrated the subtle ways in which the series highlighted the homosocial bonds between the detectives. In addition, she contends that queer subtexts were woven into the television text perhaps in an attempt to signal its relevance.[49] Similarly, *SVU* thematizes gay rape and same-sex relationships often in its attempt to strike the note of relevance. Drawing from the 'headlines' results in sensational accounts of queer lives, which help sustain audience interest in the show. Notably though male homosociality within the SVU squad is absent; erotic longings between Benson and ADA Cabot are played out only among fans, as we discuss in the following chapter. On *SVU* gay subjects appear primarily in the context of victimization or criminality.

Episodes with gay themes create a fictional universe where negative and phobic stereotypes are not only included, but are articulated specifically by the SVU detectives. At the same time that these stereotypes circulate from the legitimating point of view of SVU personnel, episode narratives often provide an opposite and more progressive valence. Themes at the narrative level are supportive of gay rights and the humanity of gay individuals. In contrast to the trans episodes, the early seasons narrate gay rape with less sensationalism and articulate a clearer vision of solidarity with LGB communities. In more recent seasons, the storylines tend to be more melodramatic and include more negative commentary on the part of the SVU team.

As we have previously mentioned, *SVU* addressed the topic of sexual diversity in its debut episode, 'Payback' (1: 1), with the walk-on character of the taxi driver Victor. Stabler dismisses him as a he/she (this phrase links his response to all forms of sexual diversity) and this retort shares intertextual links to the character Christopher Meloni plays on the HBO series *Oz*. 'Payback' does not offer a propitious representation of gay figures, as Victor is refracted through a series of stereotypes that equate sexual 'deviance' with criminality. However, subsequent storylines that center on gay characters often offer more sympathetic portrayals that resolutely assert the violability of male bodies as well as their humanity.

Sexual Citizenship

Notably in the early seasons, *SVU* presents a police force populated with gay officers. 'Bad Blood' (1: 11) features a white police officer, Joe Bandolini, who could offer valuable testimony to the SVU squad about a murder but refuses. 'I've managed to keep my personal life and job completely separate. No one in my squad knows, not even my partner, and I'd like to keep it that way.' He is certain that his career would end if his sexual identity were revealed. The storyline highlights the homophobia within the police force that may compel a gay officer to remain in the closet. Simultaneously, though, it reveals the support system that exists within the force. When Officer Bandolini arrives at the SVU squad he is accompanied by a member of the Gay Officers' Action League (GOAL) to reiterate his decision of non-cooperation. Two seasons later 'Sacrifice' (3: 7), includes a gay black cop who cooperates with SVU personnel and is not concerned about his sexuality. He proclaims, 'I don't advertise, but I'm out to my captain and my partner.' Although these two officers are fleeting figures they permit a 'one of us' theme, one that focuses on the officers' similarity with other officers, including the SVU team, rather than emphasizing difference through sexual orientation.

'Bad Blood' opens with SVU detectives called to a murder scene, where Stabler and Benson discover that the victim is Seth Langdon, the son of a well-known conservative who believes that homosexuality is an abomination. The detectives realize that Seth was sexually assaulted and assume from the start that he is gay. Seth's father verifies this hunch, pointing out that his son was going 'through a rebellious phase' and had been 'cured' of this 'unnatural' tendency after attending a 'sexual rehabilitation center.' The detectives' revulsion at such remarks cues viewers to the series' openness to sexual diversity. In addition, editing strategies undercut the relevance of the father's remarks. Langdon senior's comments are juxtaposed with detectives speaking to a polite, wealthy interracial gay couple, who cooperate with the police. Furthermore, several of the SVU team members make gay-friendly statements. Captain Cragen announces that, 'one out of every ten men is gay.' Benson declares that being gay is 'wired' in a person, while Stabler highlights the rejection and discrimination gays encounter to argue that no one would 'choose' such a life. These statements are however leavened by Officer Bandolini's anxieties about being an openly gay police officer, which we outlined above. After these opening salvos about homophobia and tolerance, the rest of the episode is focused on tracking the murderer. This episode uses the anti-gay conservative to make explicit the squad's politics, but the crime uncovered has nothing to do with gay men or same-sex desires. Similarly, 'Sacrifice' (3: 7) starts as though it was about the assault of a gay man but the storyline focuses on a heterosexual couple who are part of the pornography industry. In the early seasons, *SVU* deployed gay characters to underscore the progressive credentials of the team. There is little reference to gay culture or queer communities. Instead, the narratives offer what Sarah Lamble terms as a narrowly defined sexual citizenship; gay citizenship status is equated with the police's willingness to imprison other people on their behalf.[50]

Precarious Lives

In more recent seasons, *SVU* has started to limn better-developed gay victims and criminals. These storylines underscore what Judith Butler has termed as precarity, a 'politically induced condition in which certain populations suffer from failing social and economic networks of support and become differentially exposed to injury, violence, and death.'[51] 'Closet' (9: 16) features an executive who is found dead in his bed by his personal assistant. As the detectives follow various leads they discover that the dead executive had volunteered at a shelter for homeless gay youth.[52] While the detectives initially suspect a teen from this shelter, the presence of this institution is narratively more significant because it underscores the presence of a thriving gay support structure even as it speaks to the 'precarity' of gay life. This precarity is highlighted when the detectives discover that the dead man's husband is a closeted football superstar, Lincoln Haver. Once his sexual identity is revealed, Haver is beaten up outside his apartment and the SVU detectives are unable to protect him. Having begun the episode as a paragon of male athleticism and beauty, Haver spends the remainder as a helpless invalid in a hospital bed. The storyline punctuates this blatant homophobia with smaller humiliations, such as a lost advertisement contract. For Haver, the penalty for being gay is severe, entailing emotional, physical, and financial loss; he is also accused of the murder. Unlike in the previous episodes we have discussed, in this instance gay identity is the central cause of the murder. Ultimately, the detectives discover that the real murderer is Haver's agent, who murdered the husband fearing the ramifications of his star player's gay identity on his own career. Although Haver is acquitted of the crime, the narrative concludes with his sports career at an end. This theme of gay victimization is repeated in several other storylines ('Lessons Learned' 14: 8; 'Gridiron Soldier' 15: 15). These storylines showcase key feminist insights about sexual assaults but also offer a melancholic future for those who defy the principles of compulsory heterosexuality.

SVU's world of gays and lesbians is predominantly white.[53] The one notable exception to this is Ken, Fin's son. The detective's initial reluctance to accept his son's erotic choices permits the series to articulate the stereotype of homophobia in the black community. During the course of a murder investigation in 'Strain' (7: 5) Fin discovers that his son is gay. In later episodes Fin gradually comes to embrace his son's sexuality and proselytizes the need for tolerance with other people of color ('Learning Curves' 13: 21). Echoing this idea of black homophobia, storylines describe closeted African-American characters as being on the downlow whereas analogous white figures are described as closeted. These gestures illustrate once again *SVU*'s inability to address the intersections of race, sexuality, and gender successfully.

In the early seasons, the decision to incorporate gay sexual assault in storylines was indicative of the liberal feminist understanding the series deploys. In subsequent seasons, the storylines are more problematic even as they normalize sexual citizenship. 'Strain' (7: 5) identifies barebacking, having sex without a condom while being HIV positive, as a sex crime. During the murder trial the narrative moves into hyperbole with the ADA positioning barebacking as a terrorist act and AIDS as a dirty bomb. But equally importantly in a manner akin to what Jasbir Puar has identified as homonationalism, the defense lawyer justifies the murder proclaiming, 'You walk out of the court and see Osama bin Laden holding a dirty bomb. You have a gun. Will you shoot him to save millions of lives?' Puar coins the term homonationalism to think through how American tolerance and acceptance of gays and lesbians have become barometers for national sovereignty. Specifically she challenges feminist formulations that have presented gays and lesbians as exiles from the national project. Instead she posits that in the post 9/11 era, race and class complicate queer politics since queers of color, particularly Muslims, have come to be recognized as 'excessively queer and dangerously premodern.'[54] 'Strain' taps into these sentiments by seamlessly folding in the figure of the barebacking gay man onto that of a dirty bomb wielding Osama bin Laden. As we have pointed out in previous chapters, in this instance once again the global becomes the site of displacement. By raising the specter of the man believed to be responsible for the 9/11 attacks in the US, the narrative effectively translates barebacking as terrorism. Gay sex without a condom is thereby elevated beyond a sex crime.

In several episodes, *SVU* presents homophobia as a hate crime and represents sympathetically the ways in which gays and lesbians are discriminated against in both private and public spheres ('Alien' 7: 11; 'Home Invasions' 13: 14; 'Closet' 9: 16). Simultaneously though *SVU* operates within the terrain of what Lisa Duggan has termed as homonormativity.[55] Gay men's preference for young men is repeatedly presented as pedophilia ('Confession' 10: 2). Similarly, 'Home Invasions' (13: 14) offers a radical twist on our understanding of hate crimes. In this storyline, a teenager hires someone to kill her lesbian activist mother and father. The killer adds graffiti to the crime scene to misdirect investigators into believing a hate crime has been committed. The storyline unravels to present the mother as a queer activist who was so preoccupied with those concerns that she ignored her husband's rape of her daughter. In this instance the mother is presented as violating the rules of homonormativity by being overinvested in queer activism, as well as the rules of heteronormativity. Her neglect of her daughter's rape is presented as an explanation for the murder, with the detectives' responses offering affective cues to the viewer.

Lipstick Lesbian

One of the most striking erasures in *SVU*'s engagement with issues of sexuality and the technologies of gender is the absence of narratives of lesbian women. In the 16 seasons we have identified fewer than five episodes engaging with lesbians, with most of them cast as benighted victims or as in 'Home Invasions' already dead when the episode begins. 'P.C.' (11: 13) represents the rare instance that centers on lesbians and is one of the few storylines whose scripting directly engages with feminist discourse. Babs Duffy, played by Kathy Griffin, is a lesbian activist who mobilizes her group to protest police inaction when one of the members of her community is raped and murdered. While she is cast as a strident and belligerent activist, the episode depicts a vibrant lesbian community. Led by Duffy the group invades the SVU squad room where they chant 'We're dykes; we're pissed; and we're not leaving; till we get results' (see Figure 5.2). Duffy introduces herself to the SVU

Figure 5.2: Actor-comedian Kathy Griffin guest stars as leader of the lesbian activist group LesBeStrong in 'P. C.' (11: 13). Here she and her group confront SVU detectives in the squad in the room. Screenshot of *Law & Order: SVU*, NBC, 2010.

squad as the president, founder, and spokeswoman of LesBeStrong.com. She gives Benson a business card with the group's name resplendent in rainbow colors and a logo of a clenched fist. Duffy corrects Benson when the detective identifies LesBeStrong as a gay rights group, pointing out that it is a lesbian rights group. In a startling difference from the other gay-themed episodes, the activist is able to mobilize lesbians in the community to action. Equally importantly she charges the SVU squad with helping to maintain the 'heteronormative paradigm.' Duffy uses language which is reminiscent of feminist scholarship, which is readily dismissed by Stabler as political correctness. (This representation of a feminist character is similar to that of the feminist professor we described in the Introduction). After another rape, and a few twists and turns, the detectives finally arrest the rapist-murderer, a neighborhood white heterosexual man who feels threatened by the visible presence of lesbians. The criminal is provided very little narrative space but there is little doubt that he is homophobic and misogynist.

The episode is striking because it displays a range of women who identify as lesbian, some who appear very feminine and others who exhibit masculine traits. Tellingly one suspect will speak only to Benson and midway through the questioning declares that 'straights will never understand people like me.' Nevertheless the presence of the strident Duffy, who accuses Stabler of shoring up 'the power structure perpetuating male control,' undoes some of the discursive spaces the storyline opens. More significantly, though, by narrative's end Duffy has to confess that she has a male lover and she is forced to come out of the 'reverse closet' to her community as a bisexual. It is disappointing to have one of the strongest representatives of an activist community confess to be a liar, and the narrative undoes any positive representation of lesbians when at the end of the episode Duffy kisses Stabler on the lips, asking him to call her. The storyline misses the opportunity to present sexuality as fluid and flexible and instead presents Duffy as a dissembler. This idea of lesbian sexuality as subterfuge is reinforced when Benson chooses to interrogate the rapist-murderer by speaking as though she (Benson) is a lesbian. The detective taunts the rapist until he confesses his hatred of lesbians and his desire to 'correct' them. Viewers are used to seeing Benson and Stabler roleplay in the interrogation room, often adopting stereotypical gender roles to incite a confession. This performance by Benson is different. Earlier in the episode, Duffy tries to kiss Benson but is rebuffed. Echoing some of the fan responses we discuss in the next chapter, Duffy declares, 'you're just like Ellen, Joan Crawford, and Calamity Jane all rolled into one.' Before interrogating the suspect, Benson anxiously asks Stabler if she exudes a 'gay vibe.' Later in the interrogation room she wears a LesBeStrong sticker on her shirt, behaves aggressively, and deliberately positions herself as part of the lesbian community. This part of the narrative comes across as a superficial response to *SVU* fan culture, which has repeatedly identified Benson as a lesbian, as we discuss in Chapter 6. Duffy is also presented as a one-dimensional caricature of a lesbian, someone who hates men and at one point punches Stabler.

As we noted in the episodes dealing with trans subjects, rape itself disappears from view as the politics of gender are foregrounded. In 'P.C.' early in the narrative Duffy inveighs against the police for neglecting hate crimes, but by narrative's end, when the detectives find their rapist-murderer, there is no discussion of charging him with a hate crime.[56] *SVU* has started to offer complicated depictions of gay men, representing them as complex figures who possess agency and are also restrained by social institutions. In effect the series has elaborated on how the technologies of gender shape gay men's lives. The series has been less generous in its depiction of lesbians, offering two-dimensional caricatures.

Biological Immutability

SVU has addressed the politics of gender and sexuality with a fair degree of nuance; its representations of science and medicine may be staid but they help redefine the nature of crime, criminality, and gender. Like other crime dramas, *SVU* participates in the iconicization of DNA and genes; there is a gritty realism that is in sharp contrast to the CGIs of the *CSI* franchise.[57] *SVU* produces a fictional science, wherein science is figured as an aesthetic and with a dense aura of authority.[58] Scientific visuals are mobilized to shore up the authority of the detectives, what Derek Kompare calls 'heightened verisimilitude' wherein overt visual spectacle is mixed with elements of a realist aesthetic.[59] Given the content of the series though the effects of such fictional forms revise our understandings of rape and sexual assault, locating the cause in biology and brains. As we have illustrated *SVU* promotes a forensic neuroscience, wherein medical personnel argue that neurological impairment prevented the criminal from controlling their actions. In a move that allows the series to distance itself from feminist theories of rape and sexual assault, it has increasingly started to assert that biology is destiny. Consequently, rape is transformed from an exercise of power into a pathology. The ambivalence of consent, so central to mainstream definitions of rape, is overridden by scientific evidence about the body. The deviant and non-normative body is now reproduced through a scientific turn. Visions of science are invoked as an ordering principle, reminding us of the true nature of things, reassuring us by providing us the illusion of fullness and the sense that enough facts can produce knowledge. Effectively these narratives absolve individuals of responsibility for acts they have committed.

Outside the scientific optic, *SVU*'s representations of sexuality and gender mark a significant shift in televisual practices. From its first season, *SVU* storylines have depicted gays (and less frequently lesbians) as sympathetic subjects. The criminals may be homophobic but the squad conceives of gays as fully assimilated sexual subjects; citizens on behalf of whom the detectives are willing to wield the power of the state. On *SVU*, trans subjects have come to occupy the narrative space of ambivalence that was previously accorded to gays. We do not place this argument within a teleological progress arc, but we wish to highlight that on *SVU* it is trans subjects who now participate in a 'coming out' narrative. It is trans subjects who become the locus for a categorization of various forms of transphobia. The storylines call out for a sentimental inclusivity but always from within the matrix of cisnormativity. Trans people are seldom presented as subjects for whom the state will wield violence. Instead they are always-already exiles of televisual citizenship.

In this chapter we have outlined *SVU*'s engagement with a variety of feminist understandings. In its evocation of the scientific optic, *SVU* has not turned to feminist science studies but instead science and technology have become the fulcrum to articulate an anti-feminist understanding of sexual assault. The scientific turn permits storylines to locate the cause of criminality in disease and somatic functions instead of the operations of power. *SVU* storylines have been adept at displaying technologies of gender, but do so quite unevenly. In representing gays, *SVU* narratives hew closely with ideas prevalent in queer theory; its depictions of lesbians are problematic (if not homophobic) even when sexual assault itself is presented thoughtfully. Storylines featuring gender nonconforming subjects reveal the contradictory poles of feminism the series draws on simultaneously. In line with a broad school of transgender scholarship, *SVU* storylines highlight the prevalence of transphobia and violence. However, the narratives also repeatedly question the ontological status of trans subjectivity drawing on a strand of transphobic feminist scholarship.[60] From within this cacophony of feminisms, the series crafts an internally contradictory, protean theory of sexual assault, which acknowledges victimization but oscillates between rewriting and stabilizing current understandings of crime and criminality.

As indicated in the past four chapters, depending on the entry point into the series there are different forms of feminism that *SVU* engenders. It is worth reiterating that *SVU* does not proclaim it is a feminist show. Rather we contend that the series' depictions of sexual assault are entangled in a variety of feminist ideas pertaining to gender-based violence. The series does not promote a singular definition of sexual assault nor does it engage with feminist ideas about rape in a static and monolithic manner. Instead the series permits the airing of a cacophony of feminisms and often in any given episode feminist perspectives are entangled with anti-feminist sensibilities. Nevertheless, cumulatively the series becomes the staging ground for an inchoate and protean theory of sexual assault. In the early seasons episodes routinely reiterated feminist mantras that rape is not about sex but power and that No means No. In more recent seasons, storylines have tapped into a millennial postfeminist sensibility to cast doubt about rape claimants, to question the logic of incarceration, and to sympathetically depict gay and trans victims. Race and racism are glossed over even as the foreign male is demonized and the foreign woman cast as needing to be rescued. Similarly, the episodes have offered a multiplicity of explanations as the cause of sexual assault: prevalent rape culture, institutional practices, neurological ailments, pathological individuals, monstrous mothers, and so on. At the same time almost every episode lacks the moral resolution of the melodramatic imperative. Even when a criminal is apprehended, the storyline provides the unsatisfactory feeling that there are larger forces at play that remain unresolved. These gaps within the narrative are taken up and addressed by fans and viewers in their transmedia interactions. In the next chapter, we outline some of these engagements and enfold these responses in *SVU*'s theory of sexual assault.

6

Paratexts and the Afterlife of *SVU*

In the last five chapters, we have offered an academically inflected account of *SVU*'s appeal. We have argued for its significance as it has engaged with a variety of feminisms, what we call a cacophony of feminisms, in discussing sexual assaults. Over the years, *SVU* has acquired a life that extends far beyond the television set, including New York City tours that focus on sites the series has shown repeatedly, and a very active social media presence that has helped sustain and deepen viewer interest in the series. In this chapter we supplement our readings of the series with an accounting of these engagements, or what some scholars have identified as paratexts, the products and practices that expand the boundaries of the television text. Since *SVU* has existed alongside the growth of digital media, many of the materials we discuss in this chapter are the result of these new technologically inflected responses. Significantly, many of them identify themselves or affiliate themselves with feminist perspectives. An analysis of these engagements with the show is important because they indicate that we cannot assess the significance of the series purely through how avid viewers respond. Instead we suggest that when pop star Taylor Swift decides to name her new kitten Olivia as homage to Benson, or when the children's program *Sesame Street* mocks the show, *SVU* has become part of the cultural psyche. In this chapter we outline some of the modalities through which contemporary culture has responded to *SVU*. We begin the chapter with fan responses to particular *SVU* characters, notably Benson and Cabot, and themes explored by the series. We contend that these are productive fantasies of representation, directing our attention to the limits of network programming as well as generic demands, and should not be dismissed. We then offer a broad overview of some of the participatory culture evidenced by websites and social media sites that engage with *SVU*. We end the chapter with a brief analysis of the HBO documentary, *Sex Crimes Unit* (Lisa Jackson, 2011) which may have been designed as a corrective, offering audiences a view of the real life of a prosecutorial sex crimes unit in the District Attorney's office in New York City, but in effect is paying homage to the series.

Fan enthusiasm, particularly on the part of women, for a program that often focuses on the victimization and brutalization of feminized bodies, opens up a range of interesting questions about gender, spectatorship, and fans. Students, scholars, and those involved with real-world victims have noted that in many ways *SVU* presents a skewed portrait of the attention and interests of the police in investigating cases of sexual assault, giving real-world victims the mistaken impression that vast resources and personal energy will be expended in the pursuit of justice on their behalf. Hannah Gold's *Salon* article lists similar concerns with the generally unrealistic success rate of arrest and prosecution in programs like *SVU*, when the real-world conviction rate is still dismally low.[1] Notwithstanding the unreasonable expectations the series sets up, popular press articles and blogs have offered up a range of answers to the question about the show's popularity among women viewers, including the idea that the program offers a more sensitive portrayal of victims of sexual assault than most television programs, provides a sense of support for survivors, and includes a strong independent female character at the center of the action.[2] These assessments of *SVU*'s fidelity to the real and its effects on society are part of a much larger, repeatedly rehearsed conversation about media–society relationships. As mentioned in the previous chapter, in describing how forensic-centered crime dramas have altered people's understanding of judicial processes, especially the kinds of evidence needed to achieve conviction, scholars have coined the phrase *CSI effect*. We suggest that there is a similar *SVU effect* that has evolved around the series, which helps set unrealistic expectations about the police and judiciary processes dealing with sexual assault. However, in this chapter, we do not explore these effects, because while they may be exacerbated by *SVU*, unrealistic representations of police and prosecutorial responses to crimes of sexual assault can certainly be found in other mass mediated representations. Instead, here we offer a very broad cartography of mediated responses to the series, responses that are often at some remove from the immediate content of a given episode.

As we describe in this chapter, the gamut of fan and viewer responses to the series has ranged from online fictional rewritings to social media engagements and documentary productions. Despite the multimedia sites of responses, we use the phrase *reading position* to describe them. In what follows, we draw on two very broad strands of scholarship to make sense of these paratexts. Within the field of cultural studies Stuart Hall was among the first to argue against the idea of a passive media audience.[3] The active audience he postulated, instead, was deeply historicized and enmeshed in the social. Hall suggested that depending on the viewer's social location and identity he/she could understand a media product as the producers intended (dominant reading), see in it the exact opposite of the intended (oppositional reading), or leaven the producer's intentions with their individual experiences (negotiated reading). Since this original formulation scholars have examined individual media products to render more complex and nuanced this tripartite reading position. A second school of thought draws on the psychoanalytically inflected work of the phenomenologist Michel de Certeau to think more broadly about people's everyday engagements with mass media. De Certeau's work helps scholars account for the productive and consumptive ways in which audiences engage with media in their everyday lives. In the analysis that follows we draw upon both strands of scholarship to offer our account of *SVU*'s life beyond the television screen, or what we term its afterlife. With our use of the term afterlife, we wish to underscore how fan responses to the series transcend the materials aired, yet these discourses would make no sense without the continued presence of the TV series. In much of the analysis that follows, we trace this delicate balance fan productions navigate, going beyond the series and yet tethered to it.

Paratexts and the Afterlife of *SVU*

Figure 6.1: Mariska Hargitay's image from the opening credits in the first season. Screenshot of *Law & Order: SVU*, NBC, 1999.

Figure 6.2: The youthful feminine image of Hargitay featured in the first season was replaced with a more masculine style, popular with some fans, in season 3. Screenshot of *Law & Order: SVU*, NBC, 2002.

We investigate a range of reading positions in relation to the show suggested by previous scholarship on television, genre, spectatorship, and fans. Ultimately, this chapter shows how audience engagement with *SVU* has been complex and multivalent, and has shifted over time. Fans have responded

Figure 6.3: Hargitay's image in the opening credits of season 15. Screenshot of *Law & Order: SVU*, NBC, 2013.

to the specific content of an episode and the broad subject matter of sexual assault. They have also honed in on the stars of the show and the ensemble cast that has peopled the series. Although the interests of fans have been varied, this chapter argues that, in addition to the plethora of mainstream romance sites and fan productions focusing on an Eliot/Olivia romance, some of the important fan activity surrounding *SVU* has evidenced a new breed of fandom in part enabled by the show's unique properties and in part the result of a shifting media environment during its lengthy run. The show has inspired a range of creative production focused on lesbian relationships among the female characters of *SVU*. This stream of fan fiction has in many ways worked to fill in gaps and missing pieces of the characterizations and interactions that the series includes, inventing intimate relationships and elaborate backstories that do not exist on the show.

At the surface level, Mariska Hargitay and her character Olivia Benson provide a focus for intense fan attachments. The character is strong and no-nonsense, and she seems to represent someone that cannot be pushed around or belittled by men. *TV Guide*'s '7 Reasons Why Women Love *Law & Order: SVU* So Much' lists 'Olivia Benson' as number 2, noting that 'She's the audience surrogate. She's the hero … She'll do anything to protect the victims she encounters … She's perfect.'[4] *Elite Daily*'s 'The 24 Reasons Why

Every Woman Loves "Law & Order: SVU"' include '#1 Olivia Benson Takes No Prisoners,' and '#13 Strong Female Role Model.'[5] She is a character worthy of identification by viewers (see Figures 6.1, 6.2 and 6.3). Among the hundreds of television detectives over the past several decades, very few have been women, and even fewer have been able to hold their own in a male-dominated workplace.[6] Benson stands out among the full range of historical characters for her independence and ability to empathize with victims. Other reasons for women fans to love the series include its optimistic reading on the potential for justice as compared with the real world, and the fact that it 'offers a source of solidarity for victims.'[7]

Cyberfans and Fandom

A quick Google search using the keywords *SVU* and fan fiction will produce hundreds of sites. A visit to Livejournal reveals dozens of online communities devoted to the show and to the *Law & Order* franchise. Although not on a par with the fandom of shows like the *X Files* (Fox, 1993–2002) *SVU* has certainly generated a significant volume and range of fan interest. Previous scholarship on television fan communities has addressed a fandom that is qualitatively and quantitatively different. Until the late 1990s most online fan responses were conducted on fairly cumbersome private listservs or mailing groups. The still earlier print fandom relied on an even more stratified mode of production and circulation. *SVU*'s online fandom is more viral in its circulations and more 'democratic,' allowing anyone to enter and exit conversations. Furthermore, the long run of the series has elicited a very different kind of fan response than programs such as *The X-Files* or *Star Trek* (CBS, 1966–9), which inspired avid fan activity in earlier eras.

Some of the most active discussions and prolific sites, especially from the early years were those featuring romantic storylines based on two characters from *SVU*: Benson and Cabot. Of course, fan sites have also explored the possibilities of romance between Olivia and Eliot, although these are somewhat less interesting in the sense that the series knowingly invites viewer speculation and even hope with regard to the possibility of this heterosexual pairing. Given this book's interest in the feminisms generated by a mainstream crime drama, we have chosen to explore the female romances and female relationships viewers have produced. Thus we examine the question of how early fans made use of *SVU*, a somewhat standard crime drama and one in which female characters seldom interact, to produce femslash that addressed some of the omissions of the source material. As we have indicated in earlier chapters, the series barely passes the Bechdel test, since for many years Olivia does not have a female colleague on the SVU squad, and the named women figures do not discuss anything besides the crime propelling that particular episode. Within such a transmedia context, fan interest in a Benson/Cabot romance takes on greater salience. Although many excellent studies of online fandom and slash fiction have been published, there has been too little attention paid to what is known as 'femslash'; stories that place two female characters from source material into a romantic and/or sexual relationship.[8] We provide answers to a range of questions surrounding femslash fictions, drawn both from previous literature on television fandom and also from a close reading of stories fans have produced.

In the past four chapters, we have indicated how the series has addressed issues pertaining to gender, race, national identity, and sexuality. We have repeatedly indicated that *SVU* does not adopt a singular approach when addressing any of these issues. Moreover, over its many seasons there have been discernible shifts in the kinds of narratives *SVU* explores and the approaches it adopts. While early seasons were notable for their refusal to visualize sexual assault, this commitment has dwindled in recent years and could no longer be considered an important selling point for viewers. Just as the series itself has shifted over the seasons, there have been different trends in fan fictions. As the show has expanded its purview to address issues such as reproductive rights, it has drawn appreciation from a different kind of feminist fan.[9] These audiences evince a sophisticated capacity to critique the series' representation of sexual assault even as they praise its efforts in another opposite direction. In the section that follows we explore the narratives and meanings generated during an early period of fan activity, when the Benson/Cabot romance was developed. Although fictions based on female–female pairings are still being written, more recently fans became openly perturbed by how the series has portrayed Olivia Benson as well as how Mariska Hargitay has characterized her role. There is as well a shift in the nature of responses including those that contain lesbian content – the early fan fiction is deeply immersive and sincere while the more recent seems fleeting and marked by irony. Our analysis of the early period of female–female fan fiction engages with several key questions. How is it that source material with almost no overt lesbian content has produced so much interest and so much femslash production? What did lesbian fans see in *SVU* and how did they see it? On what was this interest based, and where did it lead? Finally, what were fans writing about that was lacking in the original series? The first part of this chapter addresses these questions, followed by a discussion of contemporary online fan communities and activities. We trace the development of these online fan discourses, highlighting significant shifts, elaborating on a number of key directions over the past several seasons.

Many early fan sites were devoted to female–female pairings (which focus primarily on Benson/Cabot but have included Benson/Novak as well as others). Based on our reading of these fictional productions, we argue that at least this form of early *SVU* 'fandom' can be characterized somewhat differently from the fandoms studied by previous scholars, for reasons we outline.[10] Tracing shifts in fan cultures, we show that contemporary audience responses have more to do with the content that is already available in the series, such as Benson's new role as a parent, and does not require the creative engagements entailed in femslash production. The second part of the chapter is devoted to an examination of these contemporary audience engagements with the series. Finally, we examine intersections between *SVU* and other cultural products and phenomena beyond the confines of the series to elaborate on some of the important ways in which the program has enabled an afterlife in contemporary media culture.

Fan Cultures

Predating the cultural studies focus on audiences, de Certeau's work helped rewrite key ideas about mass culture and popular texts. Shunning the idea of passive audiences, theoretical understandings of fan culture usually take de Certeau's work *The Practice of Everyday Life* as a starting point.[11] De Certeau calls attention to the idea that readers of mass cultural texts make their own use of these products (which he calls 'tactics'). One of his key contributions to the idea of an active reader is that of 'textual poaching,' a practice of borrowing elements from the texts as given and transforming them into other uses either not intended by, or not even consistent with, the use in the original. Developing the idea of creative resistance in the context of mass-produced cultural products, he distinguishes between the concepts of strategy and tactics. Strategies refer to the institutions and structures of power that produce products with specific rules and procedures. Individuals inhabit environments created by strategies. They however use the rules and products that are already in culture in a way that is influenced by but never determined by those in power. De Certeau's emphasis is on an ideological struggle between those who have the power to make mass-produced cultural products and those who must make do by shaping those products to their own needs. Elaborating on the creative resistance central to this ideological struggle, de Certeau notes that 'we are directed toward a reading no longer characterized merely by an "impertinent absence," but by advances and retreats, tactics and games played with the text.'[12] Media theorists such as John Fiske, Henry Jenkins, Constance Penley, Christine Scodari and Jenna Felder, Karen Hellekson and Kristin Busse, and others have taken up these concepts to make sense of audience responses to contemporary media products.[13] We are informed by these ideas as we spell out the details of *SVU*'s femslash productions.

Elaborating on de Certeau's concept of textual poaching, Jenkins comments on fans' choice of texts from which to 'poach,' asserting that '[f]ans seem to have chosen these media products from the total range of available texts precisely because they seem to hold special potential as vehicles for expressing the fans' pre-existing social commitments and cultural interests.'[14] But Jenkins goes on to say something that does not apply in the case of much of the fiction produced by *SVU*'s lesbian fan writers: 'there is already some degree of compatibility between the ideological construction of the text and the ideological commitments of the fans and therefore, some degree of affinity will exist between the meanings fans produce and those which might be located through a critical analysis of the original story.'[15] While *SVU* femslash does adhere somewhat to the personalities and settings provided in the series, much of the fan work seems quite openly critical of the 'ideological commitments' of the show. In many cases, fans deliberately distanced themselves from the producer, writers, actors, or scenarios found in *SVU* itself. In essence, the fan fictions we highlight in this chapter are at some odds with most fan fiction; they adopt what can be best characterized as an oppositional reading to heteronormativity. We contend that *SVU* fan fiction diverges from its contemporary counterparts along at least two vectors: first, a majority focuses on the female characters although the ensemble cast continues to be male dominated, and second, sexuality and private aspects of the characters' lives are developed in a manner absent in the series. These fan productions tap into a wide body of queer feminist understandings of sexual desires and pleasure but do not address issues such as carceral feminism.

Although there is a long history of crime drama fandom, especially in relation to Arthur Conan Doyle and Sherlock Holmes, little attention has been focused on online fan fiction with crime dramas as source material.[16] This chapter begins to sketch the character of crime drama online fandom by highlighting some of the implications of the crime genre on slash fiction as well as some of the ways in which femslash differs from traditionally male/male slash fiction. We repeatedly signal the minimal relationship between *SVU* as source material and femslash fictions based on its central female character. In many ways the series becomes irrelevant, while fans focus primarily on character development, emotions, and relationships that are only tangentially related to *SVU*. In earlier chapters, we have characterized the series as promoting a misogynist feminism in its family-centered storylines; the femslash we analyze offers a palliative account of a non-normative family.

Crime Drama and Lesbian Fans

In her landmark book on the crime serial *Cagney & Lacey*, Julie D'Acci observed that the series was an important one for lesbian viewers.[17] In discussing the lesbian fan interest in the show (which did not include any lesbian or gay series regulars and which often went out of its way to establish the heterosexuality of the two female protagonists), D'Acci emphasized the regular emotional intimacy and physical proximity of the two principal characters as well as specific moments in the show's storylines during which Cagney and Lacey would be involved in an intimate mutual gaze. D'Acci observed that 'Many scenes between the two women, particularly those containing the expression of physical intimacy, were singled out by lesbian viewers and "canonized" in informal repertoires that cast a lesbian slant on potent mainstream depictions."[18] Such scenes were sometimes emotionally laden and included one taking place after Lacey's surgery for breast cancer. D'Acci argues that *Cagney & Lacey* enabled feminist and lesbian readings in large part because of its focus on two strong, independent female characters who were colleagues, friends, and confidantes. In addition, the series also featured emotionally significant scenes that placed the central characters in close physical proximity. Although explicit lesbian characters and scenarios were absent, these elements suggested the potential for an intimate same-sex relationship.

D'Acci's emphasis on the importance of central female characters who share friendship and at least some form of physical intimacy *within the source material* is supported by Alexander Doty's understanding of a 'lesbian' text as one in which most of the central characters are female and interactions are mostly among women, such that the entrance of a male character is a disruptive moment in the narrative. Using Doty's definition, *Cagney & Lacey* might qualify as a 'lesbian' text. Doty's own analysis includes programs such as *I Love Lucy* and *Laverne and Shirley* under this rubric.[19] However, the case of *SVU* is clearly different. The program definitely would not qualify as a lesbian text even using Doty's broad definition. Furthermore, significant intimate gazes and emotional meaning between female characters are almost completely absent from the show. Yet, dozens of websites, femslash stories, and listservs devoted to female/female *SVU* pairings emerged within the first few seasons of the show. Fans have created femslash based on almost completely unrealized potential drawn from their imaginations rather than suggested by the series itself.

Slash Fiction and *SVU*

In previous chapters we have discussed the ways in which the dearth of regular female characters on *SVU* means that there are seldom meaningful interactions among them. With the elimination of Monique Jeffries in season 2, Olivia Benson became the sole female detective in the Unit, with only ADA Alex Cabot (and later Casey Novak) as potential female colleagues. Later, in season 13, Amanda Rollins joined the cast but by then Benson was too senior to treat her as a peer. This is in distinct contrast to the nearly constant interaction between Cagney and Lacey. Further, the limited roles of the ADAs as well as the limitations of storylines on *SVU* have consistently meant that female characters interact very little. When they do, true to generic expectations, the subject matter of conversation is focused on case-related topics and almost never veers off into areas considered 'personal' or 'political.' On one notable occasion when Benson has a rare conversation with ADA Novak in her office, it is about the difficulties of SVU work. When Benson leaves on a brief errand, Novak is violently attacked and stabbed. The narrative thus forecloses the possibility of the nascent female friendship. This is an important difference from *Cagney & Lacey*, a program in which the main characters often discussed personal, political, and feminist issues. What scholars such as Bonnie Dow and Christine Scodari have called 'women's issues' are approached almost solely through the criminal cases in *SVU*, not through the interpersonal experiences or connections of the protagonists. Instead fans have used these absences and erasures productively to generate narratives that offer an accounting of *SVU* that is unavailable on television. As many observers have noted, at least for the first eight seasons, Benson's private life was seldom explored and almost nothing of her was known other than that she was the product of rape and that her mother was an alcoholic. These characteristics and omissions were certainly noticed by female fans, who were often looking for interactions that could be culled for emotional, political, or sexual meaning. Later seasons have included a bit more personal time for Benson, featuring her doomed romantic relationship with Brian Cassidy, followed by her more recent adoption of a baby boy.

In the absence of productive veins of material within the series, *SVU* fan culture tends to be very inventive. In her analysis of *Blake's 7* fans, Camille Bacon-Smith has documented female fan authors' desires for female characters of a particular sort, characters who are not only absent from source material, but also difficult to create within fan writings:

> which signals a continuing dissatisfaction with the options available to women characters and to women in society. In spite of the radically different social organization of their community life, an overwhelming number of fan readers and writers continue to believe at some level that respect, honor, and happiness

should come to them with a fulfilling career and extended matriarchal family ... At the same time, experience teaches them that they can have none of these things – that they will pass through lives not of their own making, often with less than interesting jobs and with families in which they are the dependent, not the powerful, member. Not yet ready to take on the role of woman warrior, they have grown bitter and cynical about the only other model they have.[20]

Similarly, in individual studies Rhiannon Bury, Henry Jenkins and Cornel Sandvoss outline some of the challenges female fans face when participating in male-dominated online fan communities.[21] 'Slash writing has ... enabled female fans to break into the male domain of science fiction fandom and establish their own distinct space of reception, productivity and discussion,' Sandvoss observes.[22] Soshana Green, Cynthia Jenkins, and Henry Jenkins quote a fan author who elaborates on the appeal of slash fiction:

> We create the fiction we want to read and, more importantly, we allow ourselves to react to it. If a story moves or amuses us, we share it; if it bothers us, we write a sequel; if it disturbs us, we may even re-write it! We also continually recreate the characters to fit our images of them or to explore a new idea. We have the power.[23]

Analogously early slash fiction based on *SVU* can be understood as having two central characteristics. First, *SVU* fan writers seemed to borrow characters and quickly moved beyond or away from the source material of the show itself. With very few exceptions, writers of female/female *SVU*-based fiction have not tried to argue that the characters were well placed within the show to begin a romantic or sexual relationship (as were the 'Shipper' fans in their Mulder/Scully *X-Files* fiction). While elements of backstory and setting may be borrowed as well, the *SVU* fans have been largely unconcerned with trying to make their fictionalized relationships appear consistent with canon (that is, with what actually happened in the series). In his analysis of fan cultures, John Fiske notes that some fans 'see through' to the production processes normally hidden by the text and thus inaccessible to the non-fan.'[24] Thus, '[f]andom typically lacks ... deference to the artist and text ... so soap opera fans often feel that they could write better storylines than the scriptwriters and know the characters better.'[25] We see this occur repeatedly in *SVU* femslash: the fans seem to develop aspects of Benson's and Cabot's characters that the series' writers omit. For many of these femslash producers the series is simply an archive into which they tap while crafting narratives and characters of their own making.

Much of the earlier *SVU* femslash fandom was characterized by a playful element hinting at the fact that these fans did not take the show particularly seriously, but more as a source of material to be poached and enjoyed. Fans posted 'drabbles' (short 100 word stories) and 'drabble challenges' (words or themes that had to be included in the responding drabbles) and enjoyed writing within set parameters (for example, the story must include an umbrella and a bottle of scotch). Much of the fiction can be characterized as 'fluff' (romance without much plot) or 'smut' (stories with explicit sex between Benson and Cabot or Benson and Novak). However, it mostly goes beyond the sheer pornographic in that it includes elements of emotionality, motivation, and story elements that are not at all related to sex and romance (such as what is going on for the characters at work). Explicit stories have often carried a disclaimer to the effect that the content involves two consenting adults ... 'don't like it, can't handle it, don't read it.'

These *SVU* fans want the characters developed differently, in a way that clearly will never happen within the show itself. Indeed, a *Daily Mail* item notes that the episode 'P.C.' (11: 13) featured a kiss between Benson and Babs Duffy, but that the kiss was edited out.[26] The episode does include a scene featuring Babs kissing Stabler. Fans were frustrated with this and many elements of the original material. However fan authors were looking for at least some character elements that could suggest the potential for female/female relationships, and when this potential could no longer be found, many abandoned the series, at least temporarily. Fans have been quite conscious of the status of a fictionalized Benson and Cabot pair (and later Benson/Novak) as a representation of strong, independent, professional women working together. For some fans, it is as if these characters were really the only interesting things about the show. They borrow the pair and the setting, moving quickly into new territory that might include, for example, the two living as a happily married couple with children. Christy Carlson has noted that 'much Alex/Olivia fan fiction can be categorized as 'missing scene' fiction, a genre that functions to fill the gaps between the scenes of particular television episodes.'[27]

A second, but related characteristic of *SVU* femslash fiction is that fan writings have tended to compensate for elements that were lacking in the original series. They have generated elaborate personal backstory for Benson and constructed intricate emotional scenarios involving such topics as illness, feelings about family, and personality issues such as an inability to be vulnerable or to self-disclose. Finally, for a good portion of the femslash community – that is those writing and maintaining websites and listservs for the main purpose of purveying *SVU* femslash – the label 'fan' may be a misnomer. Much of the *SVU* female fandom has not exhibited characteristics of trying to 'fix' or rationalize elements from the show itself. Rather, their fictions could be understood as examples of participatory culture that can include overt critiques of the show's limitations, developing elements that remained under-developed in the original material.

As many scholars of fan culture have demonstrated, fans are usually not marginalized fanatics who mindlessly adore mass cultural icons and products. Rather, they are sophisticated consumers and, to use de Certeau's phrase, 'textual poachers' who borrow from mass culture, shaping its offerings to fit their individual desires, fantasies, and needs. What these early fan fictions seem to be telling us about *SVU* is that what is really new and different about this show compared to others in its genre was the presence of two strong, professional female characters perhaps unparalleled in previous police/crime dramas (with the possible exception of *Cagney & Lacey*). The notable lack of backstory for Benson and Cabot provided a fertile ground for the imagination of fan fiction writers, and could perhaps even be understood as an advantage in comparison to the provision of ample personal narratives in the case of *Cagney & Lacey*. In short, *SVU* has provided a unique combination of characteristics for femslash writers: the existence of at least two strong, independent women about whom very little is known, and who apparently enjoy very little emotional or personal life at all.

What *SVU* is Missing

The fan fiction we read often emphasized *SVU*'s weakness in the areas of emotionality and personal information or backstory, particularly for

Benson, Cabot, and Novak (of course *SVU* includes narratives related to Stabler's personal life quite regularly, but these are not of interest to the femslash fans). Fan fiction added these elements and in many instances focused on them, and this focus often resulted in personal and emotional growth for the characters within the confines of the slash narratives. The most common theme of personal growth is Benson's need to learn to trust and be more open and vulnerable. Numerous stories feature a Benson gradually more able to talk about her personal feelings and fears. These fans are not relocating Benson within the sphere of traditional femininity but seem to be struggling against the series' devaluation of the feminine (what we have termed misogynist feminism), and against the one-dimensional characterization of Benson's personality and motivations.

Of course, detective and crime genres are known for their formulaic nature, their reliance on decisive action and violence to propel the storylines, their clear moral distinctions between bad guys and good guys, and their traditional focus on masculine heroes whose emotional lives are not relevant to the successful resolution of the narrative. In recent decades, television crime dramas have added some characteristics of more 'feminine' genres including the move to ensemble casts combining men and women working together, as well as male protagonists who reflect the traditional generic characteristics in combination with some more feminine character traits such as empathy, ability to be emotionally expressive, sensitivity, and understanding of women's (or even feminists') point of view. As discussed in previous chapters, Stabler's character is unique for the emphasis placed on his personal life and its impact on his work. However, as a clear representative of the traditional crime drama genre, *SVU* still lacks emotional depth and has certainly steered clear of emotional topics in relation to the female protagonists except in their relation to victims of crime.

Fan fiction culled from the many websites linked by xenawp (a now-defunct indexing website) provides backstory for the female protagonists along with the emotional complexity and depth that might naturally accompany it. In one story, for example, details about Olivia's childhood with her alcoholic mother are filled in: 'All those trips she'd missed; first because her mother had been too drunk to sign the permission slips or had lost them and later because her mother had forbidden the trips, fearing that Olivia would use them as a jumping off point and leave her for good … All that frustrated childhood excitement had surged back on this trip.'[28] Other stories include details on Olivia's feelings about previous cases, memories of events that took place between various female characters on the show, and information about the relationship histories of the protagonists.

SVU fanfiction and listservs also included significant storylines exploring experiences that might be natural for gay characters placed in the professional situation of Benson or Cabot or Novak, in ways that (as fans know very well) will not likely be shown on prime time detective fiction any time soon. Although the niche market Showtime series *The L Word* did offer new patterns of lesbian representation for television, and prime time broadcast offerings including *LA Law*, *Ellen*, and *Roseanne* have included lesbian characters, these series have been critiqued for their limited range of lesbian (and gay) representations. *SVU* femslash goes well beyond these inadequate televisual representations.

Fan fictions place Benson and Cabot (or Benson and Novak) in intimate/sexual relationships in various degrees of 'coming out.' In some stories, Benson confides in Stabler and talks to him about her feelings, soliciting his advice about how to handle the accompanying office politics. In others, Benson and her female ADA romantic partner are able to be open about their relationship. In one, Benson and Cabot live together and have two sons. In another, Benson and Novak are quite open to colleagues about their budding romance as they go off together to Novak's family home so that Benson can 'meet the parents.' Reese's story 'Interrogation' includes an extended discussion of Stabler's thoughts in trying to decide whether Benson might be gay: 'Watching Olivia at work wouldn't give him any clue about her sexual orientation at all, so he resorted to observing her interactions with other women. He studied her drinking coffee … he watched her in court with judge Lena Petrovsky and he observed heated discussion about a warrant with A.D.A. Alex Cabot.'[29]

These stories fill in a world of possibilities never broached on prime time. They do not (always) represent fantasy narratives in terms of their content (i.e. what is the best scenario two lesbians could find), but could be understood as fantasies of representation. They articulate, through their variety and scope, the wide range of possibilities foreclosed by prime time's directives in general, and the tightly constrained *SVU* world in particular. What is it like when two women fall in love at the office? What is like when they think it best to keep their relationship a secret? What about when one has a male confidant at work? What if they can be open about the developing relationship? What kinds of comments and jokes would be shared if their colleagues were homophobic? What if they did not find anything unusual about the relationship? What if they were already married and living out an accepted and acceptable nuclear family lifestyle? These fan stories offer an alternative way of conceiving of Benson's/Stabler's/Novak's world as well as an indictment of the source material and its severe limitations. In an important way, this work says that there is no point in waiting for, or enumerating the gay and lesbian characters on television because such characters cannot be placed in any of the relationships and scenarios common to many viewers' experiences.

Who Cares About Canon? *SVU* Femslash

Many of the fan postings we read include elements of irony, sarcasm, cynicism, and realism in their treatments of the show and its creators and certainly could not be characterized as slavish devotion to anything about the show. While some include commentary about violence and issues of assault and recovery, a sense of play with the episodes, stories, and shows is evident. Many fan fiction authors write about multiple shows and even multiple genres and/or write 'crossover' fiction that involves relationships between characters from different shows.

Previous scholarship on fan fiction, particularly those in the genres of science fiction (such as *Star Trek*) and Gothic (such as *Blake's 7*), have found that fans derive pleasure in writing about sexual relationships between characters who, within the confines of the original show ('source material') do not and will not be involved with each other in an intimate or sexual way. Constance Penley's work on *Star Trek* is particularly significant in its discussion of female fans writing stories of intimacy and sexual contact between Kirk and Spock. This story type was known within fan culture as K/S, or Kirk Spock 'slash.' Penley and others found that female fans of *Star Trek* were writing stories that contained elements the fans believed they could never find in this or any other source material.[30] Fans were not so much looking for explicit same-sex relationships as they were in search of meaningfully emotional and intimate scenarios taking place between what they considered people of equal status. They chose male characters because, simply put, there were no interesting, complex, or empowered female characters with whom to work. This explanation provides a partial understanding of what we believe is significant about *SVU* femslash, although Penley's insights do not fully explain the production patterns of the *SVU* fans who wrote Benson/Cabot (and also Benson/Novak) femslash.

Christine Scodari and Jenna Felder examined online fan cultures of *The X Files* and arrived at a different conclusion. *X Files* fans often try to find evidence of their own (sometimes peculiar or far-fetched) perspective in the original program, they observed. They also found that female fans, who favor a romantic relationship between the protagonists Dana Scully and Fox Mulder, enjoy the fact that the male FBI agent appreciates his partner for her intellect, effectiveness, and competence. They specifically want to see a romantic relationship between these two because the characters first worked together in the public sphere, and learned to respect, depend on, and care for each other in that context. The fans believed that these mutual experiences could be a solid basis for a romantic relationship of mutual respect. In addition, whenever the television series veered away from fans' desires and expectations they tried to 'fix' the narratives. For instance, Scodari and Felder found that when a storyline threatened to have Mulder find his 'true love' in a new walk-on character after Scully's demise, *X Files* fans sought to correct it. Jenkins echoes this idea of fan 'ownership' of narratives and characters, noting that 'erratic fluctuations in characterizations ... are undesirable; fans call such inconsistencies "character rape".'[31] Shippers (fans who wanted Mulder and Scully to get together) also found that there was enough evidence within the show of a potential blossoming romance that it was worthwhile to mine the details of 'canon' – storylines, dialogue, events, and backstory found within the original show. These explanations might apply to fan fiction placing Benson and Stabler in romantic relationship with each other, but hardly to the femslash narratives. In the case of *SVU* femslash, we found that, while there is very little tendency to dwell on canon, either to mine out evidence in support of the idea of lesbian relationships among the characters or to argue that particular storylines are 'inconsistent,' some fans have pursued these directions. A discussion thread related to Benson's sexuality is arguably the best developed of these.

Fan discourse and mainstream discourse often play on the idea of Mariska Hargitay/Olivia Benson as a lesbian. In an interview with a late night TV host Conan O'Brien, Hargitay recounts a story of walking down the street with her husband Peter Herman and being hailed with 'hey, I thought you were a lesbian!' Hargitay laughingly notes that 'everybody thinks that, and I don't know why.'[32] Fan discussion sometimes notes with dismay or disgust the times that Hargitay has distanced herself from lesbianism; these discontented voices echo Kristina Busse's arguments that lesbian fans 'feel marginalized by a culture that permits a masquerade of queer discourse and thereby trivializes queer identities and queer experiences.'[33] Hargitay's status as a lesbian icon, however, can hardly be disputed. As an article by Angie B. published on AfterEllen.com notes:

> Although there are no explicitly lesbian characters on any of the Law & Order shows, SVU's Detective Olivia Benson (played by Mariska Hargitay) has attracted a large following. Although the fictional New York cop is not out or even directly hinted to be gay, she is one of the few characters on TV to exhibit what are often considered to be dyke characteristics – with short hair, a leather jacket, and a gun at her hip, Olivia sits with legs apart, commanding the space around her. She is the protector of the victims who come through her department, a strong woman in a profession filled with men, and often physically or verbally dominates 'perps.' Her uniform includes t-shirts, sweaters, slacks and sensible shoes – no heels, no frills, and little jewelry except for what appears to be a man's watch.[34]

Rather than cite evidence from the show indicating that Benson is gay, Angie B. reviews the potential for fans to appropriate her as a lesbian. She further notes that:

> the detective has had a few unsuccessful dates with men … What little we have seen of Olivia's romantic life has led us to believe she's straight, but the fact that those references are few and far between makes it easier for viewers to speculate about the character's sexuality.

Angie B. also quotes Co-Executive Producer Ted Kotcheff about how it 'never worked' to give Olivia a boyfriend and that the audience also did not want her to have a boyfriend. Angie B. concludes, '[w]hile the producers

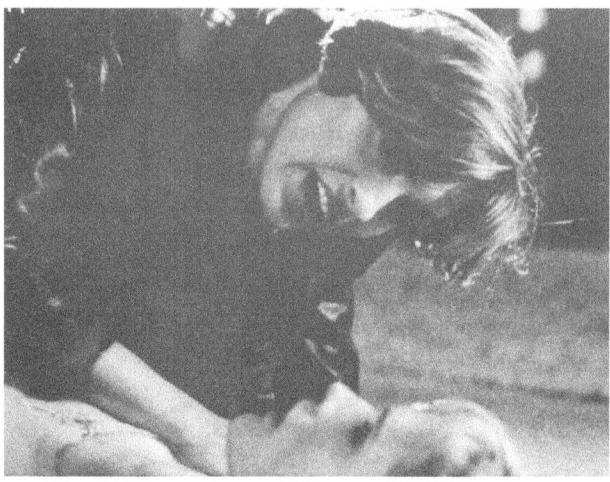

Figure 6.4: This image from the episode 'Loss' (5: 4) features an intimate gaze between Olivia Benson and Alex Cabot, alibied by Benson's effort to stanch the flow of blood from Alex's shoulder after a gunshot wound from close range. Screenshot of *Law & Order: SVU*, NBC, 2003.

might not understand why a strong androgynous female character works better without a boyfriend, we do.' These *SVU* fan discourses are akin to the queer spectatorship engendered by the series *Smallville*, a program that was also devoid of openly gay characters.[35]

In her study of fan responses on USA Network's online *SVU* discussion board, Julia Russo points out that:

> by relentlessly thematizing the investigation of desire through watching for signs, searching for clues, interrogating recalcitrant suspects, and fabricating plausible stories to fit the evidence, *SVU* is training its viewers to do the same ... Given a series whose premise is discovering clandestine sexual transgressions, how can we not be ever-vigilant, as an audience, for even the subtlest signs and clues.[36]

Online author Sally Forth's 'An Olivia Benson Rave' includes a section entitled Reasons to Think Olivia is Gay.[37] These include flirtatious behavior and gazing at women in specific episodes, the way she looks, some gay-friendly dialogue in the episode 'Abomination' (5: 8), and her tenderness toward the (apparently) dying Alex Cabot in 'Loss' (5: 4) (see Figure 6.4). Although speculation and discussion about Olivia's sexuality is commonplace, identification of specific evidence from episodes supporting her (hoped-for) lesbianism is rare. The central exception to this is fan obsession with the episode 'Loss,' arguably the only episode understood to provide the kind of moment 'canonized' by the lesbian *Cagney & Lacey* fans D'Acci discusses. The status of this episode as an exception to the near-total ban on female–female intimate gazes is indicative of the dearth of source material available to fans hoping to find evidence of lesbian desire within the text. Another short commentary by Mallory Ortberg in *Toast* entitled 'Femslash Friday: Olivia Benson, Alex Cabot, and Hope' recaps some of the key moments in their 'relationship' on the series. Ortberg captions a (different) shot of Olivia gazing at Alex, noting that it is from the episode 'Whereof We Do Not Speak' – where Alex has to join the Witness Protection Program and leave *SVU* (aside from a few later, disappointing guest turns).

> Olivia is a *wreck*. She's soft. She's vulnerable. She's been filleted. Her voice cracks, her jaw wobbles, her eyes fill with tears. It's the episode that launched a thousand ships, and they still won't give us *one goddamn kiss*. Olivia never leans over and pulls Alex's glasses off. The top of Alex's desk never gets swept clean and christened. Their voices never get close and husky until they turn off from a dark, quiet kiss. Olivia never takes off her leather jacket and lets down her guard and takes a fistful of Alex's hair in her hands.[38]

Most fans have given up or have never tried to find such evidence. Rather, fans start with the idea of Olivia (+ Alex or Casey) as lesbian and move on to write their own stories.

So, while it is certainly true that there is some level of obsession in talking and thinking about Olivia's possible sexuality, most fan discourse (with notable exceptions quoted above) focused on creating stories that include and even dwell on what fans believe cannot and will not be found in the show. These *SVU* fans are not interested in saying they know the characters better than the show's writers. They just want the characters developed differently, in a way they know will never happen.

The Demise of the Fandom

Although much of the early femslash takes the characters into areas that could not reasonably be considered consistent with the show's potential trajectories, and although many fans were articulate about their understanding of prime time's limitations with respect to gay and lesbian material, the balance between fan cynicism and the pleasures of poaching was apparently upset in seasons 6 and 7. Although lesbian fans were avidly scanning the series for even the smallest signs that Olivia might not be straight, many were turned away by their perception of Mariska Hargitay's hostility toward lesbian fandom. The femslash fandom abated when, as they understood it, storylines, gestures, dialogue, hair style, and wardrobe were manipulated to move Benson's character further away from potential lesbian readings. Discussion boards and fansite postings degenerated into energetic 'snark' (a combination of 'snide' and 'remark') about 'Oliska,' a character understood by fans to be created through the invasion of the character Olivia Benson by the actress Mariska Hargitay. Overt critique of Mariska Hargitay from this period is easy to find. The content of such postings makes it clear that fans consider themselves fans only of the character, not of the creator (Dick Wolf) or the actor who plays the character. The specifics of Mariska's 'invasion' of Olivia Benson included changes in hairstyle (longer and sprayed into place, referred to as a 'femullet') and wardrobe, new storylines featuring Benson undercover as a prostitute and undercover on a 'speed-dating' assignment. Fans reference the 'infamous Pink!outfit of doom' from an episode in season 6 in which Olivia poses as a would-be buyer of counterfeit handbags. Snark postings include 'screencaps' (short video clips from the show itself) illustrating Olivia's new 'hair flip,' her showdown with a moving vehicle while dressed in a tight pink-and-white striped shirt, and her touchy-feely approach to men. Most of these screencaps would be offered without comment. They were designed to illustrate the way in which Benson was 'not herself' anymore. Fans lamented the loss of the 'real' Benson, the one who wore a leather jacket and roughed up perps on a regular basis. A livejournal snark similarly focuses on the difficulty in locating the old Olivia Benson in the new characterization:

> Alex glanced around, waiting for her knight in shimmering leather to sweep her off her feet. When nothing happened, she glared at the feminine woman who had taken over her desk.

'So where the hell's my girlfriend?'
'She went searching for you. But she never returned.' Fin said quietly. He nodded towards the woman with the femullet.
'Have you met her replacement, Detective Hargenson?'[39]

It could be argued that the more recent tumblr sites or gifs that reimagine Benson are a continuation of this kind of fan production, although the technology and creative input enable very different kinds of readings and responses. These moving visual images often place Benson alongside other strong independent women, producing images of power and confidence. Some post still images with significant text over them, expressing a range of opinions about episodes, narratives, characters, and events within the series. Fans comment on a truly wide range of subjects including feminism, sexuality, victimization, and plot suggestions. Noting that the episode 'Fault' (7: 19) was better than the rest of that season, fangirl lamented the early death of Olivia Benson and included a poem critiquing the shifts in her character.

The terms of critique are clearly humorous, tongue-in-cheek, and also sincere. These fans clearly saw something they liked and to some extent identified with in the original Benson character. Willing to some extent to make do with a few elements that comprised the dykon (dyke icon) of Olivia Benson, they conclude that the removal of these few gestures, lines, and wardrobe elements leaves nothing for them. Their interest in the show was based very little on specific cases or program content and very much on the Benson/Cabot and Benson/Novak working pairs. The seemingly deliberate shifting of the character away from their interests signals the death of the fandom. Short hair, a leather jacket, and a few tough scenes were really all Olivia Benson had to offer. Without these, there is no dykon and not much left for lesbian fandom.

Contemporary Online Fandom

While lesbian fandom focusing on the creation of Benson/Cabot and Benson/Novak femslash died down significantly after season 7, subsequent narrative elements within the series feebly addressed the interests of lesbian fans, as we have recounted in Chapter 5. Contemporary online *SVU* fandom is characterized less by the production of slash and more by the proliferation of charts, links, quizzes, graphs, quotes, and favorites. Fans display their proficiency of knowledge regarding *SVU* through contributions of jokes, one-liners, challenges, screenshots, screencaps, and opinions. While more in-depth writings can still be found, the contemporary fanscape is arguably different in tenor, and certainly more visual than that of ten years ago. This is a reflection of the new social media platforms that enable quick fan productions and rely on formats that are marked by their brevity. Although much of this discourse is less intense, it also attests to an avid fan following based on intimate knowledge of the series and its characters.

In addition to the more facile expressions of knowledge, inside jokes, and quick quizzes and lists, there is also a significant production of thoughtful, analytical reviews of the series. Posts at sites including the *Huffington Post* and allthingslawandorder.blogspot, as well as tvtropes – the wikia site detailing every episode aired so far – aceshowbiz, and many others, provide detailed analyses and criticism of plots, relationships, treatment of characters, and narrative trajectories. These productions offer a level of detail and attention to minutiae that we cannot offer. Indeed we have often turned to these websites for their summaries and transcripts of episodes. It is important also to note that NBC has actively participated in producing a fan collective, with official Twitter and Facebook presences as well as merchandising of memorabilia, including handcuffs. *SVU*'s fan culture is at some distance from those earlier media scholars analyzed; the lines distinguishing *SVU* publicity and fan productions are thoroughly blurred.

NBC has used social media very actively to market the series and also to draw a new internet-based audience. There are Facebook sites for the series and each individual character, tumblr accounts for the series, Twitter feeds and also accounts for *SVU* writers as a group (@SVUWriterRoom). NBC has been so successful in developing these social media sites that Nielsen ratings list it very favorably in Twitter ratings. Each week *SVU* producers create a hashtag for users to follow along with each episode, creating a social media buzz before, during, and after an episode. According to media critics, their Twitter handle is constantly engaging with users tweeting at them. Thus at any given moment the social media space has officially sanctioned conversations such as #SaveBabyBenson and those produced by fans #NewGuy and #SVUDieHards. In addition, this buzz of online conversations includes *SVU* writers' responses to fan comments on Twitter or blog sites. They often characterize their fans and followers as 'detectives.' NBC and *SVU*'s official online engagements deepen the branding exercise, but they also clear the space for a conversation about specific aspects of the series.

Similar to the critical remarks of the lesbian fans in the earlier seasons, which essentially asked for a specific style for Benson's character, these contemporary critiques have the potential to engage with those involved in the show. Perhaps the most significant focus of recent critique, for example, has been around the repeated and sometimes prolonged victimization of Benson. These fan conversations engage directly with the topic of sexual assault and challenge the series' ideological commitments. This strand of fan culture fits with Stuart Hall's characterization of oppositional reading. Discussions about the series are common on mainstream blogs and social media sites, such that there is an ongoing public conversation about the plot and characters. The attacks on Benson, which account for two of 'The 24 Reasons Why Every Woman Loves *Law & Order: SVU*,'[40] seem to anger fans who see the detective's victimization as detracting from her image of power and independence. The *Huffington Post* noted that the biggest problem with season 15 was that 'Benson, a heroic character who until now has never been completely broken,' was broken three times in this one season.[41] The author, Erin Whitney, finds that Benson has now too often been cast as a 'weakened victim,' and that all of the scenarios of vulnerability for Benson are certainly dramatic, but also unnecessary. Whitney notes that:

> while watching Benson put a revolver to her head, I couldn't help but feel betrayed. I'd watched this character prevail for 14 seasons, and now her show kept breaking her down in the most brutal of ways. What kind of message was 'SVU' trying to send about rape, victims and survivors?

Another recent example of controversy surrounding content decisions on *SVU* involved the casting of convicted rapist Mike Tyson, in 'Monster's Legacy' (14: 13), which we discuss in Chapter 3, as Reggie Rhodes, a man convicted of murdering his childhood abuser, in part due to incompetent legal representation.[42] Critics of this episode pointed to the problematic stunt casting[43] and to a petition to block the episode.[44] The episode effectively recasts a convicted rapist as a sympathetic victim, and in addition provided a forum for Tyson to continue to proclaim his innocence in relation to his rape conviction. In each of these instances audiences deploy the internet and social media to challenge the series' storyline development and casting choices. While femslash destabilized the heteronormativity of the series, these social media engagements offer an equally radical critique of the series' gender politics.

Activism

In addition to the steady production of easily accessible commentary on the show, several official or semi-official sites also foster a connection between the series and the real world. Significant among these is Hargitay's Joyful Heart Foundation website, which posts news about its own events, which in turn often center on real-world causes and initiatives. The site archives news about a range of issues related to interpersonal violence including domestic violence, child abuse, teen dating violence, and sexual assault. It reports on developments in policy and procedures for handling these issues, and on smaller initiatives such as the development of an app designed to help parents understand and respond to teen dating violence. An important example, highlighted in a feministing post by Vanessa on October 1, 2010, was a screening of the episode 'Behave' (12: 3), which features Benson's discovery of a rape kit backlog at an evidence warehouse. The Joyful Heart screening event was designed to call attention to the backlog issue, and the page includes links to information about real-world efforts to address the backlog issue including a link to endthebacklog.org.[45] Also included is a photo of Hargitay testifying at a congressional hearing on the subject. All of these efforts, including the Joyful Heart Foundation website as well as the proliferation of discussions about the program's content, foster the close relationship between the fictional world of *SVU* and efforts beyond the program to address issues of violence and victimization that disproportionately affect women and girls. Feministing writer Vanessa notes, 'Didn't think I could love Law & Order: Special Victims Unit (especially Mariska Hargitay *swoon*) more until I found out that the actress and executive producer Neal Baer blogged about their episode this week that addressed the backlog of rape kit testing.'[46] Baer and Hargitay wrote about the episode and the subject of rape kit backlogs in the *Huffington Post*.[47]

These discourses beyond the confines of the fictional episodes serve as clear and deliberate engagement with feminists and feminist discourses. Meanwhile, the episode 'Behave' exhibits many of the exaggerated dramatic elements that were characteristic of the series while Baer was showrunner. The episode's narrative focuses on a woman who has been virtually trapped in her apartment for years in fear of being victimized once again by a man who has been following her and periodically raping her. The episode takes the idea of victimization to an extreme, and in the end makes the point that all victims can find voice and empowerment, as Vicki Sayers (played by Jennifer Love Hewitt) is finally able to testify against her tormenter and see the case through to successful prosecution. The narrative elements of the story are extreme rather than typical or even realistic. As is often the case with *SVU*, the facts of the fictional case push toward the limits of possibility, in this case pushing the idea of victimization so far that the victim is prevented from making basic choices about her life for decades. The extreme parameters of the case serve to highlight the potential significance of the rape kit backlog, as well as the need for a solution to the problem. However, most of the analytical discussion of the actual problem and efforts to address it take place outside of the confines of the series.

SVU clearly engages with feminist discourses both within its fictional confines and in forums outside of and beyond the fictional series itself. The afterlife of the fictional world is also evidenced by the production of the 2011 HBO production *Sex Crimes Unit*, which provides a documentary insider's look at the work depicted in fictional form in SVU.

Lisa Jackson's *Sex Crimes Unit*

Lisa Jackson's documentary film *Sex Crimes Unit* takes a close-up look at the real-world Unit of the Manhattan District Attorney's office. We contend that it is *SVU*'s sustained popularity and longevity that has created the conditions for the (production and) distribution of this series on HBO. Indeed many reviews of the film inevitably suggest that it offers insights into the reality behind the television series. The 84-minute film centers on the prosecution of two rape cases involving radically different victims, one a prostitute who is never named, and the other Natasha Alexenko, whose on-screen interview footage provides articulate first-person accounts of a survivor's perspective.

The film methodically tracks the day-to-day activities undertaken by the Unit to build a case, the kinds of evidence mobilized, and the interactions between detectives and attorneys. The suspenseful narratives of the two cases are interspersed with a wealth of information about the Unit: the social context that led to its formation in 1974, legal reforms that have made possible rape prosecution as well as the obstacles that continue to hamper the attorneys. It offers a compelling account of the significance of the Unit and the heroic work conducted by the small group of dedicated professionals.

The film's opening shots echo the familiar montage sequence of *SVU*, beginning with an aerial view of Manhattan Bridge, which leads to a bird's eye view of Manhattan, while a rape victim's voice recounts her experiences of violation. Aesthetically *Sex Crimes Unit* at first seems to mimic the prime time series, but the documentary functions as a corrective that highlights the complicated and long-drawn processes involved in prosecuting sexual assault cases. Many of the reviews of the award-winning documentary describe it as a film about the 'real-life' *SVU*.[48] Indeed several of the Unit personnel laughingly highlight how different their job is from the fictionalized account NBC airs on a weekly basis. The contrast between the scripted series and the work of the Unit is most starkly made by the talking head interviews Jackson conducts with DA Lisa Friel and her staff of ADAs. The film praises the work of those in the District Attorney's office, depicting their commitment to the work as well as the mundane routines and challenges that comprise it. It expounds feminist discourses related to rape, sexual assault, victimization, and criminality, through the words of Friel and her staff members.

In this section, we discuss some of the important ways in which Jackson's film indirectly exposes limitations of the representational characteristics of *SVU* through its inclusion of these very elements. *SVU*'s engagement with feminism within the confines of its episodes is, we argue, at a distant remove from the exposition of feminist arguments and history elaborated in Jackson's documentary. However, in its ability to engage with popular forums and discussions, the series provides an occasion for immediate discussion of a range of contemporary issues of interest to feminists and to women more generally.

Sex Crimes Unit enables the elaboration of feminist arguments through three central means. First, the film focuses a great deal of attention on the individual members of the DA's office, identifying them by name and including lengthy segments in which they discuss not only their work, but also their understanding of the issues they deal with on a daily basis. At different points in the film, these individuals discuss, for example, their commitment to a prostitute victim whose testimony eventually leads to the conviction of her rapist, the correct means for hospital workers to communicate respectfully with sexual assault victims, and the difficulty of obtaining convictions based only on the victim's word in cases of sexual assault. These sections make for feminist argumentation in more detail and at greater length than can generally be found in the fictional series. The ADAs are not only able to recite their commitment to these ideals, but are also in a position to teach others. Indeed, Friel is shown in instructional mode at several points in the film. It is clear, in *Sex Crimes Unit*, that the work performed by Friel and her staff could not be carried out successfully without a feminist sensibility and willingness not only to stand behind, but also to defend and proclaim, the truthfulness of feminist understandings of sexual assault and rape. This fundamental relationship between feminism and key functions such as empathetic support of victims and survivors, which in turn fosters the strength and commitment of victim/witness testimony, is clear in *Sex Crimes Unit*, but is largely absent in *SVU*, which is far more likely to produce intriguing case profiles that explore the boundaries between feminist politics and other viewpoints. While Jackson's film depicts actual individuals such as Friel's predecessor Linda Fairstein, who are identifiable as feminists, and who are able to spell out the importance of changes in laws and procedures related to sexual assault and rape, *SVU* usually does not include identifiable feminist characters. While Friel's office is revealed to be predominantly female, the professionals in the police and DA's office imagined in *SVU* are still predominantly male.

A second area in which *Sex Crimes Unit* can be understood as supporting feminist positions is in its exposition of the history of prosecutions of sex crimes. This material is developed through the words of Fairstein and Robert Morgenthau, another of Friel's predecessors in the role of District Attorney. Morgenthau and Fairstein provide significant historical background on the poor techniques of prosecution and the abysmal conviction rate prior to the advent of rape law reform, including a discussion of the important role played by the DA's office, and the shift in the usefulness of evidence in rape kits after the advent of the John Doe indictment. However, as Cuklanz has previously argued, even Jackson's documentary seems to omit reference to feminist activism of the past and to locate feminist politics in the present squarely within the confines of governmental institutions and efforts.[49] *Sex Crimes Unit* places feminism within institutional structures, providing an example of what Janet Halley has described as governance feminism.[50] Although *Sex Crimes Unit* locates both the arguments and the historical credit for these shifts within the DA's office and/or the government more generally, *SVU* predictably largely omits references to the historical trajectory of change in relation to crimes of this type. As we have argued in previous chapters, *SVU*'s engagement with feminism is intermittent and mixed with textual elements that are anti-feminist. The extra-textual engagement with contemporary policy and law related to the rape kit backlog issue helps raise awareness and gain support for the issue at present, although historical background is largely absent.

As these representative examples attest, *SVU* has become the focus of myriad paratexts including a proliferation of both critical and adulatory online discourses. These references range from superficial and playful, to politically outraged, to insightful analysis and critique. Due in part to the deliberate efforts of Hargitay and others involved with the show, the afterlife of the series frequently engages with feminists and feminist discourses. Even if it does not itself delve deeply into historical background and policy debates, *SVU* has inspired, or at least provoked, commentary and analysis on a wide range of issues related to gender and gendered violence. These engagements have at times been explicitly feminist, and have offered opportunities for the expression of feminist arguments and viewpoints at greater length than evidenced within *SVU* itself.

Conclusion

The Story Continues

In this book, we have argued against a simplistic celebration or dismissal of *SVU*. Through our analysis of various aspects of the series we have argued that it offers a wide range of understandings of sexual assault. In the contestation of definitions of crime, criminality, and victimization, *SVU* has become one of the sites from which a protean theory of sexual assault is being crafted. This understanding of sexual violence contains some of the legacies of 1970s feminist definitions of rape, but they have been reformulated to speak to contemporary neoliberal concerns. Thus, the violence and violation of sexual assault is depicted as traumatic and reprehensible. Yet sexual violence and its prevention are depicted foremost as issues that are individual concerns. As a police procedural, *SVU*, not surprisingly, has proclaimed a fairly strident call to incarceration of potential and proven sex offenders. It is in the delineation of the causes of sexual assault that *SVU* treads new ground. Over 16 seasons, the series has identified psychopaths as well as individuals whose biology compels their actions as assailants. Even as each individual episode identifies a criminal to be apprehended, cumulatively the series offers a diffuse and scattered field as the cause of sexual assault. *SVU* broadens the horizon of the criminal from the monstrous maternal to the closed culture of the military and feminists. By expanding the causes of sexual assault beyond an individual to institutions the series simultaneously complicates and simplifies the way forward. Feminists have argued that social reform is an appropriate solution to end sexual assault and *SVU* storylines echo this sensibility. Yet the series also advocates a dangerous overreach, arguing for the imprisonment of would-be offenders and cultivating the conditions for a robust, carceral feminism. The series seldom discusses rape-prevention strategies; on the rare instance when an episode addresses it the strategy is limited to self defense.

All-American Crime Drama has offered a multiplicity of points of entry to analyze the series. Our central aim was to indicate the rich and productive insights that can be generated by examining the crime drama with a focus on gender, race, national identity, or scientific truth claims. *SVU*, we have argued, functions as a site for the negotiation of various feminist and anti-feminist understandings of sexual assault. With its commitment to topicality, the series is well poised to help viewers track shifting American anxieties about the topic. Equally significantly, internet and social media sites offer insights into how audiences respond to the series' provocations. Cumulatively these cross-cutting, transmedia interactions reveal how sexual assault remains a contested topic.

Individual storylines have given voice to an emerging neoliberal feminist sensibility whose commitments are to a retributive model of punishment rather than to enabling social change based on social or structural analysis. Indeed, *SVU* reveals over and over again that neoliberal conditions hail a feminist subject, as Catherine Rottenberg has described it.[1] The women of *SVU*, protagonists and bit players, are aware of their violation and craft their own terms of empowerment without enabling broader social change. (Men who are subject to victimization are certainly not the central focus of the series, and they tread a more ambivalent path from their states of injury.) Femininity becomes the site from which *SVU* draws attention to a particular kind of inequality, one that is calibrated along the axis of sexual violation. The *SVU* brand of feminism draws attention to violence (individual and structural) but circumscribes the parameters of critique.

In recent years much of the television analyses emanating from a cultural studies perspective has lamented mainstream media's ideological limits. Scholars have cautioned against such a limited critique that repetitively underscores the anemic potential of mainstream popular culture.² We have heeded these voices and in our project have supplemented an ideological critique with a multifaceted engagement of an enduringly popular series. Given *SVU*'s status as a crime drama airing on commercial network television, it would be unwise to expect the series to offer a revolutionary representation of sexual assault. We have instead highlighted how the topic of sexual assault necessarily forces the series to engage with a range of ideas that were first developed by feminists. Even if a given storyline were to endorse an anti-feminist perspective on sex, race, gender, and sexuality, nevertheless in its depiction of rape the series provides the space for a public airing of feminist understandings. In addition, because of its ripped from the headlines formula, *SVU* has proven to be a very productive site from which the scripted episodic series has tapped into a number of topical concerns, such as the problem of the carceral state or biases in eyewitness testimony and cross-racial identification, without fully engaging with them. Given that the police procedural necessarily voices issues from the point of view of the policing institution, *SVU* limits the ways in which these topical concerns are addressed.

'Intimidation Game' (16: 14) encapsulates some of the characteristic multivalent responses to feminism and feminist thought that we have identified throughout this book. Drawing on the gamergate scandal that has dominated the news, 'Intimidation Game' offers a fictionalized version of the sexism prevalent in the gaming industry. The storyline offers a poignant account of the threats (physical and emotional) women in the video game industry experience. Nevertheless the resolution of the story and the solutions it offers are deeply problematic. In Chapter 3, 'The Violence of Race,' we highlighted the limited roles assigned to women of color: dead victim or silent victim. 'Intimidation Game' goes against these expectations. A woman of South Asian heritage whose race is never commented on, but who is visibly brown skinned, is the protagonist game developer. An amalgam of key figures in the gamergate scandal – Brianna Wu, Zoe Quinn, and Anita Sarkeesian – the game developer, Raina Punjabi, is the person whose victimization propels the narrative. When 'Intimidation Game' begins, Punjabi is a strong, confident woman who refuses to be intimidated by her 'haters.' She is a neoliberal feminist subject par excellence: empowered, aware of her choices, unwilling to be cowed by social expectations, and an enthusiastic participant in the capitalist enterprise. Even as the SVU detectives and her fiancé urge her to be cautious, Punjabi is determined to launch her game, Amazonian Warrior, on schedule; heeding the threats would be considered a victory for the cyberterrorists, she declares. During the course of the episode the game developer is kidnapped, tortured, and raped by males in the gaming community; the kidnappers model their actions on video games. The kidnappers live-stream Punjabi's assault and the once-confident woman appears bruised and weeping. 'I realize now that gaming is no place for females.' Although mediated by a computer screen, viewers see her pleading with her kidnappers not to rape her. As is true for the majority of *SVU* episodes, 'Intimidation Game' does not depict the assault on screen, but the vivid visual representation of her abject status effectively transforms her from strong feminist subject to terrorized victim. The storyline concludes once the detectives have rescued her and successfully apprehended her assailants (killing one of them). By narrative's end the once determined game developer leaves the industry and tells SVU detectives that the 'cyberterrorists' have won. A resolute woman violated and intimidated into retreat by her assailants undoes some of the feminist ideas promulgated earlier in the episode. This storyline nevertheless moves beyond previous representations of women of color. Punjabi is an articulate, speaking subject victimized but still alive. At narrative's end she opts out of the industry, signaling that for her there is no gaming life after rape. Punjabi is a speaking woman of color who gives voice to a pre-feminist understanding of rape as the end point of her life. She represents both pre-1970s and millennial ideas of (vulnerable) femininity. She remains disconsolate and incapable of moving beyond injury to the crime drama climax of a restored social order. Within the space of the episode Punjabi moves from advocating a neoliberal feminism to a place where the tenets of empowerment and self-care have no purchase. Here again we see *SVU* encountering the limits of its color-blind feminism.

The episode has been the subject of a great deal of online criticism for its problematic ending by viewers whose understanding of empowerment, even for fictional characters, does not include capitulation to violence and intimidation. Brianna Wu and Anita Sarkeesian took to Twitter to criticize the episode. Sarkeesian characterized it as sickening and trivializing,[3] while Wu claimed that the most implausible thing was that the police responded to a woman's complaint of an online threat.[4] These and other viewer responses reveal the ways in which *SVU* paratexts facilitate a feminism that exceeds the series; these voices highlight the ideological limits of a prime time series.

In Chapter 5, 'Images of Truth,' we honed in on the series' scientific optic and singled out the problematic ways *SVU* deploys an optical empiricism to engender understandings of sex, gender, and sexuality that are at odds with feminism. In a similar vein, the pre-credits section of 'Intimidation Game' begins with Benson at her therapist's office. She describes at length her experiences raising her foster-son Noah. She elaborates that he is 'such a boy'; on a playdate with two girls he broke their tea set and split his lip. The therapist reassures her, 'You know boys run around. They break things. They hurt themselves. It's all in their DNA.' Notwithstanding the authoritative position from which he speaks, viewers could dismiss the therapist's remarks. But the remainder of the episode, with specific sets of on-screen actions, reiterates the therapist's insight about the innate violence of men/boys by showcasing the misogyny of the men in the gaming industry. The episode depicts groups of men chanting violent slogans at a television screen; viewers also see some of them attack a woman violently; and viewers see them assault Punjabi through their live feeds. These actions of the men seem to reiterate the therapist's opinion of violence being genetically coded in men. Such an understanding locks society into existing rape scripts, with the police and incarceration as the only available solutions. The possibility that video games could be altered to produce different social outcomes, as the game developer had hoped to do with her new game, are foreclosed. What is made intelligible in the episode is that it is DNA rather than culture that produces crime.

The storyline's depiction of the misogyny in the gaming industry is undertaken in broad brushstrokes. Numerous viewer comments on blogsites have mocked the crude way in which the storyline throws in acronyms and slang terms from the gaming subculture to register a sense of authenticity. Notwithstanding these excesses in the script, 'Intimidation Game' is problematic for its binarized gender depictions. Apart from the detectives, women who have screen time are all victimized. The men in the gaming industry, with the exception of Punjabi's fiancé, are portrayed as vulgarly misogynist, incapable of distinguishing between reality and games. The cultural impasse such a scripting of gender roles produces inevitably results in a narrative of violence and violation.

The early scenes of the episode tap into a vast body of feminist scholarship that posits a media–society relationship wherein media images shape the horizons of social possibilities. The limited gender roles in video games shape the players' perceptions and practices of real-life gender roles. These understandings of enculturated violence are brought into contest with biological explanations by the end of the episode. The narrative's conclusion with Detective Rollins urging Punjabi to pursue charges is reminiscent of liberal feminism's faith in existing systems of law and justice as sites of redress, and also reminiscent of the familiar formula of police and crime dramas in which the police urge witnesses to come forward, but are often frustrated or even prohibited from performing their work when crime victims refuse or are unable to do so. In some of its most searing storylines, *SVU* has questioned the belief that victims can repair their damaged lives, but in 'Intimidation Game' the central conceit of crime drama (and its underpinning racial logic) forces such a restaging of narrative closure. In the end, this episode reiterates the familiar notion that while the police are willing to put all available energies into the pursuit of justice for crime victims, it is often only the victim's own limitations and decisions that prevent the delivery of this justice. While structural barriers to justice are hinted at through the inclusion of sexist and simplistic beliefs that accompany violent behaviors on the part of the gamer/attackers, in the end there appears to be no solution at all.

Missing in this episode is a sense of collective action, community activism and outrage, and limit-setting to extreme beliefs and behaviors that condone and enable gender-based violence. For instance, Zoe Quinn established the group Crash Override Network to assist victims of online harassment and intimidation, but this kind of community activism is starkly absent in 'Intimidation Game.'[5] Ironically, although not surprisingly given our discussion of paratexts in Chapter 6, many of the elements missing from the episode itself could be found in the online discussions of the episode in the days and weeks that followed its broadcast. One blogger, who identifies as active in the gaming community, lamented that:

> By depicting only the worst possible version of harassment, it [the storyline] diminishes the pain that real victims go through,

and it gives harassers an easy out – *at least I'm not like that!* If there's a bright side to 'Intimidation Game,' though, it's that it underscores how poorly the old stereotypes about insular and homogenous basement-dwellers are starting to hold up.[6]

A Jezebel writer offered a more scathing critique:

> You exploited an ongoing crisis that threatens the lives of real people for entertainment, made law enforcement the 'heroes' in a situation *where they've done virtually nothing*, made women the broken, passive victims in a situation where they've actually showed remarkable strength and courage, and managed to piss off, well, everyone. That takes real skill.[7]

These online posts and commentaries, though quite critical of the episode's content, are well positioned to illustrate a key aspect of our analysis in this book: even when it does not articulate a feminist understanding of victimization, the series serves as a site for the expression and consideration of feminist views on a range of related subjects (for this episode harassment, intimidation, sexual violence and rape, victim response, gendered power, and workplace environments were topics taken up in the subsequent online discussions). We have argued that this is in large part because through the long run of the show, its many plotlines and characters have engaged not only with subject matter central to feminists, but also with feminism and feminist arguments related to these very issues. In debating over the details of how *SVU*'s depiction relates to similar real-world situations, the various online commentators start with the notion that the show has something relevant to offer, that there is a need to engage with its version of events, and that the show can do better. *Law & Order: Special Victims Unit* has become a central site for the production and consideration of discourse about rape, sexual assault, rape culture, and victim experience. For good and for bad it has become a key referent in contemporary US discussions of sexual assaults and sexual violence, and in this way it has become a fulcrum around which new understandings of rape and sexual assault are emerging.

Notes

Introduction: All-American Crime Drama

1. Despite Wolf's preference for the term 'brand', in this book we use the term 'franchise' to address the panoply of programming that shares features with the original *Law & Order* series. We do this primarily because most cultural critics and television scholars recognize that the Wolf empire of programming hews closely to the defining features of a franchise.
2. Jennifer Uffalussy, 'Law & Order: SVU Bends the Conventions of the Cop Show', *The Guardian* (November 6, 2014): http://www.theguardian.com/tv-and-radio/2014/nov/06/law-order-svu-bends-cop-show-convention (accessed on March 24, 2015).
3. Emily Nussbaum, 'Trauma Queen: The Pulp Appeal of Law & Order: SVU', *New Yorker* (June 10, 2013): http://www.newyorker.com/magazine/2013/06/10/trauma-queen (accessed on March 24, 2015).

1 A Very American Story

1. Alexis Williams cited in Carol King, 'The Real Life SVU: Lisa Jackson's "Special Crimes Unit"', *Ms. Magazine* (June 19, 2011): http://msmagazine.com/blog/2011/06/19/inside-the-real-life-svu/ (accessed on March 24, 2015).
2. Catherine Rottenberg, 'The Rise of Neoliberal Feminism', *Cultural Studies* 28, no. 3 (2014): 418–37.
3. The original series aired for 20 years, between 1990 and 2010. Its spinoffs include *Law & Order: Criminal Intent* (2001–11); *Law & Order: Trial by Jury* (2005–6);

Law & Order: LA (2010–11), and all aired on NBC. The British adaptation of the original series, *Law & Order: UK* (2009–?), has been on a hiatus since June 2014.

4 Starting in the late 1970s, sex crimes investigation squads were added to police forces across the US and sex crimes units were established by the judiciary in response to feminist activism demanding different responses to rape investigations. Lisa Jackson's documentary, *Sex Crimes Unit* (HBO, 2011), offers a glimpse into the operations of the Manhattan prosecutorial unit. We discuss the film in greater detail in Chapter 6.

5 Charles McGrath, 'Law & Order & Law & Order & Law & Order & Law & Order …,' *New York Times Magazine* (September 21, 2003): http://www.nytimes.com/2003/09/21/magazine/21LAWORDER.html (accessed on March 24, 2015).

6 Television critics believe that this syndication policy has changed the 'architecture for series financing and has served as a template for repurposing.' See Bill Tush, '"Special Victims Unit" puts a Dark Spin on "Law & Order",' CNN (December 10, 1999): http://www.cnn.com/1999/SHOWBIZ/TV/12/10/special.victims/ (accessed on March 24, 2015).

7 In 2008, the three networks alone offered a total of 19 crime dramas during the prime time hours of 7 pm and 10 pm. See Gayle Rhineberger-Dunn, Nicole Rader, and Kevin Williams, 'Constructing Juvenile Delinquency through Crime Drama: An Analysis of *Law & Order*,' *Journal of Criminal Justice and Popular Culture* 15, no. 1 (2008), 94–116.

8 Susanna Lee, '"These Are Our Stories": Trauma, Form and the Screen Phenomenon of *Law & Order*,' *Discourse* 25, nos 1–2 (2004): 81–97.

9 Mark Seltzer, 'Murder/Media/Modernity,' *Canadian Review of American Studies* 38, no. 1 (2005): 11–41.

10 Yvonne Tasker, 'Television Crime Drama and Homeland Security: From *Law & Order* to Terror TV,' *Cinema Journal* 51, no. 4 (2012): 44–65.

11 *SVU* follows this practice. To our knowledge 'Serendipity' (5: 5) is the lone episode where the series announces its indebtedness to true crime. The normal disclaimer was modified as 'Although inspired in part by a true incident, the following story is fictional.'

12 The original *Law & Order* series featured Lieutenant Anita van Buren (played by S. Epatha Merkerson) as the head of the police unit; Benson's role thus had a precursor within the franchise but the lieutenant had significantly less screen time than Benson.

13 Julie D'Acci, *Defining Women: Television and the Case of Cagney and Lacey* (Raleigh: University of North Carolina Press, 1994). In an international context the British series *Prime Suspect* starring Helen Mirren, especially in its first three series, has thematized the issue of workplace discrimination. See Deborah Jermyn, *Prime Suspect* (London: BFI Films, 2010).

14 Todd Gitlin, *Inside Prime Time*, 2nd edn (Berkeley: University of California Press, 2000).

15 Sue Turnbull elaborates on the different ways in which UK, Australian, and Scandinavian television crime dramas have foregrounded women. See her book *The TV Crime Drama* (Edinburgh: Edinburgh University Press, 2014).
16 Amanda Lotz, 'Postfeminist Television Criticism: Rehabilitating Critical Terms and Identifying Postfeminist Attributes,' *Feminist Media Studies* 1, no. 1 (2001): 105–21; Jane Arthurs, '*Sex and the City* and Consumer Culture: Remediating Postfeminist Drama,' *Feminist Media Studies* 3, no. 1 (2003): 83–98.
17 Her elevation to sergeant in season 14 is also underscored in the sartorial register: she appears in full dress uniform for her promotion.
18 This taxonomy of feminisms indicates the nuanced ways in which different groups of feminists have comprehended the concept of gender disparities as well as the redressals they offer. Facebook executive Sheryl Sandberg's 2013 book *Lean In* garnered a lot of publicity for highlighting persistent gender inequities in the work place. Her advocacy of individual solutions in lieu of systemic changes has been characterized as lean-in feminism. Earlier, Amy Richards and Jennifer Baumgardner used the term girlie feminism to refer to those who embrace a feminist politics at the same time as traditionally feminine pastimes such as cooking, fashion, and crafting. See Sheryl Sandberg, *Lean In: Women, Work, and the Will to Lead* (New York: Random House, 2013); Amy Richards and Jennifer Baumgardner, *Manifesta: Young Women, Feminism, and the Future* (New York: Farrar, Strauss and Giroux, 2000).
19 Linda Mizejewski, 'Dressed to Kill: Postfeminist Noir,' *Cinema Journal* 44, no. 2 (2005): 121–7, 124.
20 Susan Douglas, *The Rise of Enlightened Sexism: How Pop Culture Took Us from Girl Power to Girls Gone Wild* (New York: St. Martin's Griffin, 2010).
21 Women comprised a little over 17 percent of the 35,000-strong NYPD in 2012 and only 46 serve at the rank of captain or higher. See http://www.policemag.com/channel/women-in-law-enforcement/news/2012/03/26/nypd-honors-policewomen-for-women-s-history-month.aspx (accessed on March 24, 2015).
22 Melissa Schaub, *Middlebrow Feminism in Classic British Detective Fiction: The Female Gentleman* (New York: Palgrave Macmillan, 2013).
23 Hargitay has received Golden Globe and Emmy awards for her portrayal of Benson. In season 15 she directed her first episode, 'Criminal Stories' (15: 18); in season 16 she directed a second episode.
24 Charlotte Brunsdon, *The Feminist, the Housewife, and the Soap Opera* (London: Clarendon Press, 2000), 101.
25 Former showrunner Neal Baer has described in numerous interviews though that he intended to depict Benson as the empathetic figure and Stabler as the enraged one. Bill Harris, 'Against the Law: There are No Plans for Benson and Stabler to Lock Lips Any Time Soon,' *Toronto Sun* (February 20, 2007).
26 'Payback' (1: 1).

27 The captain is a cross-over figure from the original *Law & Order*. His presence as a widower battling alcoholism permits a physical continuity between *SVU* and the franchise.
28 When *Law & Order* first aired NBC officials asked Wolf to include female characters to improve audience ratings among women. Wolf reluctantly acceded to this demand and saw the ratings of the original series improve dramatically. See Jonathan Nichols-Pethick, *TV Cops: The Contemporary American Television Police Drama* (New York: Routledge, 2012).
29 Like Dann Florek's character, John Munch permits *SVU* to draw its lineage with viewers' intertextual memories of the NBC series *Homicide* (1993–9).
30 The DVD box set of the initial seasons includes extra materials called police sketches wherein the individual actors limn the characters they play. These sketches flesh out some background material for the supporting characters that are never disclosed in the storylines.
31 We use the term Latino over Hispanic consciously; we are aware of the different connotations and populations covered by each of the terms. We opted for Latino since the US census has deployed the term since 2000.
32 This test is attributed to the work of graphic novelist Alison Bechdel and her comic strip *Dykes to Watch Out For*.
33 Enterprising tourist companies offer tours of the main sites featured in the *Law & Order* series. See http://onlocationtours.com/locations/law-order-series/ (accessed on March 24, 2015).
34 Kim Akass and Janet McCabe (eds), *Reading 'Sex and the City'* (London: I.B. Tauris, 2003); Serena Daalmans, '"I'm Busy Trying to Become Who I am": Self-entitlement and the City in HBO's Girls,' *Feminist Media Studies* 13, no. 2 (2013): 359–62.
35 According to critics, the dominant character in the *Law & Order* franchise is New York City: 'The show has caught the rhythm and personality of the city in its on-the-street shooting style.' See Bill Carter, 'Spin-off No. 2: Story is Still King, Ka-Ching,' *New York Times* (September 30, 2001): http://www.nytimes.com/2001/09/30/tv/cover-story-spinoff-no-2-story-is-still-king-ka-ching.html (accessed on March 24, 2015).
36 Donald Pease, *The New American Exceptionalism* (Minneapolis: University of Minnesota Press, 2009).
37 The location cards provide on-screen identification of where the scene occurs and are almost always accompanied by the signature chung-chung sound.
38 Amy Chozick, 'Dick Wolf's Drama: This is His Story,' *New York Times* (October 5, 2012): http://www.nytimes.com/2012/10/07/arts/television/chicago-fire-and-the-changing-dick-wolf.html (accessed on March 24, 2015).
39 Charlotte Brunsdon, 'The Attractions of the Cinematic City,' *Screen* 53, no. 3 (2012): 209–27.

40. As we illustrate in Chapter 5, *SVU*'s representation of trans subjects is radically different from their representation in *Sex and the City*.
41. Lisa Cuklanz, *Rape on Prime Time: Television, Masculinity, and Sexual Violence* (Philadelphia: University of Pennsylvania Press, 2000).
42. Sarah Projansky, *Watching Rape: Film and Television in Postfeminist Culture* (New York: New York University Press, 2001).
43. Sujata Moorti, *Color of Rape: Gender and Race in Television's Public Spheres* (Albany: State University of New York Press, 2002).
44. Eric Reitan, 'Rape as an Essentially Contested Concept,' *Hypatia* 16, no. 2 (2001): 43–66.
45. Raymond Williams, 'Base and Superstructure in Marxist Cultural Theory,' *New Left Review* 82 (1973): 3–16.
46. Joanna Bourke offers a good summary of feminist efforts in the US and UK to transform mainstream understandings of rape. See her book *Rape: A History from 1860 to the Present* (London: Virago, 2007).
47. Charlie Savage, 'U.S. to Expand its Definition of Rape in Statistics,' *New York Times* (January 6, 2012): http://www.nytimes.com/2012/01/07/us/politics/federal-crime-statistics-to-expand-rape-definition.html (accessed on March 27, 2014).
48. 'America's Unjust Sex Laws,' *The Economist* (August 6, 2009): www.economic.com/node/14165460 (accessed on March 27, 2014).
49. Carrie Rentschler has documented how the growth of the victims' rights movement and the concept of second victim have helped increase the reach of the police state. See her *Second Wounds: Victims Rights and the Media in the US* (Durham, NC: Duke University Press, 2011).
50. Rhonda Copelon, 'Gendered War Crimes: Reconceptualizing Rape in Time of War,' in *Women's Rights, Human Rights: International Feminist Perspectives*, edited by Julie Peters and Andrea Wolper (New York: Routledge, 1995), 197–214; Claudia Card, 'Rape as a Weapon of War,' *Hypatia* 11, no. 4 (1996): 5–18.
51. Kristin Bumiller, *In an Abusive State: How Neoliberalism Appropriated the Feminist Movement Against Sexual Violence* (Durham, NC: Duke University Press, 2008); Bourke, *Rape*.
52. Linda Fairstein notes that the original squad had 25 detectives who were to 'investigate all allegations of first degree sexual assault.' See her *Sexual Violence: Our War Against Rape* (New York: Berkeley Books, 1995), 83.
53. David Garland, *The Culture of Control: Crime and Social Order in Contemporary Society* (Chicago: University of Chicago Press, 2003); Loic Wacquant, *Prisons of Poverty* (Minneapolis: University of Minnesota Press, 2009).
54. Michel Foucault, *Discipline and Punish: The Birth of the Prison*, trans. Alan Sheridan (New York: Random House, 1979).
55. Marie Gottschalk, *The Prison and the Gallows: The Politics of Mass Incarceration in America* (London: Cambridge University Press, 2006).

56 Wacquant, *Prisons of Poverty*, xv.
57 Michelle Alexander, *The New Jim Crow: Mass Incarceration in the Age of Colorblindness* (New York: New Press, 2012).
58 In a special issue on incarceration, *New York Times Magazine* included a Norwegian prison which is centered on the principle of rehabilitation. See Jessica Benko, 'The Radical Humaneness of Norway's Halden Prison,' *New York Times Magazine* (March 26, 2015): http://www.nytimes.com/2015/03/29/magazine/the-radical-humaneness-of-norways-halden-prison.html?_r=0 (accessed on March 26, 2015).
59 David Harvey, *A Brief History of Neoliberalism* (New York: Oxford University Press, 2007).
60 Nancy Fraser, *Fortunes of Feminism: From State-Managed Capitalism to Neoliberal Crisis* (New York: Verso, 2013).
61 Elizabeth Bernstein, 'Militarized Humanitarianism meets Carceral Feminism: The Politics of Sex, Rights and Freedom in Contemporary Antitrafficking Campaigns,' *Signs* 36, no. 1 (2010): 45–71.
62 Derived from Sheryl Sandberg's book, *Lean In*, this movement seeking gender equity is confined to the workplace and women's empowerment within it.
63 Janet Halley, *Split Decisions: How and Why to Take a Break from Feminism* (Princeton: Princeton University Press, 2006); and Bernstein, 'Militarized Humanitarianism.'
64 Stabler similarly realizes that he helped incarcerate an innocent man in 'Unstable' (11: 1). He also spends a day in solitary confinement to get a taste of this form of punishment in 'Solitary' (11: 3). At the end of the episode he pleads successfully with the ADA not to send a criminal to solitary confinement. These moments offer cracks in the carceral feminism promoted by the show but are not pursued to offer a real critique.
65 In recent seasons, the series has started to stage the assault in progress during the pre-credits segment. Often this assault is technologically mediated so the detectives watch the live-streaming of an assault or a surveillance camera recording of an assault.
66 Peter Lalor, 'Twists and Turn on a Disturbing Journey,' *Weekend Australian* (March 22, 2007): 36.
67 Respondents overwhelmingly believed the professor was not guilty (60 percent), while only 20 percent believed the rape claimant.
68 Feminist media scholars have argued that liberal feminism is the most prevalent form of televisual discourse. Valerie Bryson clarifies this as a strand of feminism that 'concentrates on rights in the public sphere and does not analyze power relationships that may exist in the home or private life.' See her *Feminist Debates: Issues of Theory and Political Practice* (New York: New York University Press, 1999), 3. Also see Bonnie Dow, *Prime-Time Feminism: Television, Media*

Culture, and the Women's Movement since the 1970s (Philadelphia: University of Pennsylvania Press, 1996); Lauren Rabinovitz, 'Sitcoms and Single Moms: Representations of Feminism on American TV,' *Cinema Journal* 29, no. 1 (1989): 3–19.

2 Family Matters: Criminal Mothers and Fathers

1 Muriel Cantor asserts that the ideal family on prime time traditionally featured a husband, wife, and non-adult children. It is worth noting that most of the abusive families in *SVU* are non-traditional or, according to Cantor's parameters, less than ideal. See her 'Prime Time Fathers: A Study in Continuity and Change,' *Critical Studies in Mass Communication* 7 (1990): 275–85.
2 Other work has emphasized the way in which male characterizations on television can serve an anti-feminist purpose. Mary Vavrus shows how the figure of the stay-at-home dad on prime time television typically shows his satisfaction and positive attitude, thus undermining feminist critiques of the drudgery and monotony of housework. See her 'Domesticating Patriarchy: Hegemonic Masculinity and Television's "Mr. Mom",' *Critical Studies in Mass Communication* 19, no. 3 (2002): 352–75.
3 Angela McRobbie, *The Aftermath of Feminism: Gender, Culture, and Social Change* (Thousand Oaks, CA: Sage, 2009); Rosalind Gill, 'Postfeminist Media Culture: Elements of a Sensibility,' *European Journal of Cultural Studies* 10, no. 2 (2007): 147–66.
4 Angela McRobbie, 'Post-Feminism and Popular Culture,' *Feminist Media Studies* 4, no. 3 (2004): 255–64, 255.
5 Lisa Cuklanz and Sujata Moorti, 'Television's "New" Feminism: Prime Time Representations of Women and Victimization,' *Critical Studies in Media Communication* 23, no. 4 (2006): 302–21.
6 Erica Scharrer, 'More than "Just the Facts"?: Portrayals of Masculinity in Police and Detective Programs Over Time,' *The Howard Journal of Communications* 23 (2012): 88–109. Scharrer traces the evolution of the male detective figure, including the increasing ability of these characters to feel and express emotions, traditionally feminine qualities.
7 Previous scholarship has documented the ways in which fathers in prime time situation comedies are often ridiculed or criticized. However, no matter how foolish or problematic their parenting may be, they are seldom required to atone or apologize. See Erica Scharrer, 'From Wise to Foolish: TV Portrayals of the Sitcom Father, 1950s–1990s,' *Journal of Broadcasting and Electronic Media* (Winter 2001): 23–40; Kimberly Walsh, Elfriede Fursich, and Bonnie Jefferson, 'Beauty and the Patriarchal Beast: Gender Role Portrayals in Sitcoms Featuring Mismatched Couples,' *Journal of Popular Film and Television* (2008): 123–32.

8 Suzanne Enck-Wanzer, 'All's Fair in Love and Sport: Black Masculinity and Domestic Violence in the News,' *Communication and Critical/Cultural Studies* 6, no. 1 (2009): 1–18, 2.
9 Barbara Creed, *The Monstrous-Feminine: Film, Feminism, and Psychoanalysis* (New York: Routledge, 1993).
10 E. Ann Kaplan, *Motherhood and Representation: The Mother in Popular Culture and Melodrama* (London: Routledge, 1992).
11 Bumiller, *In an Abusive State*, 86.
12 While a maternal story angle was added in 'Chameleon,' an episode based on the Aileen Wuornos case, there is little relationship between real-life cases of murderous mothers and *SVU* episodes. However, general issues such as childhood vaccinations and mercy killing may remind viewers of real-life debates, and the narrative parameters of episodes such as 'Mercy' (4: 14) and 'Selfish' (10: 19) also bear resemblances to specific real-life cases. 'Selfish' depicts a mother who inadvertently causes the death of her child through a refusal to vaccinate. The episode's harmful mother is played by Missi Pyle, whose physical resemblance to real-life anti-vaccination spokesperson Jenny McCarthy was noted in several online discussion threads. 'Taboo' (7: 14), an episode about a young woman who has abandoned a second newborn baby in a trashcan, echoes some of the elements of the case of Kenisha Berry, an African-American woman from Texas who was charged with the murder of her baby and neglect of a second infant. The *SVU* version, however, features a white criminal and elements of consensual incest to the storyline.
13 Hannah Hamad, *Postfeminism and Paternity in Contemporary U.S. Film: Framing Fatherhood* (New York: Routledge, 2013).
14 Narratives about abusive fathers are almost exclusively focused on Caucasian characters, even when the accusations are false. For an analysis of black fatherhood on television, see Debra Smith, 'Critiquing Reality-Based Televisual Black Fatherhood: A Critical Analysis of Run's House and Snoop Dogg's Father Hood,' *Critical Studies in Media Communication* 25, no. 4 (2008): 393–412.
15 This episode, starring Jeremy Irons as the therapist, is also discussed in Chapter 5.
16 This episode is also discussed in Chapter 5.
17 This characterization of mother and father as equally at fault in child abuse is echoed in 'Cage' (8: 8) in which a foster mother and father use a cage to discipline unruly foster children in their care.
18 In 'Transitions' (10: 14) the father is similarly exonerated. His actions are not presented as abusive but rather those of an overprotective, misguided father who does not understand how to parent a transgender child.
19 In 'Lessons Learned' (14: 8), a father who is unable to accept his son's homosexuality fails to realize that his son is being abused while at private school.

20 The theme of man–boy love is raised for shock value in other episodes as well.
21 In 'Sugar' (11: 2), a man who neglected his daughter to the point that she becomes a murderer tries to regain some lost ground by trying to take the blame for the murder she has committed.
22 'Inheritance' is further discussed in Chapters 3 and 5.

3 The Violence of Race

1 In 2007, staff associated with the series charged *SVU* co-executive producer Ted Kotcheff with directing racist and sexist invective. See Matt Mitovich, 'SVU Biggie Charged with Racism, Sexism,' *TV Guide* (April 26, 2007): http://www.tvguide.com/news/svu-biggie-charged-15903.aspx (accessed on March 24, 2015).
2 Herman Gray, 'Race, Media, and the Cultivation of Concern,' *Communication and Critical/Cultural Studies* 10, nos 2–3 (2013): 253–8.
3 Our work on this manuscript was conducted amidst the syncopated sounds of protests against structural racism and the murders of African Americans at the hands of the police, such as Michael Brown, Edward Garner, Freddie Gray, and Sandra Bland. We have no doubt that *SVU* episodes in season 17 will incorporate these events in their storylines, but it is unpredictable how the series will address them.
4 Eduardo Bonilla-Silva, *Racism without Racists: Colorblind Racism and the Persistence of Inequality in Racial America* (New York: Rowman and Littlefield, 2003); Michael Brown et al., *Whitewashing Race: The Myth of a Colorblind Society* (Berkeley: University of California Press, 2003).
5 Judges, staff from the judiciary, and other bit parts are also allocated to guest actors. But our focus in this chapter is on the depictions of crime and criminality.
6 Various internet sites have documented the actors who acted on *SVU* before attaining fame. See http://www.buddytv.com/slideshows/law-and-order-svu/most-memorable-guest-stars-of-law-amp-order-svu-99907.aspx; http://www.backstage.com/news/59-actors-who-have-been-law-order-special-victims-unit/; http://www.glamour.com/entertainment/blogs/obsessed/2014/09/law-and-order-svu-celeb-cameos (all accessed on March 24, 2015).
7 Helen Benedict, *Virgin or Vamp: How the Press Covers Sex Crimes* (New York: Oxford University Press, 1993).
8 As we discuss in Chapter 5, a black school guidance counselor is identified as an assailant in 'Transitions' (10: 4). Highlighting how her experiences while transitioning gender motivated her actions, the storyline recasts her as the

archetypal Hollywood mammy, a woman willing to sacrifice her life to secure the happiness of the white child who is her responsibility.
9. Officially this unit was 'responsible for matters of taste and violence' in network programs. The mandate was ambiguous enough that under the guise of 'taste' the office would censor programs that may offend some portion of the viewing public. See 'NBC and CBS Reduce Role of Self Censors,' *New York Times* (August 20, 1988): http://www.nytimes.com/1988/08/20/business/nbc-and-cbs-reduce-role-of-self-censors.html (accessed on March 24, 2015).
10. According to a *Wall Street Journal* article Dick Wolf believes that viewers are more interested in storylines with white, wealthy people as victims. 'He limits the number of shows containing minority victims, including blacks and Muslims to four or five episodes a season.' See Rebecca Dana, 'Law and Disorder,' *Wall Street Journal* (July 12, 2008): http://www.wsj.com/articles/SB121582018406147559 (accessed on March 24, 2015).
11. Ten seasons later, in 'Unstable' (11: 1), a black suspect, Mark Foster, repeats the same sentiments when SVU detectives question him: 'white woman gets raped in the area and every brother within 20 blocks gets rounded up.'
12. Several tumblr sites ironically document the limited scope of Fin's character. See https://www.tumblr.com/tagged/fin-tutuola (accessed on March 24, 2015).
13. By depicting most sexual assaults as intraracial *SVU* narratives undo some foundational popular culture myths (such as the rapes represented in *Birth of a Nation* and *Gone with the Wind*).
14. 'Hooked' (6: 15) features a similar storyline of a dead white teenager; the father is shocked and grieves his daughter's death but does not feel the need to kill her lover. There is an unarticulated presumption that the police and judiciary would work on his behalf.
15. Sherene Razack, *Casting Out: The Eviction of Muslims from Western Law and Politics* (Toronto: University of Toronto Press, 2008).
16. 'Presumed Guilty' (14: 10) features a previously convicted sex offender falsely accused of assault. The suspect is Fin's brother-in-law. The detective is convinced of his relative's guilt although his colleagues are unable to find evidence to support this conviction. Similarly, a black ADA is tougher on this black man arrested on false charges than he is on white suspects. The storylines do not offer African-American officials the same complex reactions to men-of-color assailants that are afforded their white counterparts.
17. See Tricia Rose, *Black Noise: Rap Music and Black Culture in Contemporary America* (Middletown, CT: Wesleyan University Press, 1994).
18. Ironically, the episode was originally scheduled to air the same day as the One Billion Rising global campaign, a movement designed to raise awareness about gender-based violence. At least three online petitions protesting Tyson were organized through the website change.org. NBC aired the episode

a week earlier but the criticisms continued unabated. See Emine Saner, 'Why is Mike Tyson to Star in a Crime Drama about Rape?' *The Guardian* (28 January 2013): http://www.theguardian.com/society/2013/jan/28/mike-tyson-star-in-rape-drama (accessed on March 24, 2015).

19 Mike Tyson served three years of a six-year prison sentence for his conviction in the 1992 rape of Miss Black America pageant contestant Desiree Washington. Addressing the various protests surrounding his inclusion in *SVU*, Tyson denied raping Washington and claimed that he was in the episode 'to do a service.' See William Keck, 'Mike Tyson discusses his Controversial Role in *Law & Order: SVU*,' (January 29, 2013): http://www.tvguide.com/News/Mike-Tyson-SVU-1060070.aspx (accessed on March 24, 2015).

20 Kimberlé Crenshaw, 'Mapping the Margins: Intersectionality, Identity Politics and Violence against Women of Color,' *Stanford Law Review* 43, no. 6 (1990): 1241–99.

21 Ramping up the celebrity quotient of this episode, Ed Asner plays the role of the summer camp pedophile.

22 *SVU* showrunner Warren Leight took to Twitter to defend his casting choice and urged audiences to 'keep an open mind.' Since it was over two decades after the conviction Leight believed that Tyson's presence would 'provoke discussion and awareness.' See 'Mike Tyson Responds to "Law & Order: SVU" Guest Role Controversy,' *Huffington Post* (January 30, 2013): http://www.huffingtonpost.com/2013/01/30/mike-tyson-svu-controversy_n_2579207.html (accessed on March 24, 2015). Producer Dick Wolf praised the episode as one of the strongest episodes of the previous five years and refused to comment on the petitions or criticisms. See Nellie Andreeva, '"Law & Order" Boss Dick Wolf Praises "SVU" Episode featuring Mike Tyson,' (February 2, 2013): http://deadline.com/2013/02/law-order-boss-dick-wolf-praises-svu-episode-featuring-mike-tyson-420349/ (accessed on March 24, 2015).

23 The series and the actor highlight the Joyful Heart Foundation, a non-profit organization Hargitay has started to assist sexual abuse victims. While *SVU* may have cast Mike Tyson in the show expecting viewers to tap into their intertexual knowledge of the boxer's conviction, unintentionally viewers may also tap into Hargitay's real-life advocacy efforts to read the episode as problematizing Tyson's real-life conviction. Notably, the Joyful Heart Foundation apologized to viewers who felt betrayed and condemned the casting choice but did not reference Hargitay. For more on the concept of intertextuality and its centrality to making sense of television narratives see Robert Deming, 'Theorizing Television: Text, Textuality, Intertextuality,' *Journal of Communication Inquiry* 10 (1986): 32–44; Hamid Naficy, 'Television Intertextuality and the Nuclear Family,' *Journal of Film and Video* 41, no. 4 (1989): 42–59.

24 It is worth noting that in episodes prior to this one, 'Beautiful Frame' (14: 11) and 'Presumed Guilty' (14: 10), falsely accused people are sent to jail. The Tyson episode builds on this thread.
25 David Leonard has highlighted how a color-blind racism has shaped mainstream society's appreciation of these black athletes' talents and simultaneous disavowal of their 'monstrous' masculinities. See Leonards' 'The Next M. J. or the Next O. J.? Kobe Bryant, Race, and the Absurdity of Colorblind Rhetoric,' *Journal of Sport and Social Issues* 28, no. 3 (2004): 284-313.
26 Amanda Edgar, 'R&B Rhetoric and Victim-Blaming Discourses: Exploring the Popular Press's Revision of Rihanna's Contextual Agency,' *Women's Studies in Communication* 37, no. 2 (2014): 138-58.
27 Karen Fields and Barbara Fields, *Racecraft: The Soul of Inequality in American Life* (New York: Verso, 2012).
28 'Funny Valentine' aired on the same day media coverage depicted a reconciliation and rekindled romance between Rihanna and Chris Brown, four years after the 2009 assault case.
29 Erica Meiners, 'Never Innocent: Feminist Trouble with Sex Offender Registries and Protection in a Prison Nation,' *Meridians* 9, no. 2 (2009): 31-62.
30 In 'Unstable' (11: 1), the new executive ADA cautions SVU detectives that '75% of wrongful convictions' result from mis-identifications. She later reminds them that '53 convictions had been overturned in the state' because detectives did not do their jobs effectively.
31 Alexander, *The New Jim Crow*.
32 Walker's character is played by Billy Porter who received a Tony award for his role in the Broadway production of *Kinky Boots*. In this instance, Porter's celebrity appealed to a very different audience than those episodes featuring athletes or rap stars.
33 Mary Fellows and Sherene Razack, 'The Race to Innocence: Confronting Hierarchical Relations among Women,' *Journal of Gender, Race and Justice* 1 (1998): 335-52.
34 Mary Beltran argues that the increasing prevalence of multiracial casts and actors is a trend reflecting contemporary shifts in US ethnic demographics and ethnic identity, while subtly reinforcing notions of white centrism. See Beltran's 'The New Hollywood Racelessness: Only the Fast, Furious, (and Multiracial) Will Survive,' *Cinema Journal* 44, no. 2 (2005): 50-67.
35 The storyline draws attention to the distinctions between Mandarin and Cantonese, which SVU detectives gloss over in their invocation of Chinese.
36 Emily Nussbaum describes him as a dandy. See her, 'Trauma Queen: The Pulp Appeal of "Law & Order: SVU",' *New Yorker* (June 10, 2013): http://www.newyorker.com/magazine/2013/06/10/trauma-queen (accessed on March 24, 2015).

37 Jennifer Rudolph uses the term masculatinidad to characterize the tensions and unities that are papered over in the phrase Latino masculinities. See Rudolph's *Embodying Latino Masculinities: Producing Masculatinidad* (New York: Palgrave Macmillan, 2012).
38 Hamilton Carroll, *Affirmative Reaction: New Formations of White Masculinity* (Durham, NC: Duke University Press, 2011), 10.
39 Gloria Hull, Patricia Scott, and Barbara Smith (eds), *But Some of us are Brave: All the Women are White, All the Blacks are Men* (New York: Feminist Press, 1993).

4 A Foreign Affair: The Global Turn to Gaze at the Self

1 Cuklanz and Moorti, 'Television's "New Feminism"'; Moorti, *Color of Rape*.
2 Bumiller, *In an Abusive State*.
3 Susan Jeffords, 'Rape and the New World Order,' *Cultural Critique* 19 (1991): 203–15; Judith Stiehm, 'The Protected, the Protector, the Defender,' *Women's Studies International Forum* 5, nos 3–4 (1982): 367–76.
4 We derive our understanding of cosmopolitan from Kwame Anthony Appiah who uses it to designate a community wherein individuals from different locations (geographic, cultural, class) enter relationships of mutual respect despite their differing beliefs. See his 'Cosmopolitan Patriots,' *Cultural Critique* 23, no. 3 (1997): 617–39.
5 Shilpa Davé, *Indian Accents: Brown Voice and Racial Performance in American Television and Film* (Chicago: University of Illinois Press, 2013).
6 We are not making a causal connection but wish to signal a conjuncture. It is likely that *SVU* showrunners were responding to online viewer comments which berated a turn to the elsewhere when there are plenty of sex crimes at home to address.
7 For more on the belief that the US is unique and qualitatively different from other nations see Pease, *The New American Exceptionalism*.
8 Foucault, *Discipline and Punish*.
9 Deborah Jaramillo, 'Narcocorridos and Newbie Drug Dealers: The Changing Image of the Mexican Narco on US Television,' *Ethnic and Racial Studies* 37, no. 9 (2014): 1587–604, 1587.
10 Alex Cabot's death is an emotionally weighted moment in the series. In Chapter 6, we explore how viewers responded to this event.
11 'Risk' (4: 12) features a white businessman who is operating a cocaine ring. He travels to Mexico but there is no other aspect of the foreign attached to him, making him an All-American criminal who is different from the others we examine in this section.

12 In 'Gambler's Fallacy' (15: 16) an undercover police officer acts as an Irish mercenary. He secures this foreign identity by modifying his accent, not his appearance.
13 The Polaris project is a notable NGO in this arena; more recently the Department of Homeland Security has established a Blue Campaign to combat trafficking while the UN has its own Blue Heart project. In addition, pressure groups have helped pass laws at the federal and state levels to combat trafficking in the US (for a comprehensive list of these laws see http://www.polarisproject.org/what-we-do/policy-advocacy/national-policy/current-federal-laws). New York City has instituted a series of laws to address all forms of trafficking, see http://www.criminaljustice.ny.gov/pio/humantrafficking/humantrafficking.htm (accessed on March 24, 2015).
14 For feminist critiques of the rescue and rehabilitation efforts see Rutvica Andrijasevic, 'Beautiful Dead Bodies: Gender, Migration and Representation in Anti-trafficking Campaigns,' *Feminist Review* 86 (2007): 24–44; Nandita Sharma, 'Anti-trafficking Rhetoric and the Making of a Global Apartheid,' *NWSA Journal* 17, no. 3 (2005): 88–111; Gretchen Soderlund, 'Running from the Rescuers: New US Crusades against Trafficking and the Rhetoric of Abolition,' *NWSA Journal* 17, no. 3 (2005): 64–87; Bernstein, 'Militarized Humanitarianism.'
15 In 'Slaves' (1: 22), Munch carefully elaborates on the phenomenon known as Stockholm Syndrome and informs his colleagues about its origins in 1970s Sweden. He also elaborates on the evils of the Ceausescu regime in Romania.
16 The coffin-like structure resembles the Iron Maiden torture device Naomi Wolf references in *The Beauty Myth: How Images of Beauty are Used against Women* (New York: William Morrow, 1990).
17 'Ace' (11: 22) features a baby trafficking ring where Bulgarian women are raped, impregnated, and forced to give up their babies for adoption while 'Hothouse' (9: 12) is about the trafficking in Ukrainian women. In both instances the trafficking centers around white people but race remains silenced. Erica Johnson documents the popularity of Russian women in cross-border marriages while Kristen Ghodsee shows how Bulgarian women have coped with the economic shifts in East Europe following the collapse of the Soviet Union. See Erica Johnson, *Dreaming of a Mail-Order Husband: Russian–American Internet Romance* (Durham, NC: Duke University Press, 2007); and Kristen Ghodsee, *The Red Riviera: Gender, Tourism, and Postsocialism on the Black Sea* (Durham, NC: Duke University Press, 2005).
18 The one instance when African-American men figure in a trafficking storyline is in the trade of exotic animals. In 'Wildlife' (10: 7), the people who purchase these animals are depicted as hip-hop artists invested in making ostentatious claims of distinction. The episode includes a guest appearance by Big Boi, a member of the hip-hop group Outkast. The presence of recognizable hip-hop

stars functions as an authenticating device for the series but also simultaneously complicates its racial politics. They also facilitate an aural level of recognition among viewers.
19 Gina Marchetti, *Romance and the Yellow Peril: Race, Sex and Discursive Strategies in Hollywood Fiction* (Berkeley: University of California Press, 1994).
20 In 'Merchandise' (12: 4), SVU detectives point out that when trafficking is domestic the only charge that can be made is that of prostitution, not that of trafficked subjects. In effect the trafficked person is the criminal in a domestic context.
21 The detectives initially identify Sofia as Indian. The slippage between two South Asian identities while seemingly innocent also hints at how much Pakistan and Islam have become associated with terrorism in the US imaginary.
22 Amal Amireh, 'Palestinian Women's Disappearing Act: The Suicide Bomber through Western Feminist Eyes,' in *Arab and Arab American Feminisms: Gender, Violence, & Belonging*, edited by Rabab Abdulhadi et al. (Syracuse: Syracuse University Press, 2010), 29–45.
23 For a summary of feminist responses to this organization see Gayle Rubin, 'Thinking Sex: Notes for a Radical Theory of the Politics of Sexuality,' in *Pleasure and Danger*, edited by Carole Vance (New York: Routledge & Kegan, Paul, 1984), 143–78.
24 Erika Alexander, an actor familiar to television viewers, plays the consular agent. Her foreignness is signaled through her heavily accented English and her dress.
25 Laura Mulvey, 'Visual Pleasure and Narrative Cinema,' *Screen* 16, no. 3 (1975): 6–18; and Griselda Pollock, 'Modernity and the Spaces of Femininity,' in *Feminism, Femininity and the Histories of Art* (New York: Routledge, 2003), 50–90.
26 E. Ann Kaplan, *Looking for the Other: Feminism, Film and the Imperial Gaze* (New York: Routledge, 1997); Meyda Yegenoglu, *Colonial Fantasies: Toward a Feminist Reading of Orientalism* (London: Cambridge University Press, 1998).
27 The use of the term wilding takes on additional meaning for viewers who recall that it was the predominant word used to characterize the alleged gang rape of the 'Central Park Jogger' in 1989. In that real case a Wall Street banker was raped, beaten, and left for dead in Central Park and five teenagers of color were arrested and jailed. Wilding became a shorthand term to describe the brutality of the rape and the alienness of the teenagers' actions. The five accused were subsequently found to have been innocent of the rape after another man was found to have been responsible for the assault. In 2002, a couple of years after this episode first aired, the teenagers' convictions were vacated after they had served their sentences. For more on the Central Park case see Moorti, *Color of Rape*; Natalie Byfield, *Savage*

Portrayals: Race, Media and the Central Park Jogger Story (Philadelphia: Temple University Press, 2014); and the documentary *Central Park Five* (Sarah Burns, 2012).

28 Anthropologist Lila Abu-Lughod contends that the term honor crime sets a culturally specific form of violence as distinct from other forms of intimate partner violence and the culture itself is presented as the cause of criminal violence. Honor crime functions as a comforting phantasm that empowers the West; it shifts attention to an abjected stage where caricatured people are victims of their own violent will, hence it demands self-righteous commitment to change those dysfunctional cultures. See her 'Seductions of the "Honor Crime,"' *differences* 22, no. 1 (2011): 17–63.

29 As we discuss in the following chapter, in later episodes *SVU* often verifies claims of diminished rationality through a scientific turn. In this instance *SVU* is unable to translate the brother's cultural argument of diminished rationality through a visual turn.

30 'Criminal Stories' (15: 17) features the rape of an Indian Muslim woman. In the early stages of the episode the detectives assume they are investigating a hate crime. Later they realize that the rape did not occur in Central Park nor was it motivated by a hatred of Muslims. Instead, the detectives discover that two wealthy white men assaulted the woman and she concocted the story of hate crime to save her family's honor. In this episode the haremic gaze is muted since the Muslim woman is presented as being raised in the US. She is also depicted as having some agency and autonomy. Consequently, none of the SVU staff attempt to forge a sisterhood with her.

31 Lila Abu-Lughod, 'Do Muslim Women Really Need Saving?,' *American Anthropologist* 104, no. 3 (2002): 783–90.

32 Stabler suggests that the dead woman preferred an iPhone over FGM and her refusal to adhere to tradition caused her death.

33 Dicle Kogacioglu, 'The Tradition Effect: Framing Honor Crimes in Turkey,' *differences* 15, no. 2 (2004): 118–51.

34 See Leti Volpp, 'Framing Cultural Difference: Immigrant Women and Discourses of Tradition,' *differences* 22, no. 1 (2011): 90–110.

35 Some scholars have noted that Western media representations of 'rape camps' have tended to portray the rapists as Serbians and Muslim women as vulnerable. These narratives situate gendered sexual violence in a matrix of ethno-religious difference. See Rana Jaleel, 'Weapons of Sex, Weapons of War: Feminisms, Ethnic Conflict, and the Rise of Rape and Sexual Violence in Public International Law during the 1990s,' *Cultural Studies* 27, no. 1 (2013): 115–35.

36 Elizabeth Heineman, 'The History of Sexual Violence in Conflict Zones: Conference Report,' *Radical History Review* 101 (2008): 5–21.

37 Dubravka Zarkov, *The Body of War: Media, Ethnicity and Gender in the Break-up of Yugoslavia* (Durham, NC: Duke University Press, 2007), 146–7.
38 The rape camps in the former Yugoslavia have been thematized with very different effect in the British crime drama, *Prime Suspect 6: The Last Witness* (Granada, 2002) and feature films *In the Land of Blood and Honey* (Angelina Jolie, 2012) and *As if I am Not There* (Juanita Wilson, 2010). *Prime Suspect*, starring Helen Mirren, addressed the topic with a greater degree of nuance and complexity in its four-hour narrative arc than does *SVU*. For more on this see Gary Cavender and Nancy Jurik, 'Scene Composition and Justice for Women: An Analysis of the Portrayal of Detective Tennison in the British Television Program Prime Suspect,' *Feminist Criminology* 2 (2007): 277–303; Maud Lavin, *Push Comes to Shove: New Images of Aggressive Women* (Cambridge, MA: MIT Press, 2010); and Deborah Jermyn, *Prime Suspect* (London: BFI Films, 2010).
39 *SVU* teamed with the Enough Project in both these episodes and the aim was specifically to highlight rape as a war crime. Enough Project is an NGO which seeks to end genocide and crimes against humanity. See Mariska Hargitay and John Prendergast, 'How we can all Help Women in Congo,' *Huffington Post* (May 17, 2010): http://www.huffingtonpost.com/mariska-hargitay/how-we-can-all-help-women_b_502411.html (accessed on March 24, 2015).
40 'Hell' is the first instance that television fiction was filmed inside the UN compound. See Chris Zimmer, *'Law & Order SVU*: First TV Show Filmed at UN' (March 9, 2009): http://allthingslawandorder.blogspot.com (accessed on March 24, 2015).
41 Gayatri Spivak, 'Can the Subaltern Speak?' in *Marxism and the Interpretation of Culture*, edited by Cary Nelson and Larry Grossberg (Urbana: University of Illinois Press, 1988), 271–313.
42 Yvonne Tasker has offered a very provocative account of this episode as being part of a larger trend of terror TV. Our analysis in this chapter is motivated by different goals. See her 'Television Crime Drama and Homeland Security.'
43 For more on the Western appropriation of henna and other exotic fashions see Sujata Moorti, 'Out of India: Fashion Culture and the Marketing of Ethnic Style,' in *A Companion to Media Studies*, edited by Angharad N. Valdivia (Malden, MA: Blackwell, 2003), 293–308.
44 Etienne Balibar, *We, the People of Europe? Reflections on Transnational Citizenship*, trans. James Swenson (Princeton: Princeton University Press, 2003).

5 Images of Truth: The Science of Detection

1. Jeffrey Rosen, 'The Brain on the Stand,' *New York Times Magazine* (March 11, 2007): 49–53, 70, 77–83.
2. Sue Tait, 'Autoptic Vision and the Necrophilic Imaginary in *CSI*,' *International Journal of Cultural Studies* 9, no. 2 (2006): 45–62; Derek Kompare, *CSI* (New York: Wiley-Blackwell, 2010); Kit Roane, 'The CSI Effect,' *US News & World Report* 138, no. 16 (May 2, 2005): 17.
3. Richard Sherwin, *Visualizing Law in the Age of the Digital Baroque: Arabesques and Entanglements* (New York: Routledge, 2011).
4. Franklin Melendez, 'Video Pornography, Visual Pleasure and the Return of the Sublime,' in *Porn Studies*, edited by Linda Williams (Durham, NC: Duke University Press, 2004), 401–27.
5. Walter Benjamin, 'The Work of Art in the Age of Mechanical Reproduction,' in *Illuminations: Essays and Reflections*, trans. Harry Zohn (New York: Schocken Books, 1968), 219–26.
6. Dial-up internet connections were the norm in the late 1990s when *SVU* began. The search engine Google started in 1998 and by the new millennium had become a household name. Similarly, social networking site MySpace was launched in 2003 and Facebook went public in 2007. Mobile technologies took over after 2010 and social media have since become seemingly ubiquitous. For a more detailed accounting of this dense and tangled set of innovations see 'The History of Social Networking,' http://www.digitaltrends.com/features/the-history-of-social-networking/ (accessed on March 24, 2015).
7. Melinda Warner has been a recurring cast member since the second season. Between seasons 7 and 13, she was added to the main credits and the profile photograph. Her character continues to appear in later seasons as a recurring guest actor. During its first season *SVU* featured Elizabeth Rodgers (played by Leslie Hendrix) as the medical examiner in several of the storylines.
8. José van Dijck, 'Picturing Science: The Science Documentary as Multimedia Spectacle,' *International Journal of Cultural Studies* 9, no. 1 (2006): 5–24.
9. The featured TARU technicians are mostly people of color; for over ten seasons an Asian American, Ruben Morales, was the TARU technician. Together with the medical examiner, an African-American woman, and the resident psychiatrist, these technical staff make the *SVU* landscape more diverse.
10. Scientists have questioned the liberties crime dramas take in their depiction of forensic technologies. See for instance, Lamont Wood, 'The Reality of Fingerprinting Not Like TV Crime Labs,' LiveScience (February 24, 2008): http://www.livescience.com/4843-reality-fingerprinting-tv-crime-labs.html (accessed on March 24, 2015); Claudio Rapezzi, Roberto Ferrari and Angelo Branzi, 'White Coats and Fingerprints: Diagnostic Reasoning in Medicine

and Investigative Methods of Fictional Detectives,' *British Medical Journal* 231 (December 22, 2005): 1491–4.
11 Chandak Sengoopta contends that fingerprinting was invented in colonial India as a mechanism to control 'natives.' It was transported to England where it became a key component of the British criminal court. The racist and imperial underpinnings of this forensic tool continue to haunt it, he argues. See *Imprint of the Raj: How Fingerprinting was Born in Colonial India* (New York: Macmillan, 2003).
12 Allan Sekula, 'The Body and the Archive,' *October* 39 (1986): 3–64.
13 Roland Thomas, *Detective Fiction and the Rise of Forensic Science* (London: Cambridge University Press, 1999).
14 Julie Johnson-McGrath, 'Speaking for the Dead: Forensic Pathologists and Criminal Justice in the US,' *Science, Technology and Human Values* 20, no. 4 (1995): 438–59.
15 Joy Palmer, 'Tracing Bodies: Gender, Genre and Forensic Detective Fiction,' *South Central Review* 18, nos 3–4 (2001): 54–71.
16 Neal Baer, the showrunner for 12 years, is a trained medical doctor and shaped the series' depiction of science and medicine.
17 Rosen, 'The Brain on the Stand.'
18 This episode is reminiscent of other storylines we have analyzed in Chapter 2 with female assailants and the monstrous maternal.
19 Scenes such as this one draw our attention to the limited value of labels such as pedophile and rapist. As critical scholars in sociology have pointed out, naming an act rather than labeling the person who commits the act may be more useful in thinking through the issue.
20 Anne Beaulieu, 'The Brain at the End of the Rainbow: The Promises of Brain Scans in the Research Field and in the Media,' in *Wild Science: Reading Feminism, Medicine and the Media* edited by Janine Marchessault and Kim Sawchuk (New York: Routledge, 2000), 39–54.
21 Joseph Dumit, *Picturing Personhood: Brain Scans and Biomedical Identity* (Princeton: Princeton University Press, 2004).
22 Stephen Morse, 'Brain Overclaim Syndrome and Criminal Responsibility: A Diagnostic Note' (2006). Faculty Scholarship. Paper 117. http://scholarship.law.upenn.edu/faculty_scholarship/117 (accessed on March 24, 2015).
23 Amit Prasad, 'Making Images/Making Bodies: Visibilizing and Disciplining through Magnetic Resonance Imaging (MRI),' *Science, Technology, and Human Values* 30, no. 2 (2005): 291–316.
24 Sigrid Schmitz, 'The Neuro-Technological Cerebral Subject: Persistence of Implicit and Explicit Gender Norms in a Network of Change,' *Neuroethics* 5 (2012): 261–74.

25 In the first two seasons Detectives Stabler and Benson repeatedly summarize key feminist arguments on issues as diverse as body image concerns, sexual objectification, 'female genital mutilation,' and so on. Specifically in describing rape the two repeatedly avow that No means No and that it is not about sex but about power (two quintessential liberal feminist mantras).
26 The storyline poaches key ideas and signifiers of the 1980s Born to Kill Chinatown gang which used the racism of the US Army in Vietnam to mobilize teenagers into computer thefts. Gang members wear tattoos with the Born to Kill slogan, revalorizing the slogan used by the US military in Vietnam to local conditions. In a postcolonial context such a resignifying art would be hailed as the empire writing back. See Bill Ashcroft, Gareth Griffins and Helen Tiffin, *The Empire Writes Back: Theory and Practice in Post-Colonial Literatures* (New York: Routledge, 2002).
27 Jenny Reardon, 'Decoding Race and Human Difference in a Genomic Age,' *differences* 15, no. 3 (2004): 38–65.
28 This is also in keeping with the series' disdain for intellectuals.
29 'Demons' (7: 1) features a similar dismissal of rehabilitation but in this case Stabler participates actively in making a newly released sex offender assault a girl. The sex offender is presented as a predator, a figure Loic Wacquant has characterized as providing 'an urgent and perpetually refreshed motive for the full repudiation of the ideal of rehabilitation,' *Prisons of Poverty* (Minneapolis: University of Minnesota Press, 2009), 213.
30 It also marks a radical shift from nineteenth-century detective fiction.
31 Teresa de Lauretis, *Technologies of Gender: Essays on Theory, Film, and Fiction* (Bloomington: Indiana University Press, 1987), 2.
32 As we completed this manuscript celebrity Caitlyn Jenner drew renewed mainstream attention to the trans experience, and *SVU* had already announced its intention to incorporate this event in a season 17 episode.
33 Bending a series of genres, *RuPaul's Drag Race* (Logo, 2009–present) clarifies for television audiences the nuances of drag performance.
34 John Sloop, 'Disciplining the Transgendered: Brandon Teena, Public Representations, and Normativity,' *Western Journal of Communication* 64 (2000): 165–89; Brenda Cooper, '*Boys Don't Cry* and Female Masculinity: Reclaiming a Life & Dismantling the Politics of Normative Heterosexuality,' *Critical Studies in Media Communication* 19, no. 1 (2002): 44–63.
35 K. E. Sullivan, 'Ed Gein and the Figure of the Transgendered Criminal,' *Jump Cut* 43 (2000): 38–47; Annabelle Wilcox, 'Branding Teena: (Mis) Representations in the Media,' *Sexualities* 6, nos 3–4 (2003): 407–25.
36 David Valentine, *Imagining Transgender: Ethnography of a Category* (Durham, NC: Duke University Press, 2007).

37 Rebecca Jordan-Young, *Brain Storm: The Flaws in the Science of Sex Differences* (Cambridge, MA: Harvard University Press, 2011); Cordelia Fine, *Delusions of Gender: How our Minds, Society, and Neurosexism Create Difference* (New York: W. W. Norton, 2011).
38 Scholars have characterized as monster ethics the principles underpinning medical procedures conducted on conjoined twins or intersex babies, patients considered to be 'less than human.' See George Annas, 'Siamese Twins: Killing One to Save the Other,' *The Hastings Center Report* 17 (April 1987): 27–9.
39 The episode is derived from the so-called John/Joan case. John Reimer was raised as a girl on the advice of sexologist John Money. John chose to revert to his original male identity as a teenager. He lived as an adult heterosexual male but later committed suicide.
40 Cheryl Chase cited in Elizabeth Weil, 'What if it's (Sort of) a Boy, and (Sort of) a Girl?' *New York Times Magazine* (September 24, 2006): http://www.nytimes.com/2006/09/24/magazine/24intersexkids.html?pagewanted=all (accessed on March 24, 2015).
41 Emily Skidmore has argued that transwomen of color have had to assert their femininity quite differently from their white counterparts. See 'Constructing the "Good Transsexual": Christine Jorgensen, Whiteness, and Heterosexuality in the Mid-Twentieth Century Press,' *Feminist Studies* 37, no. 2 (2011): 270–300.
42 Patricia Hill-Collins, *Black Feminist Thought: Knowledge, Consciousness, and the Politics of Empowerment*, 2nd edn (New York: Routledge, 1999); Kimberly Wallace-Sanders, *Mammy: A Century of Race, Gender, and Southern Memory* (Ann Arbor: University of Michigan Press, 2009).
43 Joelle Ryan, 'Reel Gender: Examining the Politics of Trans Images in Film and Media,' doctoral dissertation, OhioLink ETD Center (2009) (bgsu1245709749); Skidmore, 'Constructing the "Good Transsexual".'
44 Skidmore, 'Constructing the "Good Transsexual".'
45 Anne Fausto-Sterling, 'The Five Sexes, Revisited,' *The Sciences* (July–August 2000), 19–23.
46 Susan Stryker, *Queer Pulp: Perverted Passions from the Golden Age of the Paperback* (New York: Chronicle Books, 2001).
47 Suzanna Walters, *The Tolerance Trap: How Gods, Genes and Good Intentions Are Sabotaging Gay Equality* (New York: New York University Press, 2014).
48 In 2015, six states continue to specify that rape can occur only between men and women.
49 Amy Villarejo, 'TV Queen: Lending an Ear to Charles Pierce,' *Modern Drama* 53, no. 3 (2010): 350–69.
50 Sarah Lamble, 'Queer Necropolitics and the Expanding Carceral State: Interrogating Sexual Investments in Punishment,' *Law and Critique* 24 (2013): 229–53.

51 Judith Butler, 'Performativity, Precarity and Sexual Politics' (2009): http://www.aibr.org/antropologia/04v03/criticos/040301b.pdf (accessed on March 24, 2015).
52 The iconic Laverne Cox features in this brief scene as Candace.
53 Episodes tend to characterize black men as being on the down low when they refuse to claim a gay identity; white men however are presented as being closeted. These rhetorical variations reflect social stereotypes wherein down low is seen as a peculiarly black malaise.
54 Jasbir Puar, 'Rethinking Homonationalism,' *International Journal of Middle East Studies* 45 (2013): 236–9.
55 Lisa Duggan, 'The New Homonormativity: The Sexual Politics of Neoliberalism,' in *Materializing Democracy: Toward a Revitalized Cultural Politics*, edited by Russ Castronovo and Dana Nelson (Durham, NC: Duke University Press, 2002).
56 Queer scholars, such as Dean Spade, have pointed out that hate crime legislation shores up the carceral system and is not an appropriate response to violence. See 'Prisons will not protect you,' in *Against Equality: Queer Revolution, Not Mere Inclusion*, edited by Ryan Conrad (Baltimore: AK Press, 2014), 165–75; and Chandan Reddy, *Freedom with Violence: Race, Sexuality, and the US State* (Durham, NC: Duke University Press, 2011).
57 Ruth Hubbard, 'Science, Power, Gender: How DNA Became the Book of Life,' *Signs* 28, no. 3 (2003): 791–9.
58 Tait, 'Autoptic Vision'.
59 Derek Kompare, *CSI* (Malden, MA: Wiley-Blackwell, 2010), 18.
60 See Sheila Jeffreys, *Gender Hurts: A Feminist Analysis of the Politics of Transgenderism* (New York: Routledge, 2014).

6 Paratexts and the Afterlife of *SVU*

1 Hannah Gold, '8 Ways Shows Like "Law & Order: SVU" Mess with Your Head' (November 15, 2014): http://www.salon.com/2014/11/15/8_ways_shows_like_law_order_svu_mess_with_your_head_partner/ (accessed on March 16, 2015).
2 For example, see Sadie Gennis, '7 Reasons Why Women Love *Law & Order: SVU* So Much' (November 4, 2014): http://www.tvguide.com/news/reasons-women-love-svu-1088704/ (accessed on March 16, 2015).
3 Stuart Hall, *Encoding and Decoding in the Television Discourse* (Birmingham: Birmingham University, Centre for Cultural Studies, 1973).
4 Gennis, '7 Reasons.'
5 Ashley Fenn, 'The 24 Reasons Why Every Woman Loves "Law & Order: SVU"', http://elitedaily.com/women/reasons-women-love-law-order-svu/ (accessed on March 30, 2015).

6 Linda Mizejewski, *Hardboiled and High Heeled: The Woman Detective in Popular Culture* (New York: Routledge, 2004).
7 Gennis, '7 Reasons.'
8 'Slash' refers to fan fiction that features two characters in a romantic relationship with each other, with the names divided by a slash: Benson/Cabot. Stories featuring two women are sometimes known as femslash.
9 'Law & Order: SVU – The Most Feminist Show on TV,' http://feministing.com/2008/12/04/law_order_svu_-_the_most_femi/ (accessed on February 22, 2016).
10 See Henry Jenkins, *Textual Poachers: Television Fans and Participatory Culture* (New York: Routledge, 1992); Constance Penley, *Nasa/Trek: Popular Science and Sex in America* (London: Verso, 1997); Christine Scodari and Jenna Felder, 'Creating a Pocket Universe: "Shippers," Fan Fiction, and the *X-Files* Online,' *Communication Studies* 51 no. 3 (2000): 238–57.
11 Michel de Certeau, *The Practice of Everyday Life*, translated by Steven F. Rendall (Berkeley: University of California Press, 1984).
12 Michel de Certeau, *The Practice of Everyday Life*, 175.
13 John Fiske, 'Madonna,' in *Media Journal: Reading and Writing about Popular Culture*, edited by Joseph Harris and Jay Rosen (Boston: Allyn and Bacon, 1995), 281–95; John Fiske, 'The Cultural Economy of Fandom,' in *The Adoring Audience: Fan Culture and Popular Media*, edited by Lisa A. Lewis (New York: Routledge, 1992), 30–49; Jenkins, *Textual Poachers*; Constance Penley, *Nasa/Trek*; Scodari and Felder, 'Creating a Pocket Universe'; Karen Hellekson and Kristina Busse (eds), *Fan Fiction and Fan Communities in the Age of the Internet* (New York: McFarland, 2006).
14 Jenkins, *Textual Poachers*, 35.
15 Ibid., 34.
16 Louisa Stein and Kristin Busse (eds), *Sherlock and Transmedia Fandom: Essays on the BBC Series* (Jefferson, NC: McFarland, 2012).
17 Julie D'Acci, *Defining Women: Television and the Case of Cagney and Lacey* (Raleigh: University of North Carolina Press, 1994).
18 Ibid., 196.
19 Alexander Doty, *Making Things Perfectly Queer: Interpreting Mass Culture* (Minneapolis: University of Minnesota Press, 1993).
20 Camille Bacon-Smith, *Enterprising Women: Television Fandom and the Creation of Popular Myth* (Philadelphia: University of Pennsylvania Press, 1992), 144.
21 Rhiannon Bury, *Cyberspaces of Their Own: Female Fandoms Online* (New York: Peter Lang, 2005); Jenkins, *Textual Poachers*; Cornel Sandvoss, *Fans* (Cambridge: Polity, 2005).
22 Sandvoss, *Fans*, 25.
23 Shoshanna Green, Cynthia Jenkins and Henry Jenkins, '"Normal Female Interest in Men Bonking": Selections from the *Terra Nostra Underground* and *Strange*

Bedfellows,' in *Theorizing Fandom: Fans, Subculture, and Identity*, edited by Cheryl Harris and Alison Alexander (Cresskill, NJ: Hampton Press, 1998), 9–40, 36.
24 Fiske, 'The Cultural Economy of Fandom,' 43.
25 Ibid., 40.
26 'Mariska Hargitay Cools Off as She Films Law & Order: SVU with Jennifer Love Hewitt,' http://www.dailymail.co.uk/tvshowbiz/article-1301727/Mariska-Hargitay-stays-cool-films-Law-Order-SVU-Jennifer-Love-Hewitt.html (accessed on 30 March 2014).
27 Christy Carlson, 'Is This Because I'm Intertextual?' in *Queer Online: Media, Technology, and Sexuality* edited by Kate O'Riordan and David Phillips (New York: Peter Lang Publications, 2007), 177–96, 187. Carlson explains the term 'hoyay,' used by participants in the Television Without Pity forum, to mean 'homoeroticism, yay!' She provides a lengthy and detailed analysis of some of the ways in which fan fictions intersect with the televisual *SVU* text to produce combined meaning, and includes several examples of negotiated lesbian fan readings of *SVU* dialogue. She argues that, taken together, the fan fictions and televisual text in this case effectively produce a fluid and ambiguous sexuality for the characters. According to Carlson, hoyay viewer guides function 'not only to critique the show's heterocentrism but also to reveal the extent to which it is built on a thinly veiled homoeroticism' (182).
28 'The Awakening' by DiNovia, http://seftiri.livejournal.com/77920.html (accessed on March 9, 2016).
29 http://us.f517.mail.yahoo.com/ym/showletter?box=inbox (accessed on June 9, 2006, no longer available).
30 Penley, *Nasa/Trek*.
31 Jenkins, *Textual Poachers*, 103.
32 Julie Russo, 'Sex Detectives: "Law & Order: SVU's" Fans, Critics, and Characters Investigate Lesbian Desire,' *Transformative Works and Cultures* 3 (2009), http://journal.transformativeworks.org/index.php/twc/article/view/155 (accessed on February 22, 2016).
33 Kristina Busse, 'My Life is a WIP on My LJ: Slashing the Slasher and the Reality of Celebrity and Internet Performances,' in *Fan Fiction and Fan Communities in the Age of the Internet* edited by Karen Hellekson and Kristina Busse (New York: McFarland, 2006), 207–24.
34 Afterellen.com, 'SVU's Detective Benson Attracts lesbian Fans,' May 2004. (accessed on March 19, 2006).
35 Sharon Ross and Louisa Stein (eds), *Teen Television: Essays on Programming and Fandom* (Jefferson, NC: McFarland, 2008).
36 Russo, 'Sex detectives.'
37 Sally Forth, http://web.archive.org/web/20060205021701/http://www.sallyforth.info/#spoiler (accessed on March 9, 2016).

38 Mallory Ortberg, 'Femslash Friday: Olivia Benson, Alex Cabot, and Hope' (November 15, 2013): http://the-toast.net/2013/11/15/femslash-friday-olivia-alex-svu/ (accessed on March 30, 2015).
39 See http://community.livejournal.com/svu100/110669.html (accessed in livejournal archive on March 4, 2015).
40 Fenn, '24 Reasons.'
41 See http://www.huffingtonpost.com/2014/05/22/svu-season-15_n_5374096.html (accessed on March 4, 2015).
42 Emily Nussbaum, 'Trauma Queen: The Pulp Appeal of "Law & Order: SVU"', *New Yorker* (June 10, 2013): http://www.newyorker.com/magazine/2013/06/10/trauma-queen (accessed on March 24, 2015).
43 See http://www.washingtonpost.com/blogs/tv-column/post/mike-tyson-guest-gig-on-law-and-order-svu-backfires-ratings-wise/2013/02/07/4a8e5c06-7160-11e2-8b8d-e0b59a1b8e2a_blog.html (accessed on March 4, 2015).
44 See http://allthingslawandorder.blogspot.com/2013/02/law-order-svu-monsters-legacy-recap.html (accessed on March 4, 2015).
45 See http://www.joyfulheartfoundation.org/programs/policy-advocacy/rape-kit-backlog-reform (accessed on February 28, 2015).
46 'Law & Order SVU Brings Attention to Rape Kit Backlog,' http://feministing.com/2010/10/01/law-and-order-svu-brings-attention-to-rape-kit-backlog/ (accessed on February 22, 2016).
47 'Ending the Backlog,' http://www.huffingtonpost.com/neal-baer/ending-the-backlog_b_739159.html (accessed on March 2, 2015).
48 King, 'Inside the Real-Life SVU'; Al Baker, 'Focusing on Sex-Crime Unit, and Honoring Jewish Chaplains,' *New York Times* (June 9, 2011): http://cityroom.blogs.nytimes.com/2011/06/09/focusing-on-sex-crime-unit-and-honoring-jewish-chaplains/ (accessed on March 24, 2015).
49 Lisa Cuklanz, 'Creating a sense of reality in *Sex Crimes Unit*,' in *Documenting Gendered Violence: Representations, Collaborations, and Movements*, edited by Lisa Cuklanz and Heather McIntosh (New York: Bloomsbury, 2014), 25–44.
50 Janet Halley, *Split Decisions: How and Why to Take a Break from Feminism* (Princeton: Princeton University Press, 2006).

Conclusion: The Story Continues

1 Catherine Rottenberg, 'The Rise of Neoliberal Feminism,' *Cultural Studies* 28, no. 3 (2014): 418–37.
2 Brian Ott, '(Re)Locating Pleasure in Media Studies: Toward an Erotics of Reading,' *Communication and Critical/Cultural Studies* 1, no. 2 (2004): 194–212.

3 See https://twitter.com/femfreq/status/565985365119365120 (accessed on April 24, 2015).
4 See https://twitter.com/Spacekatgal/status/565746783717191680 (accessed on April 24, 2015).
5 See http://www.crashoverridenetwork.com/ (accessed on April 24, 2015).
6 See http://www.theverge.com/2015/2/12/8026175/law-and-order-svu-gamergate-episode (accessed on April 24, 2015).
7 See http://jezebel.com/gamergate-and-its-victims-hated-the-law-order-gamerga-1685386251 (accessed on April 24, 2015).

Bibliography

Abu-Lughod, Lila. 'Do Muslim Women Really Need Saving?,' *American Anthropologist* 104, no. 3 (2002): 783–90.
—— 'Seductions of the "Honor Crime",' *differences* 22, no. 1 (2011): 17–63.
Akass, Kim and Janet McCabe (eds). *Reading 'Sex and the City'*. London: I.B.Tauris, 2003.
Alexander, Michelle. *The New Jim Crow: Mass Incarceration in the Age of Colorblindness*. New York: New Press, 2012.
Amireh, Amal. 'Palestinian Women's Disappearing Act: The Suicide Bomber through Western Feminist Eyes,' in *Arab and Arab American Feminisms: Gender, Violence, & Belonging*, edited by Rabab Abdulhadi et al. Syracuse: Syracuse University Press, 2010, 29–45.
Andreeva, Nellie. '"Law & Order" Boss Dick Wolf Praises "SVU" Episode featuring Mike Tyson' (February 2, 2013): http://deadline.com/2013/02/law-order-boss-dick-wolf-praises-svu-episode-featuring-mike-tyson-420349/ (accessed on March 24, 2015).
Andrijasevic, Rutvica. 'Beautiful Dead Bodies: Gender, Migration and Representation in Anti-trafficking Campaigns,' *Feminist Review* 86 (2007): 24–44.
Annas, George. 'Siamese Twins: Killing One to Save the Other,' *The Hastings Center Report* 17 (April 1987): 27–9.
Appiah, Kwame Anthony. 'Cosmopolitan Patriots,' *Cultural Critique* 23, no. 3 (1997): 617–39.
Arthurs, Jane. '*Sex and the City* and Consumer Culture: Remediating Postfeminist Drama,' *Feminist Media Studies* 3, no. 1 (2003): 83–98.
Bacon-Smith, Camille. *Enterprising Women: Television Fandom and the Creation of Popular Myth*. Philadelphia: University of Pennsylvania Press, 1992.
Balibar, Etienne. *We, the People of Europe? Reflections on Transnational Citizenship*, trans. James Swenson. Princeton: Princeton University Press, 2003.
Beaulieu, Anne. 'The Brain at the End of the Rainbow: The Promises of Brain Scans in the Research Field and in the Media,' in *Wild Science: Reading Feminism, Medicine and the Media*, edited by Janine Marchessault and Kim Sawchuk. New York: Routledge, 2000, 39–54.
Beltran, Mary. 'The New Hollywood Racelessness: Only the Fast, Furious (and Multiracial) Will Survive,' *Cinema Journal* 44, no. 2 (2005): 50–67.

Bibliography

Benedict, Helen. *Virgin or Vamp: How the Press Covers Sex Crimes*. New York: Oxford University Press, 1993.

Benjamin, Walter. 'The Work of Art in the Age of Mechanical Reproduction,' in *Illuminations: Essays and Reflections*, trans. Harry Zohn. New York: Schocken Books, 1968, 219–26.

Benko, Jessica. 'The Radical Humaneness of Norway's Halden Prison,' *New York Times Magazine* (March 26, 2015): http://www.nytimes.com/2015/03/29/magazine/the-radical-humaneness-of-norways-halden-prison.html?_r=0 (accessed on March 26, 2015).

Bernstein, Elizabeth. 'Militarized Humanitarianism meets Carceral Feminism: The Politics of Sex, Rights and Freedom in Contemporary Antitrafficking Campaigns,' *Signs* 36, no. 1 (2010): 45–71.

Bonilla-Silva, Eduardo. *Racism without Racists: Colorblind Racism and the Persistence of Inequality in Racial America*. New York: Rowman and Littlefield, 2003.

Bourke, Joanna. *Rape: A History from 1860 to the Present*. London: Virago, 2007.

Brown, Michael, et al. *Whitewashing Race: The Myth of a Colorblind Society*. Berkeley: University of California Press, 2003.

Brunsdon, Charlotte. *The Feminist, the Housewife, and the Soap Opera*. London: Clarendon Press, 2000.

——— 'The Attractions of the Cinematic City,' *Screen* 53, no. 3 (2012): 209–27.

Bryson, Valerie. *Feminist Debates: Issues of Theory and Political Practice*. New York: New York University Press, 1999.

Bumiller, Kristin. *In an Abusive State: How Neoliberalism Appropriated the Feminist Movement Against Sexual Violence*. Durham, NC: Duke University Press, 2008.

Bury, Rhiannon. *Cyberspaces of Their Own: Female Fandoms Online*. New York: Peter Lang, 2005.

Busse, Kristina. 'My Life is a WIP on My LJ: Slashing the Slasher and the Reality of Celebrity and Internet Performances,' in *Fan Fiction and Fan Communities in the Age of the Internet*, edited by Karen Hellekson and Kristina Busse. New York: McFarland, 2006, 207–24.

Butler, Judith. 'Performativity, Precarity and Sexual Politics' (2009): http://www.aibr.org/antropologia/04v03/criticos/040301b.pdf (accessed on March 24, 2015).

Byfield, Natalie. *Savage Portrayals: Race, Media and the Central Park Jogger Story*. Philadelphia: Temple University Press, 2014.

Cantor, Muriel. 'Prime Time Fathers: A Study in Continuity and Change,' *Critical Studies in Mass Communication* 7 (1990): 275–85.

Card, Claudia. 'Rape as a Weapon of War,' *Hypatia* 11, no. 4 (1996): 5–18.

Carlson, Christy. 'Is This Because I'm Intertextual?,' in *Queer Online: Media, Technology, and Sexuality*, edited by Kate O'Riordan and David Phillips. New York: Peter Lang Publications, 2007, 177–96.

Bibliography

Carroll, Hamilton. *Affirmative Reaction: New Formations of White Masculinity*. Durham, NC: Duke University Press, 2011.

Carter, Bill. 'Spin-off No. 2: Story is Still King, Ka-Ching,' *New York Times* (September 30, 2001): http://www.nytimes.com/2001/09/30/tv/cover-story-spinoff-no-2-story-is-still-king-ka-ching.html (accessed on March 24, 2015).

Cavender, Gary, and Nancy Jurik. 'Scene Composition and Justice for Women: An Analysis of the Portrayal of Detective Tennison in the British Television Program Prime Suspect,' *Feminist Criminology* 2 (2007): 277–303.

Certeau, Michel de. *The Practice of Everyday Life*, trans. Steven F. Rendall. Berkeley: University of California Press, 1984.

Chozick, Amy. 'Dick Wolf's Drama: This is His Story,' *New York Times* (October 5, 2012): http://www.nytimes.com/2012/10/07/arts/television/chicago-fire-and-the-changing-dick-wolf.html (accessed on March 24, 2015).

Cooper, Brenda. '*Boys Don't Cry* and Female Masculinity: Reclaiming a Life & Dismantling the Politics of Normative Heterosexuality,' *Critical Studies in Media Communication* 19, no. 1 (2002): 44–63.

Copelon, Rhonda. 'Gendered War Crimes: Reconceptualizing Rape in Time of War,' in *Women's Rights, Human Rights: International Feminist Perspectives*, edited by Julie Peters and Andrea Wolper. New York: Routledge, 1995, 197–214.

Creed, Barbara. *The Monstrous-Feminine: Film, Feminism, and Psychoanalysis*. New York: Routledge, 1993.

Crenshaw, Kimberlé. 'Mapping the Margins: Intersectionality, Identity Politics and Violence against Women of Color,' *Stanford Law Review* 43, no. 6 (1990): 1241–99.

Cuklanz, Lisa. *Rape on Prime Time: Television, Masculinity, and Sexual Violence*. Philadelphia: University of Pennsylvania Press, 2000.

―― 'Creating a Sense of Reality in *Sex Crimes Unit*,' in *Documenting Gendered Violence: Representations, Collaborations, and Movements*, edited by Lisa Cuklanz and Heather McIntosh. New York: Bloomsbury, 2014, 25–44.

Cuklanz, Lisa, and Sujata Moorti. 'Television's "New" Feminism: Prime Time Representations of Women and Victimization,' *Critical Studies in Media Communication* 23, no. 4 (2006): 302–21.

D'Acci, Julie. *Defining Women: Television and the Case of Cagney and Lacey*. Raleigh: University of North Carolina Press, 1994.

Daalmans, Serena. ' "I'm Busy Trying to Become Who I am": Self-entitlement and the City in HBO's Girls,' *Feminist Media Studies* 13, no. 2 (2013): 359–62.

Dana, Rebecca. 'Law and Disorder,' *Wall Street Journal* (July 12, 2008): http://www.wsj.com/articles/SB121582018406147559 (accessed on March 24, 2015).

Davé, Shilpa. *Indian Accents: Brown Voice and Racial Performance in American Television and Film*. Chicago: University of Illinois Press, 2013.

Bibliography

Deming, Robert. 'Theorizing Television: Text, Textuality, Intertextuality,' *Journal of Communication Inquiry* 10 (1986): 32–44.

Doty, Alexander. *Making Things Perfectly Queer: Interpreting Mass Culture*. Minneapolis: University of Minnesota Press, 1993.

Douglas, Susan. *The Rise of Enlightened Sexism: How Pop Culture Took Us from Girl Power to Girls Gone Wild*. New York: St. Martin's Griffin, 2010.

Dow, Bonnie. *Prime-Time Feminism: Television, Media Culture, and the Women's Movement since the 1970s*. Philadelphia: University of Pennsylvania Press, 1996.

Duggan, Lisa. 'The New Homonormativity: The Sexual Politics of Neoliberalism,' in *Materializing Democracy: Toward a Revitalized Cultural Politics*, edited by Russ Castronovo and Dana Nelson. Durham, NC: Duke University Press, 2002.

Dumit, Joseph. *Picturing Personhood: Brain Scans and Biomedical Identity*. Princeton: Princeton University Press, 2004.

Edgar, Amanda. 'R&B Rhetoric and Victim-Blaming Discourses: Exploring the Popular Press's Revision of Rihanna's Contextual Agency,' *Women's Studies in Communication* 37, no. 2 (2014): 138–58.

Enck-Wanzer, Suzanne. 'All's Fair in Love and Sport: Black Masculinity and Domestic Violence in the News,' *Communication and Critical/Cultural Studies* 6, no. 1 (2009): 1–18.

Fairstein, Linda. *Sexual Violence: Our War Against Rape*. New York: Berkeley Books, 1995.

Fausto-Sterling, Anne. 'The Five Sexes, Revisited,' *The Sciences* (July–August 2000), 19–23.

Fellows, Mary, and Sherene Razack. 'The Race to Innocence: Confronting Hierarchical Relations among Women,' *Journal of Gender, Race and Justice* 1 (1998): 335–52.

Fields, Karen, and Barbara Fields. *Racecraft: The Soul of Inequality in American Life*. New York: Verso, 2012.

Fine, Cordelia. *Delusions of Gender: How our Minds, Society, and Neurosexism Create Difference*. New York: W. W. Norton, 2011.

Fiske, John. 'The Cultural Economy of Fandom,' in *The Adoring Audience: Fan Culture and Popular Media*, edited by Lisa A. Lewis. New York: Routledge, 1992, 30–49.

——— 'Madonna,' in *Media Journal: Reading and Writing about Popular Culture*, edited by Joseph Harris and Jay Rosen. Boston: Allyn and Bacon, 1995, 281–95.

Foucault, Michel. *Discipline and Punish: The Birth of the Prison*, trans. Alan Sheridan. New York: Random House, 1979.

Fraser, Nancy. *Fortunes of Feminism: From State-Managed Capitalism to Neo-liberal Crisis*. New York: Verso, 2013.

Bibliography

Garland, David. *The Culture of Control: Crime and Social Order in Contemporary Society*. Chicago: University of Chicago Press, 2003.

Ghodsee, Kristen. *The Red Riviera: Gender, Tourism, and Postsocialism on the Black Sea*. Durham, NC: Duke University Press, 2005.

Gill, Rosalind. 'Postfeminist Media Culture: Elements of a Sensibility,' *European Journal of Cultural Studies* 10, no. 2 (2007): 147–66.

Gitlin, Todd. *Inside Prime Time*, 2nd edn. Berkeley: University of California Press, 2000.

Gold, Hannah. '8 Ways Shows Like "Law & Order: SVU" Mess with Your Head,' (November 15, 2014): http://www.salon.com/2014/11/15/8_ways_shows_like_law_order_svu_mess_with_your_head_partner/ (accessed on March 16, 2015).

Gottschalk, Marie. *The Prison and the Gallows: The Politics of Mass Incarceration in America*. London: Cambridge University Press, 2006.

Gray, Herman. 'Race, Media, and the Cultivation of Concern,' *Communication and Critical/Cultural Studies* 10, nos 2–3 (2013): 253–8.

Green, Shoshanna, Cynthia Jenkins and Henry Jenkins. '"Normal Female Interest in Men Bonking": Selections from the *Terra Nostra Underground* and *Strange Bedfellows*,' in *Theorizing Fandom: Fans, Subculture, and Identity*, edited by Cheryl Harris and Alison Alexander. Cresskill, NJ: Hampton Press, 1998, 9–40.

Hall, Stuart. *Encoding and Decoding in the Television Discourse*. Birmingham, UK: Birmingham University, Centre for Cultural Studies, 1973.

Halley, Janet. *Split Decisions: How and Why to Take a Break from Feminism*. Princeton: Princeton University Press, 2006.

Hamad, Hannah. *Postfeminism and Paternity in Contemporary U.S. Film: Framing Fatherhood*. New York: Routledge, 2013.

Hargitay, Mariska, and John Prendergast. 'How We Can all Help Women in the Congo,' *Huffington Post* (May 17, 2010): http://www.huffingtonpost.com/mariska-hargitay/how-we-can-all-help-women_b_502411.html (accessed on March 24, 2015).

Harris, Bill. 'Against the Law: There are No Plans for Benson and Stabler to Lock Lips Any Time Soon,' *Toronto Sun* (February 20, 2007): http://jam.canoe.com/Television/TV_Shows/L/Law_Order_Special_Victims_Unit/2007/02/20/pf-3647224.html (accessed on March 9, 2016).

Harvey, David. *A Brief History of Neoliberalism*. New York: Oxford University Press, 2007.

Heineman, Elizabeth. 'The History of Sexual Violence in Conflict Zones: Conference Report,' *Radical History Review* 101 (2008): 5–21.

Hellekson, Karen, and Kristina Busse (eds). *Fan Fiction and Fan Communities in the Age of the Internet*. New York: McFarland, 2006.

Hill-Collins, Patricia. *Black Feminist Thought: Knowledge, Consciousness, and the Politics of Empowerment*, 2nd edn. New York: Routledge, 1999.

Bibliography

Hubbard, Ruth. 'Science, Power, Gender: How DNA Became the Book of Life,' *Signs* 28, no. 3 (2003): 791–9.

Hull, Gloria, Patricia Scott and Barbara Smith (eds). *But Some of Us are Brave: All the Women are White, All the Blacks are Men*. New York: Feminist Press, 1993.

Jaleel, Rana. 'Weapons of Sex, Weapons of War: Feminisms, Ethnic Conflict, and the Rise of Rape and Sexual Violence in Public International Law during the 1990s,' *Cultural Studies* 27, no. 1 (2013): 115–35.

Jaramillo, Deborah. 'Narcocorridos and Newbie Drug Dealers: The Changing Image of the Mexican Narco on US Television,' *Ethnic and Racial Studies* 37, no. 9 (2014): 1587–604.

Jeffords, Susan. 'Rape and the New World Order,' *Cultural Critique* 19 (1991): 203–15.

Jeffreys, Sheila. *Gender Hurts: A Feminist Analysis of the Politics of Transgenderism*. New York: Routledge, 2014.

Jenkins, Henry. *Textual Poachers: Television Fans and Participatory Culture*. New York: Routledge, 1992.

Jermyn, Deborah. *Prime Suspect*. London: BFI Films, 2010.

Johnson, Erica. *Dreaming of a Mail-Order Husband: Russian–American Internet Romance*. Durham, NC: Duke University Press, 2007.

Johnson-McGrath, Julie. 'Speaking for the Dead: Forensic Pathologists and Criminal Justice in the US,' *Science, Technology and Human Values* 20, no. 4 (1995): 438–59.

Jordan-Young, Rebecca. *Brain Storm: The Flaws in the Science of Sex Differences*. Cambridge, MA: Harvard University Press, 2011.

Kaplan, E. Ann. *Motherhood and Representation: The Mother in Popular Culture and Melodrama*. London: Routledge, 1992.

Keck, William. 'Mike Tyson Discusses his Controversial Role in Law & Order: SVU.' (January 29, 2013): http://www.tvguide.com/News/Mike-Tyson-SVU-1060070.aspx (accessed on March 24, 2015).

King, Carol. 'The Real Life SVU: Lisa Jackson's 'Special Crimes Unit'," *Ms. Magazine* (June 19, 2011): http://msmagazine.com/blog/2011/06/19/inside-the-real-life-svu/ (accessed March 24, 2015).

Kogacioglu, Dicle. 'The Tradition Effect: Framing Honor Crimes in Turkey,' *differences* 15, no. 2 (2004): 118–51.

Kompare, Derek. *CSI*. New York: Wiley-Blackwell, 2010.

Lalor, Peter. 'Twists and Turn on a Disturbing Journey,' *Weekend Australian* (March 22, 2007): 36.

Lamble, Sarah. 'Queer Necropolitics and the Expanding Carceral State: Interrogating Sexual Investments in Punishment,' *Law and Critique* 24 (2013): 229–53.

Lauretis, Teresa de. *Technologies of Gender: Essays on Theory, Film, and Fiction*. Bloomington: Indiana University Press, 1987.

Bibliography

Lavin, Maud. *Push Comes to Shove: New Images of Aggressive Women*. Cambridge, MA: MIT Press, 2010.

Lee, Susanna. '"These Are Our Stories": Trauma, Form and the Screen Phenomenon of *Law & Order*,' *Discourse* 25, nos 1–2 (2004): 81–97.

Leonard, David. 'The Next M. J. or the Next O. J.? Kobe Bryant, Race, and the Absurdity of Colorblind Rhetoric,' *Journal of Sport and Social Issues* 28, no. 3 (2004): 284–313.

Lotz, Amanda. 'Postfeminist Television Criticism: Rehabilitating Critical Terms and Identifying Postfeminist Attributes,' *Feminist Media Studies* 1, no. 1 (2001): 105–21.

Marchetti, Gina. *Romance and the Yellow Peril: Race, Sex and Discursive Strategies in Hollywood Fiction*. Berkeley: University of California Press, 1994.

McGrath, Charles. 'Law & Order & Law & Order & Law & Order & Law & Order …,' *New York Times Magazine* (September 21, 2003): http://www.nytimes.com/2003/09/21/magazine/21LAWORDER.html (accessed on March 24, 2015).

McRobbie, Angela. 'Post-Feminism and Popular Culture,' *Feminist Media Studies* 4, no. 3 (2004): 255–64.

—— *The Aftermath of Feminism: Gender, Culture, and Social Change*. Thousand Oaks, CA: Sage, 2009.

Meiners, Erica. 'Never Innocent: Feminist Trouble with Sex Offender Registries and Protection in a Prison Nation,' *Meridians* 9, no. 2 (2009): 31–62.

Melendez, Franklin. 'Video Pornography, Visual Pleasure and the Return of the Sublime,' in *Porn Studies*, edited by Linda Williams. Durham, NC: Duke University Press, 2004, 401–27.

Mitovich, Matt. 'SVU Biggie Charged with Racism, Sexism,' *TV Guide* (April 26, 2007): http://www.tvguide.com/news/svu-biggie-charged-15903.aspx (accessed on March 24, 2015).

Mizejewski, Linda. *Hardboiled and High Heeled: The Woman Detective in Popular Culture*. New York: Routledge, 2004.

—— 'Dressed to Kill: Postfeminist Noir,' *Cinema Journal* 44, no. 2 (2005): 121–7.

Moorti, Sujata. *Color of Rape: Gender and Race in Television's Public Spheres*. Albany: State University of New York Press, 2002.

—— 'Out of India: Fashion Culture and the Marketing of Ethnic Style,' in *A Companion to Media Studies*, edited by Angharad N. Valdivia. Malden, MA: Blackwell, 2003, 293–308.

Morse, Stephen. 'Brain Overclaim Syndrome and Criminal Responsibility: A Diagnostic Note,' *Faculty Scholarship* (2006). Paper 117. http://scholarship.law.upenn.edu/faculty_scholarship/117 (accessed on March 24, 2015).

Mulvey, Laura. 'Visual Pleasure and Narrative Cinema,' *Screen* 16, no. 3 (2): 6–18.

Naficy, Hamid. 'Television Intertextuality and the Nuclear Family,' *Journal of Film and Video* 41, no. 4 (1989): 42–59.

Bibliography

Nichols-Pethick, Jonathan. *TV Cops: The Contemporary American Television Police Drama*. New York: Routledge, 2012.

Nussbaum, Emily. 'Trauma Queen: The Pulp Appeal of Law & Order: SVU,' *New Yorker* (June 10, 2013): http://www.newyorker.com/magazine/2013/06/10/trauma-queen (accessed on March 24, 2015).

Ott, Brian. '(Re)Locating Pleasure in Media Studies: Toward an Erotics of Reading,' *Communication and Critical/Cultural Studies* 1, no. 2 (2004): 194–212.

Palmer, Joy. 'Tracing Bodies: Gender, Genre and Forensic Detective Fiction,' *South Central Review* 18, nos 3–4 (2001): 54–71.

Pease, Donald. *The New American Exceptionalism*. Minneapolis: University of Minnesota Press, 2009.

Penley, Constance. *Nasa/Trek: Popular Science and Sex in America*. London: Verso, 1997.

Pollock, Griselda. 'Modernity and the Spaces of Femininity,' in *Feminism, Femininity and the Histories of Art*. New York: Routledge, 2003, 50–90.

Prasad, Amit. 'Making Images/Making Bodies: Visibilizing and Disciplining through Magnetic Resonance Imaging (MRI),' *Science, Technology, and Human Values* 30, no. 2 (2005): 291–316.

Projansky, Sarah. *Watching Rape: Film and Television in Postfeminist Culture*. New York: New York University Press, 2001.

Puar, Jasbir. 'Rethinking Homonationalism,' *International Journal of Middle East Studies* 45 (2013): 236–9.

Rabinovitz, Lauren. 'Sitcoms and Single Moms: Representations of Feminism on American TV,' *Cinema Journal* 29, no. 1 (1989): 3–19.

Rapezzi, Claudio, Roberto Ferrari and Angelo Branzi. 'White Coats and Fingerprints: Diagnostic Reasoning in Medicine and Investigative Methods of Fictional Detectives,' *British Medical Journal* 231 (December 22, 2005): 1491–4.

Razack, Sherene. *Casting Out: The Eviction of Muslims from Western Law and Politics*. Toronto: University of Toronto Press, 2008.

Reardon, Jenny. 'Decoding Race and Human Difference in a Genomic Age,' *differences* 15, no. 3 (2004): 38–65.

Reddy, Chandan. *Freedom with Violence: Race, Sexuality, and the US State*. Durham, NC: Duke University Press, 2011.

Reitan, Eric. 'Rape as an Essentially Contested Concept,' *Hypatia* 16, no. 2 (2001): 43–66.

Rentschler, Carrie. *Second Wounds: Victims Rights and the Media in the US*. Durham, NC: Duke University Press, 2011.

Rhineberger-Dunn, Gayle, Nicole Rader and Kevin Williams. 'Constructing Juvenile Delinquency through Crime Drama: An Analysis of *Law & Order*,' *Journal of Criminal Justice and Popular Culture* 15, no. 1 (2008), 94–116.

Bibliography

Richards, Amy, and Jennifer Baumgardner. *Manifesta: Young Women, Feminism, and the Future*. New York: Farrar, Strauss and Giroux, 2000.

Roane, Kit. 'The CSI Effect,' *US News & World Report* 138, no. 16 (May 2, 2005): 17.

Rose, Tricia. *Black Noise: Rap Music and Black Culture in Contemporary America*. Middletown, CT: Wesleyan University Press, 1994.

Rosen, Jeffrey. 'The Brain on the Stand,' *New York Times Magazine* (March 11, 2007): 49–53, 70, 77–83.

Ross, Sharon and Louisa Stein (eds). *Teen Television: Essays on Programming and Fandom*. Jefferson, NC: McFarland, 2008.

Rottenberg, Catherine. 'The Rise of Neoliberal Feminism,' *Cultural Studies* 28, no. 3 (2014): 418–37.

Rubin, Gayle. 'Thinking Sex: Notes for a Radical Theory of the Politics of Sexuality,' in *Pleasure and Danger*, edited by Carole Vance. New York: Routledge & Kegan Paul, 1984, 143–78.

Rudolph, Jennifer. *Embodying Latino Masculinities: Producing Masculatinidad*. New York: Palgrave Macmillan, 2012.

Russo, Julie. 'Sex Detectives: "Law & Order: SVU's" Fans, Critics, and Characters Investigate Lesbian Desire,' *Transformative Works and Cultures* 3 (2009), http://journal.transformativeworks.org/index.php/twc/article/view/155 (accessed February 22, 2016).

Ryan, Joelle. 'Reel Gender: Examining the Politics of Trans Images in Film and Media," Doctoral dissertation, OhioLink ETD Center (2009) (bgsu1245709749).

Sandberg, Sheryl. *Lean In: Women, Work, and the Will to Lead*. New York: Random House, 2013.

Saner, Emine. 'Why is Mike Tyson to Star in a Crime Drama about Rape?,' *The Guardian* (28 January 2013): http://www.theguardian.com/society/2013/jan/28/mike-tyson-star-in-rape-drama (accessed on March 24, 2015).

Savage, Charlie. 'U.S. to Expand its Definition of Rape in Statistics,' *New York Times* (January 6, 2012): http://www.nytimes.com/2012/01/07/us/politics/federal-crime-statistics-to-expand-rape-definition.html (accessed on March 27, 2014).

Scharrer, Erica. 'From Wise to Foolish: TV Portrayals of the Sitcom Father, 1950s–1990s,' *Journal of Broadcasting and Electronic Media* (Winter 2001): 23–40.

——— 'More than "Just the Facts"?: Portrayals of Masculinity in Police and Detective Programs Over Time,' *The Howard Journal of Communications* 23 (2012): 88–109.

Schaub, Melissa. *Middlebrow Feminism in Classic British Detective Fiction: The Female Gentleman*. New York: Palgrave MacMillan, 2013.

Schmitz, Sigrid. 'The Neuro-technological Cerebral Subject: Persistence of Implicit and Explicit Gender Norms in a Network of Change,' *Neuroethics* 5 (2012): 261–74.

Bibliography

Scodari, Christine, and Jenna Felder. 'Creating a Pocket Universe: "Shippers," fan fiction, and the *X-Files* online,' *Communication Studies* 51 no. 3 (2000): 238–57.
Sekula, Allan. 'The Body and the Archive,' *October* 39 (1986): 3–64.
Seltzer, Mark. 'Murder/Media/Modernity,' *Canadian Review of American Studies* 38, no. 1 (2005): 11–41.
Sengoopta, Chandak. *Imprint of the Raj: How Fingerprinting was Born in Colonial India*. New York: Macmillan, 2003.
Sharma, Nandita. 'Anti-trafficking Rhetoric and the Making of a Global Apartheid,' *NWSA Journal* 17, no. 3 (2005): 88–111.
Sherwin, Richard. *Visualizing Law in the Age of the Digital Baroque: Arabesques and Entanglements*. New York: Routledge, 2011.
Skidmore, Emily. 'Constructing the "Good Transsexual": Christine Jorgensen, Whiteness, and Heterosexuality in the Mid-twentieth Century Press,' *Feminist Studies* 37, no. 2 (2011): 270–300.
Sloop, John. 'Disciplining the Transgendered: Brandon Teena, Public Representations, and Normativity,' *Western Journal of Communication* 64 (2000): 165–89.
Smith, Debra. 'Critiquing Reality-Based Televisual Black Fatherhood: A Critical Analysis of Run's House and Snoop Dogg's Father Hood,' *Critical Studies in Media Communication* 25, no. 4 (2008): 393–412.
Soderlund, Gretchen. 'Running from the Rescuers: New US Crusades against Trafficking and the Rhetoric of Abolition,' *NWSA Journal* 17, no. 3 (2005): 64–87.
Spade, Dean. 'Prisons Will Not Protect You,' in *Against Equality: Queer Revolution, Not Mere Inclusion*, edited by Ryan Conrad. Baltimore: AK Press, 2014, 165–75.
Spivak, Gayatri. 'Can the Subaltern Speak?,' in *Marxism and the Interpretation of Culture*, edited by Cary Nelson and Larry Grossberg. Urbana: University of Illinois Press, 1988, 271–313.
Stein, Louisa and Kristin Busse (eds). *Sherlock and Transmedia Fandom: Essays on the BBC Series*. Jefferson, NC: McFarland, 2012.
Stiehm, Judith. 'The Protected, the Protector, the Defender,' *Women's Studies International Forum* 5, nos 3–4 (1982): 367–76.
Stryker, Susan. *Queer Pulp: Perverted Passions from the Golden Age of the Paperback*. New York: Chronicle Books, 2001.
Sullivan, K. E. 'Ed Gein and the Figure of the Transgendered Criminal,' *Jump Cut* 43 (2000): 38–47.
Tait, Sue. 'Autoptic Vision and the Necrophilic Imaginary in *CSI*,' *International Journal of Cultural Studies* 9, no 2 (2006): 45–62.
Tasker, Yvonne. 'Television Crime Drama and Homeland Security: From *Law & Order* to Terror TV,' *Cinema Journal* 51, no. 4 (2012): 44–65.

Bibliography

Thomas, Roland. *Detective Fiction and the Rise of Forensic Science.* London: Cambridge University Press, 1999.

Turnbull, Sue. *The TV Crime Drama.* Edinburgh: Edinburgh University Press, 2014.

Tush, Bill. '"Special Victims Unit" puts a Dark Spin on "Law & Order"', CNN (December 10, 1999): http://www.cnn.com/1999/SHOWBIZ/TV/12/10/special.victims/ (accessed on March 24, 2015).

Uffalussy, Jennifer. 'Law & Order: SVU Bends the Conventions of the Cop Show,' *The Guardian* (November 6, 2014): http://www.theguardian.com/tv-and-radio/2014/nov/06/law-order-svu-bends-cop-show-convention (accessed on March 24, 2015).

Valentine, David. *Imagining Transgender: Ethnography of a Category.* Durham, NC: Duke University Press, 2007.

van Dijck, José. 'Picturing Science: The Science Documentary as Multimedia Spectacle,' *International Journal of Cultural Studies* 9, no. 1 (2006): 5–24.

Vavrus, Mary. 'Domesticating Patriarchy: Hegemonic Masculinity and Television's "Mr. Mom",' *Critical Studies in Mass Communication* 19, no. 3 (2002): 352–75.

Villarejo, Amy. 'TV Queen: Lending an Ear to Charles Pierce,' *Modern Drama* 53, no. 3 (2010): 350–69.

Volpp, Leti. 'Framing Cultural Difference: Immigrant Women and Discourses of Tradition,' *differences* 22, no. 1 (2011): 90–110.

Wacquant, Loic. *Prisons of Poverty.* Minneapolis: University of Minnesota Press, 2009.

Wallace-Sanders, Kimberly. *Mammy: A Century of Race, Gender, and Southern Memory.* Ann Arbor: University of Michigan Press, 2009.

Walsh, Kimberly, Elfriede Fursich and Bonnie Jefferson. 'Beauty and the Patriarchal Beast: Gender Role Portrayals in Sitcoms Featuring Mismatched Couples,' *Journal of Popular Film and Television* (2008): 123–32.

Walters, Suzanna. *The Tolerance Trap: How Gods, Genes and Good Intentions Are Sabotaging Gay Equality.* New York: New York University Press, 2014.

Weil, Elizabeth. 'What if it's (Sort of) a Boy, and (Sort of) a Girl?' *New York Times Magazine* (September 24, 2006): http://www.nytimes.com/2006/09/24/magazine/24intersexkids.html?pagewanted=all (accessed on March 24, 2015).

Wilcox, Annabelle. 'Branding Teena: (Mis)Representations in the Media,' *Sexualities* 6, nos 3–4 (2003): 407–25.

Williams, Raymond. 'Base and Superstructure in Marxist Cultural Theory,' *New Left Review* 82 (1973): 3–16.

Wolf, Naomi. *The Beauty Myth: How Images of Beauty are Used against Women.* New York: William Morrow, 1990.

Bibliography

Wood, Lamont. 'The Reality of Fingerprinting Not Like TV Crime Labs,' LiveScience (February 24, 2008): http://www.livescience.com/4843-reality-fingerprinting-tv-crime-labs.html (accessed on March 24, 2015).

Yegenoglu, Meyda. *Colonial Fantasies: Toward a Feminist Reading of Orientalism*. London: Cambridge University Press, 1998.

Zarkov, Dubravka. *The Body of War: Media, Ethnicity and Gender in the Break-up of Yugoslavia*. Durham, NC: Duke University Press, 2007.

Zimmer, Chris. 'Law & Order SVU: First TV Show Filmed at UN,' (March 9, 2009): http://allthingslawandorder.blogspot.co.uk/2009/03/law-order-svu-first-tv-show-filmed-at.html (accessed on February 8, 2016).

Index

9/11, 8, 61, 108, 113, 128, 133, 163
30 Rock, 78

abandonment, 86, 87
abduction, 22, 48, 90, 99, 142
Abu Ghraib, 1
acquaintance rape, 12, 37
activism, 5, 36, 38, 43, 46, 105, 164, 196, 200, 206
ADA, 25–6, 28, 29, 85, 96–9, 111–12, 120, 126, 131, 144, 152, 156, 158, 159, 163, 180, 181, 186, 198, 199
African American, 25, 26, 40, 77, 83, 84, 86–8, 90–2, 97, 120, 123, 155, 162
Alexander, Michelle, 40, 94
Amaro, Nick, 23, 25, 26, 29, 62, 95, 96, 97, 98, 99, 100, 103, 130
American exceptionalism, 30, 109
Amireh, Amal, 117
Anthony, Carmelo, 78
anti-feminism, 34, 51, 53, 65, 70
Arendt, Hannah, 85
Asian American, 26, 84, 97, 98, 100, 107, 116, 146, 203
athletes, 78, 101

Baer, Neal, 4, 196, 197
Baldwin, Alec, 78
Balibar, Etienne, 132, 225, 235
Barba, Rafael, 26, 29, 96, 97, 98, 99
barebacking, 33, 163

baroque visuality, 135, 141
BDSM, 33
Beach, Adam, 26, 97, 98
Bechdel test, 28, 176
Beck, Dani, 24
Belzer, Richard, 25
Benson, Olivia, 4, 5, 12, 14, 18–29, 42–7, 52, 59, 62, 79, 86, 88, 89, 90, 91, 94, 95, 98–101, 112, 117, 120, 123–9, 140, 142, 149, 152, 153, 159, 160, 161, 165, 166, 170, 171, 174–7, 180–1, 183–93, 195–6, 205
Berger, John, 122
Bernstein, Elizabeth, 42, 43
Big Boi, 78
biology, 9, 44, 136, 137, 143–7, 154, 158, 167, 201
Bonilla-Silva, Eduardo, 77
Bosh, Chris, 78
brain overclaim syndrome, 145
brain scan, 134, 137, 143, 144, 146, 150–1
Broadcast Standards and Practices, 81
Bryant, Kobe, 91
Bumiller, Kristin, 42, 56, 106, 126
Butler, Judith, 161

Cabot, Alexandra, 28, 85, 111, 112, 126, 131, 152–4, 156, 159, 171, 175–7, 180, 183–6, 188, 190, 191, 193
Cagney & Lacey, 18, 179–81, 184, 191
carceral state, 36, 40, 41, 48, 49, 89, 94, 141, 147, 203

Index

Carroll, Hamilton, 103
casting, 18, 19, 25, 88, 89, 96, 97, 100, 195, 196
celebrity guest, 66, 78, 79
Central Park, 31, 32, 119, 123, 143
cerebral subject, 146
Certeau, Michel de, 172, 177–8
CGI, 134, 146
Chase, Cheryl, 155
child pornography, 48, 119, 140
children
    as victims, 7, 35, 48, 53–8, 60–1, 63–4, 67–74, 88, 98–9, 102–3, 110, 112–13, 118–22, 124, 132, 140, 149, 195–6
citizenship, 3, 6, 32, 40, 105, 132, 133, 160, 161, 163, 167
Civil Rights Act, 19
civil rights movement, 40, 77, 92, 93, 153
claimant, 11, 12, 35, 43, 46, 47, 48, 50, 52, 65, 92–4, 100, 101, 148, 152, 168
color-blind racism, 77, 96, 100
color-blind society, 94
Columbo, 18
competing marginalities, 96
consciousness raising, 24, 33, 36, 38
consent, 34, 37, 45, 73, 167, 183
conspiracy, 26, 65–6
conviction, 60, 68, 88–9, 94, 156, 171, 196, 199
corruption, 29, 32, 80, 116, 121
cosmopolitan, 107, 108
Cragen, Captain, 25, 27, 28, 68, 85, 114, 125, 140, 161
credibility, 101, 141
Creed, Barbara, 54
Crenshaw, Kimberlé, 87
crime drama, 3, 5, 8, 10, 12, 15, 16–17, 18, 29, 31–5, 50–1, 78–9, 97, 100, 134–5, 139, 166, 171, 175–6, 179, 184–5, 202–6
criminal insanity, 56, 66, 70
CSI, 8, 15, 31, 134–5, 171
Cuklanz, Lisa, 33, 200
custody, 57, 60, 68, 98

D'Acci, Julie, 19, 179–80, 191
date rape, 59
Davé, Shilpa, 107
Davis, Angela, 82
Deen, Paula, 93
defense, 44, 47, 58, 59, 86, 88, 93, 94, 152, 163, 202
dental, 137, 138
district attorney, 38, 128, 171, 197–8, 199
diversity, 26, 32, 37, 100, 151, 157, 160, 161
DNA, 44, 59, 71, 137, 139, 140, 146, 166, 205
domestic violence, 42, 54, 91, 196
Douglas, Susan, 21
Dragnet, 18
Dumit, Joseph, 145

Enck-Wanzer, Suzanne, 54
ensemble cast, 4–5, 17, 18, 19, 22, 25–6, 27, 77–8, 80, 98, 151, 174, 179, 185
Esparza, Raul, 26
evidence, 37–8, 46–7, 52, 55, 58–9, 63, 64–5, 71, 73, 82, 85, 95, 101, 102, 120, 134–6, 138–9, 141, 144–5, 150, 152–3, 155, 167, 171, 174, 188–91, 196, 197, 198, 200
exceptionalism, 109, 121
exoneration, 7, 50, 53–4, 60–2, 67–9, 71–4, 82, 89, 150
extortion, 59, 101

Facebook, 4, 194
fans, 4, 9, 14, 159, 166, 169, 171–95

Index

fathers, 7, 22, 24, 44, 50, 51, 53–7, 60–76, 84–6, 92, 98, 101–3, 117, 120, 124, 130, 142, 147, 149, 155–6, 160–1, 163
femininity, 7, 21, 22, 52, 90–1, 95, 97, 101, 128, 131, 157, 185, 202, 204
feminism, 5–9, 13–15, 21–3, 24, 28, 33–6, 42–4, 46–8, 51, 90, 92, 109, 118, 124, 126, 133, 151, 154, 168, 170, 175, 193, 198–200, 202–3, 205, 207
  backlash, 5
  carceral, 34, 42–3, 49, 89, 93, 97, 115, 133, 153, 179, 202
  color-blind, 7, 76, 80, 84–5, 89, 92, 100, 103, 132, 204
  embedded, 21
  girlie, 21
  governance, 43, 200
  lean-in, 21, 43
  liberal, 13, 34, 37, 42, 48, 125–6, 162, 206
  neoliberal, 15, 34–6, 41, 44, 141, 202–4
  postfeminism, 5, 15, 20–1, 23, 33–5, 51, 61, 69, 168
  televisual, 22, 51
fetishization, 21, 23, 90, 132
fingerprints, 137, 138
Florek, Dann, 25
forensic, 6, 8, 46, 52, 58, 65, 82, 95, 96, 97, 99, 120, 124, 135, 138–41, 138, 152, 167, 171
Foucault, Michel, 39, 110, 151

gamergate, 203
gaming, 141, 203–6
gangs, 83, 91, 97–8, 100, 115, 126, 146
Garland, David, 40–1
gaze, 179, 180, 191
  color-blind, 75

disciplinary, 110
  haremic, 109, 110, 115, 122, 123, 124, 127, 130
  imperial, 122
  male, 122, 123
  policing, 8, 109–12, 114, 118, 121, 122, 127, 131
genetics, 60–1, 67, 71, 84, 130, 136, 146–7, 150–1, 154, 158
Giddish, Kelli, 26
Girls, 29
Gill, Rosalind, 51
Gitlin, Todd, 19
global city, 106, 113
globality, 32, 142
globalization, 132
good cop–bad cop, 19, 23–4, 45, 95
Gottschalk, Marie, 40
grand jury, 46
grandfather, 68, 92
grandmother, 53, 57–8, 60, 68
Gray, Herman, 75

Haraway, Donna, 137
Hargitay, Mariska, 4, 9, 14, 18, 23, 30, 173, 174, 176, 189, 192, 196, 200
Harlem, 83, 86
HBO, 9, 23, 29, 160, 171, 197
hegemony, 95, 103
heteronormativity, 33, 118, 150, 156, 159, 164, 165, 179, 196
Hill Street Blues, 18, 24
Hill-Collins, Patricia, 156
homophobia, 160–3, 165, 167–8, 187
homosexuality, 71, 118, 160
Houston, Whitney, 90
Huang, Dr. David, 26, 28, 96–9, 116, 138, 143–5, 147–8, 152–3, 155, 157
Hurd, Michelle, 26

Ice-T, 26, 83–4
identity politics, 86

Index

In the Heat of the Night, 24
incarceration, 24, 35, 39–42, 77, 145, 168, 201, 205
incest, 62–3, 65–6, 71–4, 86–7, 149
insanity, 56, 66, 70
International Criminal Tribunal, 127
internet, 2–3, 136, 140, 194, 196, 202
intersectionality, 87, 93, 96
intertextual, 23, 83, 89, 91, 160

Jackson, Lisa, 9, 171, 197–200
Jackson, Michael, 77
Jaramillo, Deborah, 111
Jeffords, Susan, 106
Jeffries, Monique, 26, 27, 77, 80, 180
Jim Crow laws, 40, 82, 94
Joyful Heart Foundation, 9, 23, 196

Kaplan, E. Ann, 55
Keller, Chris, 24
kidnapping, 44, 57–8, 60, 67–8, 101, 204
Kogacioglu, Dicle, 126
Ku Klux Klan (KKK), 92–3

Lake, Chester, 26, 97
Lamble, Sarah, 161
Latino/a, 25, 26, 94, 96, 98–100, 103, 111
Lauretis, Teresa de, 28, 151, 157
Law & Order franchise, 4, 15–18, 29, 135, 175
Leight, Warren, 4
lesbian, 9, 35, 58, 148, 162–8, 174, 176–80, 186–9, 191–3, 195
LGBT, 151
Ludacris, 78, 86–7
luminol, 139

mammy role, 90, 156, 157
Manhattan, 29–30, 32, 38, 72, 114, 197, 198
Marchetti, Gina, 116
Martin, Trayvon, 93

masculatinidad, 99
masculinity, 11–12, 22, 34, 61, 69, 86–7, 90, 91, 97, 99, 101–3, 115, 121, 149
 hegemonic, 33, 51, 99, 102
 labile, 103
 victimized, 53, 102–3, 131
McRobbie, Angela, 51
media event, 79
Meloni, Christopher, 18, 23–5, 30, 160
memory
 recovered, 62
 repressed, 65, 147, 150
Miami Vice, 18
millennial, 1, 2, 5, 7, 8, 9, 13, 15, 31, 34, 77, 86, 115, 133, 168, 204
misconduct, 88
misogynist feminism, 6, 7, 46, 51, 52–3, 56–7, 59, 61, 67, 76, 92, 95, 103, 179, 185
Mizejewski, Linda, 21
Money, John, 154
monstrous maternal, 7, 51, 53, 54–8, 60–2, 67–8, 71, 73, 76, 146, 201
Moorti, Sujata, 34
Morse, Stephen, 145, 155
mothers, 7, 20, 22, 43, 50, 51, 53–62, 64–74, 86–7, 94–5, 125–6, 129, 146, 155, 163–4, 168, 181, 185
MRI, 143, 146
MTF, 152, 153, 156
multiculturalism, 7, 25–6, 28, 31, 80, 96–8, 103, 111
Munch, John, 25, 27, 28, 82
murder, 24, 30–1, 55, 57–8, 64–6, 68–70, 85–9, 93, 102, 111–12, 119–20, 125–31, 143, 146, 152–5, 160–6, 195

narco-monster, 110–12, 114
narcotics, 83, 98
nationalism, 87, 106, 163

Index

NBC, 1, 2, 4, 15, 18, 19, 28, 29, 38, 47, 79, 80, 81, 88, 103, 138, 164, 173, 174, 190, 194-5, 198
NCIS, 8, 15
neglect, 53, 57, 69, 84, 89, 99, 164, 166
neoliberalism, 6-7, 15, 28, 29, 34, 35-6, 40, 41-2, 54, 56, 103, 141, 201-4
neurobiology, 137
neurolaw, 143
New Jersey, 32
New York City, 2, 7, 15-16, 29-33, 38, 48, 83, 93, 97, 109-12, 122, 129, 131, 151, 170-1
Nielsen, Connie, 24
Nixon, Cynthia, 66, 78
'No means No', 15, 24, 168
nuclear family, 25, 51, 61, 71, 74, 187
NYPD, 44, 83, 91, 93, 94

objectification, 21, 23, 34, 122
optic, 10, 110, 132, 135-7, 139, 141, 147, 150, 152, 157, 158, 167, 205
optical empiricism, 8, 139, 141, 142, 149, 205
Orientalist, 107, 108, 109, 130
Oz, 23-4, 160

panopticon, 110
paratext, 6, 9, 22, 133, 170, 172, 200, 205-6
patriarchy, 7, 12, 35, 41, 124, 132
pedophilia, 67, 77, 95, 98, 118, 144-5, 163
perpetrator, 33-4, 51, 52, 114, 118, 151
personality disorder, 66
Pino, Danny, 23
police procedural, 1-4, 6, 8, 16, 18-19, 22, 23, 29, 33, 41, 135, 201, 203
policy, 16, 35, 39, 76-7, 117, 196, 200
postfeminist
  media culture, 34, 61
  noir, 21

post-racialism, 77, 100
Post-Traumatic Stress Disorder (PTSD), 45, 88-9, 98, 102, 130
precarity, 40, 161-2
prison, 23-4, 36, 39-42, 45, 60, 64, 68, 71, 89, 93-4, 97, 110-11, 114, 129, 149-50, 154, 156, 157, 161, 202
privacy, 63, 149, 150
Projansky, Sarah, 33
prosecution, 3, 15, 36-8, 47, 59, 78, 88, 98-9, 120, 156, 171-2, 197-9
prostitution, 38, 43, 58-9, 79-80, 84, 101, 192, 197, 199
protection scenario, 106, 109, 113, 117, 122, 127, 130, 131-3
  protected, 106, 120
  protector, 106, 109, 122, 127, 128
psychiatrist, 26, 28, 97, 116, 138, 147-8
Puar, Jasbir, 163
public sphere, 16, 36, 42, 163, 188
punishment, 6, 16, 35-6, 39-40, 48, 110, 133, 134, 202

queer
  activism, 163, 164
  community, 161
  feminist, 179
  lives, 158, 159
  subjectivity, 136
  theory, 5, 168

race, 3, 5-8, 13, 28, 36, 56, 74, 75-87, 89, 91-3, 96-8, 100, 104, 108, 119, 133, 135, 147, 151, 156, 162-3, 168, 176, 202-3
racecraft, 91
race-thinking, 8, 84-9
racial profiling, 81, 86, 94, 120
racism, 7-8, 75-8, 80-3, 85, 87, 89-94, 96, 100, 147, 168
racist institution, 77, 82

Index

rape, 1–3, 5–6, 9–13, 15, 20, 22, 33–4, 36–9, 42–8, 50–3, 58–66, 71, 79–84, 86, 88–90, 92–5, 100–1, 106, 111–12, 117–18, 123, 127–32, 136, 141–4, 146–50, 152, 154, 158–9, 163–8, 181, 188, 195–9, 201–5, 207 *see also* date rape
   culture, 10–13, 168, 207
   false claim of, 35, 50, 59, 92–3, 141
   law reform, 37, 46, 199
   rape kit, 38, 196–7, 200
   rape myth, 36, 82, 94, 100
   revenge, 128–33
Razack, Sherene, 85
rescue narrative, 8, 42, 43, 113, 117, 118, 125–9
Rihanna, 90
Rolling Stone (magazine), 10–11
Rollins, Amanda, 26, 29, 43, 48, 95, 100, 180, 206
Rudolph, Jennifer, 99

Said, Edward, 108
Sandusky, Jerry, 1
Santeria, 32, 119–20
Schaub, Melissa, 22
Schmitz, Sigrid, 146
Serbia, 31, 127
serial murder, 58
Sex and the City, 29, 78
Sex Crimes Unit, 9, 38, 171, 197–200
sex offender registry, 52, 92
sex work, 80, 100, 116–17
sexism, 15, 19–21, 137, 154, 203, 206
sexual assault, 1–16, 23–4, 31, 33–9, 42–4, 47–9, 50–2, 57, 63–4, 66–7, 71, 74, 76–80, 82, 84, 88–9, 94, 96, 101, 104–5, 115, 127, 131–2, 135–7, 139, 141–3, 146–50, 158, 162, 166–9, 170–2, 174, 176, 195–6, 198–9, 201–3, 207
sexual citizenship, 160–1, 163

Shakur, Tupac, 91
Sherwin, Richard, 135, 141
Sikh, 31
Sister Peg, 38
Skidmore, Emily, 157
Smalls, Biggie, 91
SNCC, 92
sociality, 16, 159
sociopath, 55, 59
Special Victims Squad (NYPD), 13–16, 18, 20–1, 23–5, 38, 43–4, 46, 58–60, 82, 85, 91, 95–6, 98–100, 115, 120, 134, 141–2, 144–5, 159–61, 164–5, 167, 176
Stabler, Elliot, 18–20, 23–8, 45–7, 52, 57, 61–3, 66, 68, 84–6, 94–5, 98–103, 118–20, 123–4, 126–9, 131, 144–5, 147–9, 152–3, 155–6, 160–1, 165–6, 183, 185–8
stereotypes, 59, 70, 76, 84–5, 90–1, 96–7, 109, 116, 123, 130, 159–60, 162, 165, 207
steroid use, 101–2
Stiehm, Judith, 106
stop-and-frisk, 86, 93
structures of feeling, 17
subjectivity, 21, 136, 153, 168
suicide, 46, 59, 63, 68, 84–5, 128
surveillance, 8, 37, 109–10, 112–13, 115, 118–19, 121–2, 131, 138, 140
survivor, 33, 37, 109, 126, 128–9, 171, 195, 197, 199

technology, 106, 134–9, 141, 143, 146, 147, 167, 193
terrorism, 29, 60, 90, 116–18, 132, 163, 204
Thomas, Roland, 139
trafficking, 111, 113–21, 123
transgender, 152–3, 155, 157, 168
transgressive, 25, 33, 57, 190

transmedia, 4, 133, 169, 176, 202
trauma, 2, 4, 16, 44, 88, 89, 129, 131
trial, 37, 46, 58, 86, 88, 92–4, 125, 153, 163
truth claim, 137
Tunie, Tamara, 26
Turner, Tina, 90
Tutuola, Odafin, 26, 28, 29, 83, 86
Tyson, Mike, 81, 87–9, 102, 195–6

undercover work, 24, 83, 111, 116–17, 150, 192
United Nations, 127, 129
Untouchables, 18
USA cable channel, 16

victim, 1–3, 7–8, 10–13, 15–16, 20, 23, 25, 30–8, 40–4, 46–7, 50, 52–6, 58–67, 69–70, 72–4, 77–83, 85–6, 88–91, 93, 96–7, 99–103, 106, 108–15, 117, 119, 123, 126–8, 131–2, 135–42, 146, 149, 151–2, 159–62, 164, 168, 171, 174–5, 185, 189, 193, 195–9, 201–7
Villarejo, Amy, 159
Violence Against Women Act (VAWA), 113
Virginia, University of, 10–11
visual empiricism, 139
visual sublime, 135

Wacquant, Loic, 40–1
Walters, Suzanna, 158
war on crime, 17, 39
war on terror, 17
Warner, Melinda, 26, 80, 100, 137, 138
whiteness, 75–6, 100, 115
whitewashing, 77, 85
wilding, 123
Williams, Raymond, 34
Williams, Serena, 78, 79
witness testimony, 46, 55, 86, 95, 199, 203
Wolf, Dick, 4, 15, 31, 103, 129, 192, 208
Wong, B. D., 26, 97

www.ingramcontent.com/pod-product-compliance
Lightning Source LLC
Chambersburg PA
CBHW072136290426
44111CB00012B/1884